HIKING COASTAL TRAILS OF DELAWARE, MARYLAND, AND VIRGINIA

Help Us Keep this Guide Up to Date

Every effort has been made by the authors and editors to make this guide as accurate and useful as possible. However, many things can change after a guide is published—trails are rerouted, regulations change, facilities come under new management, and so forth.

We welcome your comments concerning your experiences with this guide and how you feel it could be improved and kept up to date. While we may not be able to respond to all comments and suggestions, we'll take them to heart, and we'll also make certain to share them with the author. Please send your comments and suggestions to editorial@falcon.com.

Thanks for your input, and happy trails!

HIKING COASTAL TRAILS OF DELAWARE, MARYLAND, AND VIRGINIA

WATERFRONT HIKES FROM THE DELMARVA PENINSULA TO VIRGINIA'S TIDEWATER REGION

Erin Gifford

FALCONGUIDES

ESSEX, CONNECTICUT

For Dirk, Clare, Max, Molly, and Paul

FALCONGUIDES®

An imprint of Globe Pequot, the trade division of The Rowman & Littlefield Publishing Group, Inc.
4501 Forbes Blvd., Ste. 200
Lanham, MD 20706
www.rowman.com

Falcon and FalconGuides are registered trademarks and Make Adventure Your Story is a trademark of The Rowman & Littlefield Publishing Group, Inc.

Distributed by NATIONAL BOOK NETWORK

Copyright © 2022 by The Rowman & Littlefield Publishing Group, Inc.
Photos by Erin Gifford
Maps by The Rowman & Littlefield Publishing Group, Inc.

British Library Cataloguing in Publication Information available

Library of Congress Cataloging-in-Publication Data

Names: Gifford, Erin, 1973- author.
Title: Hiking coastal trails of Delaware, Maryland, and Virginia : waterfront hikes from the Delmarva Peninsula to Virginia's Tidewater region / Erin Gifford.
Description: Guilford, Connecticut : FalconGuides, 2022. | Includes bibliographical references.
| Summary: "This book covers 50 hikes in Delaware, Maryland and Virginia with hike sections divided by state. Hikes will highlight birding and wildlife viewing hotspots, local history and heritage, and bucket-list outdoor gems"— Provided by publisher.
Identifiers: LCCN 2021060461 (print) | LCCN 2021060462 (ebook) | ISBN 9781493064205 (paperback) | ISBN 9781493064212 (ebook)
Subjects: LCSH: Hiking—Delaware—Guidebooks. | Hiking—Maryland—Guidebooks. | Hiking—Virginia—Guidebooks. | Trails—Delaware—Guidebooks. | Trails—Maryland—Guidebooks. | Trails—Virginia—Guidebooks. | Delaware—Guidebooks. | Maryland—Guidebooks. | Virginia—Guidebooks.
Classification: LCC GV199.42.D428 G54 2022 (print) | LCC GV199.42.D428 (ebook) | DDC 796.5109751—dc23/eng/20211215
LC record available at https://lccn.loc.gov/2021060461
LC ebook record available at https://lccn.loc.gov/2021060462

♾️™ The paper used in this publication meets the minimum requirements of American National Standard for Information Sciences—Permanence of Paper for Printed Library Materials, ANSI/NISO Z39.48-1992.

CONTENTS

THE HIKES

Delaware Coastal Trails

Maryland Coastal Trails

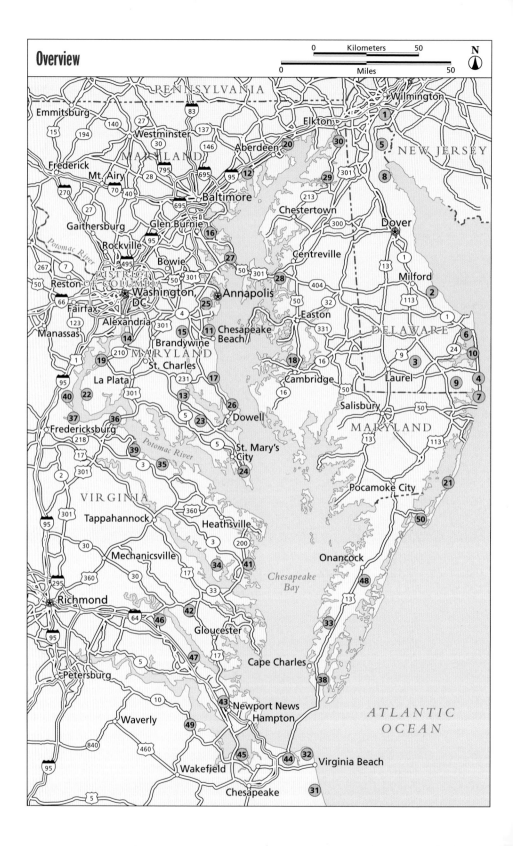

Overview

Kilometers

0   50

0   Miles   50

N

PENNSYLVANIA

Wilmington

Emmitsburg

Elkton

①

140

83

Westminster

137

Aberdeen

20

30

⑤

NEW JERSEY

15

194

27

146

MARYLAND

30

795

95

12

29

301

⑧

Frederick

Mt. Airy

28

70

40

695

213

270

Baltimore

Dover

27

695

Chestertown

300

Gaithersburg

Glen Burnie

16

Centreville

Milford

Rockville

95

Centreville

13

②

Potomac River

Bowie

27

50 301

28

404

32

113

267

7

DISTRICT

50

50

Easton

①

50

OF COLUMBIA

50 301

Reston

Washington,

DC

Annapolis

331

DELAWARE

⑥

66

25

Easton

24

⑩

Fairfax

123

4

Chesapeake

Beach

331

9

③

④

Alexandria

301

15

11

Manassas

14

Brandywine

18

16

Laurel

⑨

1

19

MARYLAND

St. Charles

16

50

⑦

210

17

Cambridge

Salisbury

95

La Plata

301

13

Dowell

13

MARYLAND

40

22

231

26

16

50

113

37

36

5

23

Dowell

Fredericksburg

218

Potomac River

5

St. Mary's

17

39

City

Pocamoke City

21

2

301

3

35

24

50

VIRGINIA

301

360

95

Tappahannock

Heathsville

Onancock

30

3

200

Mechanicsville

17

34

41

48

360

30

33

Chesapeake

13

295

Richmond

Bay

64

46

42

33

Gloucester

5

47

17

Cape Charles

Petersburg

38

43

Newport News

ATLANTIC

10

Hampton

OCEAN

Waverly

49

840

460

45

44

32

95

Wakefield

Virginia Beach

5

31

Chesapeake

Virginia Coastal Trails

ACKNOWLEDGMENTS

I want to first thank my husband, Dirk. Thank you for holding down the fort at home—with a smile—each time I took a research trip to the beach. To our kids, Clare, Max, Molly, and Paul, thank you for joining me on hiking adventures from time to time, doing your best on the buggy trails, and for helping out Dad while I was away.

A big thank-you to my editor, Katie O'Dell with FalconGuides, for your patience and flexibility, and, most of all, for helping me get this book to the finish line. Thank you also to mapmaker extraordinaire Melissa Baker. I can tell you that maps are not as easy to make as they may look.

One final shout-out to my parents, in-laws, friends, and siblings for your support. I couldn't have completed this book without you.

MEET YOUR GUIDE

Erin Gifford has been writing about travel and the outdoors for more than ten years. She has written magazine, newspaper, and online articles for such media outlets as the *Washington Post, Chicago Tribune, Family Circle, Parents,* CNN.com, *Health, Northern Virginia Magazine,* AFAR.com, and *AAA World.* She is the founder of GoHikeVirginia.com, a website she created in April 2020 to introduce fellow nature lovers to the hiking trails of Virginia, as well as Kidventurous.com, an award-winning family travel resource. In her spare time, Erin enjoys family road trips, exploring national parks, running half-marathons, and, of course, hiking. She is currently working toward completing a half-marathon in every US state. She graduated from the University of Virginia and lives in Northern Virginia with her husband, two quirky dogs, and three of her four children. Her oldest just wrapped up her freshman year as a Husky at the University of Washington in Seattle. You can find more on Erin at eringifford.com.

INTRODUCTION

Not everyone wants to climb the highest mountains in search of views for miles and miles from rocky summits—to post on Instagram, of course. And guess what, that's okay. I certainly couldn't tackle elevation hikes every day. Thankfully, many of the most beautiful vistas can be found and enjoyed closer to sea level, on breezy coastal trails across my longtime home base in the mid-Atlantic—specifically, near and alongside oceans, rivers, bays, wetlands, and creeks in Delaware, Maryland, and Virginia. The coastal hikes I've completed and shared in this book extend from the Delmarva Peninsula in the north to the Tidewater region in the south, including Newport News and Virginia Beach in Virginia.

From strolling the gentle dunes of Cape Henlopen State Park in Delaware to hunting for mollusk fossils at Calvert Cliffs in Maryland to curiously ogling the knobby knees of the bald cypress trees in the freshwater swamps at First Landing State Park in Virginia, I think you'll agree there's a lot to love about the relaxed coastal trails in these three mid-Atlantic states. Coastal hikes are easy on the eyes, good on the knees, and as scenic as any elevation-laden hike.

I love sand dunes and coastal swamps as much as the next person, but I want you to be engaged by more than the usual natural features. Prepare to be awed by wild ponies, historic lighthouses, iconic bridges, ghost ships, Native American culture, a stone quarry, former military batteries, and curious artifacts from days long gone. Of course, you'll see your fair share of sandy shores and riverbanks, too.

The coastal hikes in this guidebook are organized by state, then listed in alphabetical order, to make it easy for you to find hikes by trail or park name. The hikes that made the cut for this book have been selected for their scenic value, their relative ease, and, in some cases, their uniqueness. If you're going to drive to any of these trailheads, I want to make sure you are wowed by the hike and want to tell your friends (who will want to complete the same hike and tell their friends).

Every hike in this book has only minimal or modest elevation changes. No trail has an elevation gain of more than 300 feet and no hike is more than 6 miles. All hikes are safe, scenic, and rewarding, with engaging features like wooden overlooks, footbridges, and educational displays. Get ready to get out there and explore coastal trails across Delaware, Maryland, and Virginia.

THE HIKING REGIONS

As you can likely tell by the title, as well as by the introduction, this guidebook covers and is divided into three regions (or states): Delaware, Maryland, and Virginia. This will help you identify the location of each hike and importantly the driving distance from your home.

Delaware

Nearly all of Delaware, the second smallest state in the United States, is packed into the upper east corner of the Delmarva Peninsula. It should come as no surprise then that nearly all—if not all—of the coastal trails in this state are situated on sandy beaches that touch the Atlantic Ocean, Indian River Bay, Delaware River, or Delaware Bay.

Delaware is divided up into three regions: North, Central, and South. Thanks for keeping it simple, Delaware. The state's beaches are largely in Southern Delaware, so it only makes sense that seven of the coastal hikes in this book are in this beloved section of our first state. Many are situated at pristine wetlands a mere stone's throw from popular beaches such as Bethany Beach and Dewey Beach. Few know that these waterfront nature preserves and scenic park trails that wind across windswept sand dunes and freshwater marshes alive with wading birds even exist.

In North Delaware, the area's coastal trails allow for spectacular views across the free-flowing Delaware River. Each of the trails in this slice of the state have stories to tell, too. Fort DuPont State Park in Delaware City has a rich military history that runs from the Civil War to World War II. Concrete batteries left behind inspire visitors to learn more about the soldiers who once manned their posts here. Meanwhile, the Port Penn Wetlands Trail in Middletown educates on life in the nineteenth century for those living off the land, like fishermen and fur trappers.

Maryland

This section features low-lying hiking trails across nine counties of Maryland's Eastern Shore, which is situated in the middle of the Delmarva Peninsula, touching both the Chesapeake Bay and the Atlantic Ocean. Mingle with wild ponies at Assateague Island National Seashore or savor far-reaching views across the bay and the bluffs from atop the 35-foot-tall stucco Turkey Point Lighthouse, all the while traipsing past trailside cordgrasses and coastal loblolly pines.

In Central and Southern Maryland, scenic peninsulas elegantly extend eastward into the Chesapeake Bay, allowing for vast opportunities to explore coastal lands that extend from North East in the north to Scotland in the south. Bay views reign supreme, and visitors can soak in spectacular views of the iconic 4.3-mile dual-span Chesapeake Bay Bridge from hiking trails and soft-sand beaches on both sides of Maryland's famous estuary.

Virginia

This section features low-elevation hikes along the Chesapeake Bay and Atlantic Ocean in Virginia's Tidewater region, as well as hikes in the coastal plain region, which is divided up by four rivers, namely the Potomac, Rappahannock, York, and James. The four rivers define the three peninsulas east of the fall line: from west to east, the Peninsula, the Middle Peninsula, and the Northern Neck. Meanwhile, the 70-mile-long Eastern Shore of Virginia, which runs from Chincoteague in the north to Cape Charles in the south, is a separate coastal region. Located at the southernmost tip of the Delmarva Peninsula, this less-populous area is known for unspoiled natural beauty and abundant wildlife, like migratory birds.

As the easternmost region of Virginia, these hiking trails are on low, flat land. You will walk over freshwater cypress swamps, across wooden boardwalks, along the edge of flowing rivers, and onto sandy beaches. Hiking trails are located in state parks, wildlife refuges, nature preserves, city and county parks, and privately owned protected areas.

WEATHER

Across Delaware, Maryland, and Virginia, you can expect much the same weather in each of these largely four-season states, including rain, snow, sun, and occasional storms. Extreme weather events, like hurricanes and earthquakes, are rare to nonexistent.

The coasts tend to be milder than western regions of each state, due largely to their proximity to water, including the Atlantic Ocean and Chesapeake Bay. This is especially true on the Delmarva Peninsula, which is buffered by these two large bodies of water and is therefore less likely to be affected by significant temperature fluctuations. This also means that snow—even flurries—becomes less common. When it's snowing inland, the coastal areas generally see rain.

Coastal areas, including peninsulas, are also more likely to feel the impact of wind. Traveling over land, wind experiences more resistance from trees, mountains, vehicles, and man-made structures, like buildings. Bodies of water do little to slow down wind, leading to more gusty conditions at times on the coasts.

Oceanic currents also affect the climate, temperature, and humidity of coastal areas, due in large part to the Gulf Stream that brings warmer water up from the Caribbean along the coast of the United States, including across coastal Delaware, Maryland, and Virginia. Wind blowing across the warmed ocean waters leads to warmer overall air temperatures.

The majority of the coastal trails in this guidebook can be hiked at any time of the year. It's worth noting, however, that the wetlands, like those at Taskinas Creek at York River State Park in Virginia, will not green up until late spring. They take time to go from wintry brown to verdant green, though they are still quite beautiful even when not fully green.

Bugs are just a part of summer hiking, but their presence and impact can be amplified on hiking trails that sidle up alongside bodies of water, especially swamps, marshes, and tidal wetlands. Mosquitoes, blackflies, and gnats are the most common offenders, and they can be particularly aggressive in coastal and swampy areas. With this in mind, note that some trails in this book are not recommended in summer, largely due to aggravating blood-thirsty biting insects.

FLORA AND FAUNA

All of the hikes in this guidebook are located on the east side of the Atlantic Seaboard Fall Line, a 900-mile slope that separates the piedmont and coastal plain regions. This naturally means that you'll find habitats and wildlife associated with sandy beaches, freshwater and saltwater marshes, grassy wetlands, and tidal rivers.

Migratory waterfowl like snowy egrets, blue herons, white ibises, wood ducks, and piping plovers are common. The Delmarva Peninsula is an important stopover location for migratory birds traveling along the Atlantic Flyway, which follows Canada's Atlantic coast south to the Caribbean and on to South America. Several wildlife refuges, including Prime Hook National Wildlife Refuge in Delaware and Eastern Shore of Virginia National Wildlife Refuge, provide critical habitats and rest areas for birds on their way south and north.

While wading birds are a favorite in the coastal region, there are plenty of mammals that can be spotted along the trails, including white-tailed deer, muskrats, red and gray foxes, and eastern cottontail rabbits. The region even has its own dedicated animal, the Delmarva fox squirrel, which lives in the forested areas of the Delmarva Peninsula.

FEES AND PERMITS

Many of the state and local parks, nature preserves, and privately held organizations with hiking trails listed in this guidebook do not charge a fee. However, there are some that do, and among them, cash is typically preferred. Cash may be the only way to pay at some parks with an honor-system envelope that must be deposited into a repository when there is no manned booth.

The fee may not be the same every day or for every person. In Maryland and Delaware, state park fees depend on whether you have an in-state or out-of-state license plate. In-staters pay less, of course. In Maryland, some park fees are less for county residents. In Virginia, state park fees are the same for everyone, though they may be higher (for everyone) on in-season weekends.

Fees can change from year to year, so in this guidebook we identify fees by way of a scale:

$ = $1–$5
$$ = $6–$15
$$$ = $16–$25
$$$$ = $25+

LEAVE NO TRACE PRINCIPLES

The relative ease and relaxing nature of coastal trails may make you feel as though you're on a Sunday stroll in the park, but the seven Leave No Trace principles cannot be overlooked or forgotten. Being a first-time or new hiker is no excuse not to follow any of these guiding principles in order to preserve and protect our environment for current and future generations.

First, let's start with no-nos when on the trail:

- Getting too close to—even stalking—wildlife in their natural habitats
- Leaving trash behind, including fast-food containers, soda cans, and empty chip bags, even clothing, dirty diapers, and towels
- Carving initials into trees with pocketknives
- Stacking rocks (i.e., rock cairns) alongside the trail
- Impairing the tranquility of nature with loud noises, including music and words

The goal of the seven Leave No Trace principles is to minimize human impact on nature and the environment. Here is what you can do to reduce your footprint when on these coastal trails:

1. Plan ahead and prepare. Do not put yourself and others at risk by wearing improper footwear, not carrying enough water, wearing inappropriate clothing, and not adequately illuminating your hike (if setting off before sunrise or returning after the sunset). Poorly preparing can lead to damage of natural resources.

2. Travel and camp on durable surfaces. Essentially, this means stay on the trails. Do not go off-trail to get close to a creek or river, to visit with wildlife, or to reach an unmarked viewpoint. Stay on designated hiking trails to discourage creation of multiple routes that damage the landscape. Do not take shortcuts on switchback trails or camp on vegetation.

3. Dispose of waste properly. The forest is not your trash can or dumpster. As they say, if you pack it in, then pack it out. Some parks are trash-free parks, which means there are no trash cans, so your only choice is to pack it out. Leave with what you brought in, including single-use water bottles and snack wrappers. Do not bury anything that will not naturally decompose.

4. Leave what you find. Enjoy the sights on a hike, including wildflowers, tree leaves, mushrooms, and pine cones, but leave them be. Do not bring them home. Avoid causing harm to live plants or trees (carving your initials in a tree is a huge no-no). Unless specifically allowed and noted, do not bring home any natural or cultural objects as souvenirs.

5. Minimize campfire impacts. If you must build a fire, use a camping stove or a fire ring specifically created for campfires. Consider the severity of fire danger for the time of year and location. Also, be certain that a fire is allowed, and contemplate the potential damage to the forested region. If you build a fire, know how to properly extinguish a fire, too.

6. Respect wildlife. Do not feed the bears, or any wildlife for that matter. Do not approach wild animals, not even for an Instagram-worthy photo. Observe all wildlife from a safe and respectful distance. Sudden movements and loud noises can cause wildlife undue stress. You are in their home. Stay back, and let them go about their daily lives.

7. Be considerate of other visitors. We all need to share the trails and respect those with whom we are sharing the trails. Do not play loud music, do not scream or make loud noises, and do not let your off-leash dog run way up the trail. Control your volume and your pet so that everyone on the trail can be awed and inspired by the natural surroundings.

BEFORE YOU HIT THE TRAIL

There is so much to do along the pristine coastlines of Delaware, Maryland, and Virginia, like shelling, surfing, fishing, sunning, and, of course, walking along sun-splashed and well-shaded coastal trails. You can't spend every moment on a beach towel, you know. Every coastal hike and trail in this guidebook offers a welcome break from the beach and a new way to appreciate the region as you take in verdant wetlands, explore historic lighthouses, admire sandstone cliffs, even quietly watch wading birds hunting for tasty treasures at low tide.

All of the trails in this book are easy, engaging, and worth your time away from the waves. With this guide in hand—dog-eared to the page with the topo map you need— you're in for a relaxing and enjoyable walk that wows with water views for miles. Get your sunblock and insect repellant—it's time to get out on the trails.

As you read each hike description, you'll note that each one includes **distance** and **difficulty**. All of the hikes in this book are *easy* and can be completed by hikers of all abilities. Most hikes are quite short, under 2 miles. The longest hike is nearly 6 miles. However, all trails have a minimal **elevation gain**, so you won't be struggling to climb hills. With the exception of two or three hikes, there really are no hills that offer up any reasonable challenge. You may also notice a listing for **maximum grade**, which goes hand in hand with elevation gain. A very low number, like 1%, means that the trail is almost entirely flat. The higher the percentage, the more strenuous any hill or elevation change may be.

The **hiking time** is how long the hike may take you from start to finish, including time spent ogling views or reading historical placards. Your mileage may vary, of course, and you may take more or less time. It's your hike, take your time. No need to rush. The hiking time is just a rough baseline to give you a general idea of what to expect in terms of time spent on the trail.

For **best seasons**, this was a tough one to gauge. Most hikes are good year-round. Some, as are noted, are not good at all in summer—as in, way too buggy. If you want to go on a summer day, wear insect repellant and keep your skin covered with long sleeves and pants. Some coastal bugs can be extremely aggressive. Winter can be a great time for a coastal hike since it's more mild weather-wise on the coast and the bugs are absent. The trade-off, of course, is that views aren't quite as nice. More brown than green, you know.

Be sure to make note of the **trail surface** for each hike. Trail surface can range from grass to sand to gravel to paved, or it can be a mix of several different surfaces. Dirt trails may require encounters with roots, while sand trails may be soft and challenging to walk across, like the Life of the Dunes Trail at Assateague Island National Seashore. It's good to keep surface in mind before you home in on a specific hike.

For **maps**, many of the trails can be found on the National Geographic Trails Illustrated Topographic Map 772 (Delmarva Peninsula). You can also find nearly every trail and park listed in this guidebook online, too. When that's the case, the website address is included if you wish to print out a map or pull it up on your smartphone during your hike. All of the trails listed in this book are located in areas with reliable cell service, so you should not have a problem opening up maps on your phone while on the trail.

Not every park or trail wows with visitor-friendly amenities, like restrooms and picnic tables. Some hikes in this book have no amenities at all, but we listed the **amenities** we noticed while hiking the trails and visiting the parks to give you an idea of what to expect, or at the very least give you an indication that you'll need to find a restroom before you reach the trailhead.

GPS coordinates lead to the parking lot, so you know exactly where to go to park for your coastal hike. No need to waste time circling, trying to figure out if you are in the right lot and where the trailhead is located.

The Hike section leads with an overview of the park or nature preserve where the trail is located, including any must-see geological or historical features you won't want to miss. As the section continues, you will learn more about what you will see and at what mileage point, including turns on the trail, connections with other trails, and changes in terrain, as well as benches, picnic tables, and good spots to stop on the trail for a snack or to simply savor the views.

Each hike ends with a section of **Miles and Directions**, which features trail junctions, landmarks, and notable surface changes to help ensure you stay on the trail until the end of the hike. As a companion, you'll also find a map clearly indicating the route, parking area, local roads, and must-see spots, like overlooks and observation blinds.

To maximize use of this guide, we suggest you keep it on your night table so that it's the last thing you see at night and the first thing you see when you wake up. These delightful coastal hikes will always be on your mind, as will the need to flip through to find the perfect hike for your next escape to the coast of Delaware, Maryland, or Virginia.

ACKNOWLEDGING NATIVE LANDS

This book is intended to support your exploration. Readers will come away with a deeper knowledge of the area, and the opportunity to connect more closely and experience more fully the wonders these lands offer. We respectfully acknowledge that this book covers the traditional land of Native Peoples.

TRAIL FINDER

BEST HIKES FOR GREAT VIEWS
Hike 2: Boardwalk and Dike Trails
Hike 3: Bob Trail
Hike 6: Gordons Pond Trail
Hike 7: James Farm Ecological Preserve
Hike 11: Beverly Triton Nature Park
Hike 16: Downs Park
Hike 21: Life of the Dunes, Forest, and Marsh Trails
Hike 23: Myrtle Point Park
Hike 24: Point Lookout State Park
Hike 26: Red and Orange Trails, Calvert Cliffs State Park
Hike 27: Sandy Point State Park
Hike 30: Turkey Point Lighthouse Trail
Hike 31: Back Bay National Wildlife Refuge
Hike 33: Beach Trail, Savage Neck Dunes Natural Area Preserve
Hike 35: Big Meadow Trail
Hike 39: George Washington Birthplace National Monument
Hike 41: Hughlett Point Natural Area Preserve
Hike 42: Interpretive Trail, Machicomoco State Park
Hike 45: Ragged Island Wildlife Management Area
Hike 46: Taskinas Creek Trail

BEST HIKES FOR CHILDREN
Hike 1: Battery Park Trail
Hike 2: Boardwalk and Dike Trails
Hike 3: Bob Trail
Hike 6: Gordons Pond Trail
Hike 7: James Farm Ecological Preserve
Hike 9: Seahawk Trail
Hike 11: Beverly Triton Nature Park
Hike 12: Black Marsh Loop
Hike 16: Downs Park
Hike 17: Duncan's Pond and North Ridge Trails
Hike 20: Katie and Wil's Trail
Hike 21: Life of the Dunes, Forest, and Marsh Trails
Hike 22: Mallows Bay Hiking Trail
Hike 23: Myrtle Point Park

BEST HIKES FOR SANDY BEACHES

BEST DOG-FRIENDLY HIKES

Hike 3: Bob Trail
Hike 6: Gordons Pond Trail
Hike 7: James Farm Ecological Preserve
Hike 11: Beverly Triton Nature Park
Hike 12: Black Marsh Loop
Hike 16: Downs Park
Hike 18: Ferry Point Landing Trail
Hike 23: Myrtle Point Park
Hike 24: Point Lookout State Park
Hike 25: Quiet Waters Park
Hike 26: Red and Orange Trails, Calvert Cliffs State Park
Hike 27: Sandy Point State Park
Hike 28: Terrapin Nature Park
Hike 36: Boyd's Hole Trail
Hike 41: Hughlett Point Natural Area Preserve
Hike 43: Noland Trail
Hike 44: Pleasure House Point Natural Area
Hike 46: Taskinas Creek Trail
Hike 49: Windsor Castle Park Trail

BEST HISTORICAL HIKES

Hike 1: Battery Park Trail
Hike 5: Fort DuPont State Park
Hike 6: Gordons Pond Trail
Hike 8: Port Penn Wetlands Trail
Hike 12: Black Marsh Loop
Hike 13: Blue Trail, Greenwell State Park
Hike 14: Chapman State Park
Hike 21: Life of the Dunes, Forest, and Marsh Trails
Hike 22: Mallows Bay Hiking Trail
Hike 24: Point Lookout State Park
Hike 30: Turkey Point Lighthouse Trail
Hike 38: Butterfly Trail
Hike 39: George Washington Birthplace National Monument
Hike 40: Government Island Park
Hike 42: Interpretive Trail, Machicomoco State Park

BEST HIKES FOR SOLITUDE

Hike 4: Burton Island Nature Preserve
Hike 5: Fort DuPont State Park
Hike 8: Port Penn Wetlands Trail
Hike 9: Seahawk Trail
Hike 10: Thompson Island Nature Preserve
Hike 14: Chapman State Park

Map Legend

Municipal

≡⟨95⟩≡ Interstate Highway

≡⟨301⟩≡ US Highway

≡⟨24⟩≡ State Road

═══ Local/County Road

= = = = Unpaved Road

├──┼──┤ Railroad

··─··─·· State Boundary

Trails

▪▪▪▪▪▪ Featured Trail

─ ─ ─ ─ Trail or Fire Road

Water Features

⬭ Body of Water

Marsh

River/Creek

Waterfall

Land Management

National Monument

National Seashore

Symbols

Boat Launch

Bridge

▪ Building/Point of Interest

▲ CampgroundTrailhead

✪ Capital

† Cemetery

•─• Gate

Lighthouse

🅿 Parking

Picnic Area

Restrooms

Scenic View

||||||||| Steps/Boardwalk

○ Town

① Trailhead

Visitor/Information Center

State/County Park

Preserve/Refuge

1 BATTERY PARK TRAIL

In historic New Castle, this easy hike along a paved trail rewards with far-reaching views across the Delaware River, as well as sandy coastline and plenty of relaxing benches.

Start: Wharf in historic New Castle
Elevation gain: 43 feet
Maximum grade: 1%
Distance: 3.7 miles out and back
Difficulty: Easy
Hiking time: 1.5 to 2 hours
Best seasons: Year-round
Fees and permits: Free
Trail contact: Delaware Greenways, 1910 Rockland Rd., Wilmington, DE; (302) 655-7275; delawaregreenways .org
Dogs: Yes, on a leash no longer than 6 feet

Trail surface: Paved
Land status: County park
Nearest town: New Castle
Maps: National Geographic Trails Illustrated Topographic Map 772 (Delmarva Peninsula). A trail map is also available online at delawaregreenways.org/trail/ battery-park-trail.
Other trail users: Cyclists
Amenities: Porta-potty, picnic tables, playground, walking distance to restaurants
Cell service: Reliable

FINDING THE TRAILHEAD

The trail starts to the right of the wharf parking area in New Castle. GPS: N39°39'28.1" / W75°33'43.3"

THE HIKE

The paved Battery Park Trail in historic New Castle for pedestrians and cyclists begins in Battery Park and gently meanders alongside the flowing Delaware River. This historic park is best known as the site where William Penn came ashore in 1682, taking his first steps on the soil of America, on land granted to him by King Charles II. Today, the park is adjacent to the New Castle Historic District, a four- or five-square-block town made up of historic homes, gardens, shops, museums, and churches. Before or after a stroll along the Battery Park Trail, walk the cobblestone streets, even pop into a tavern before brushing up on colonial history at First State National Historical Park on Delaware Street.

The Battery Park Trail begins to the right of the parking circle for the wharf on the waterfront. Before you take your first steps, look right to see a marker for the New Castle and Frenchtown Railroad, one of the first railroads in the country, as well as a historic ticket office. As the paved trail extends along the shoreline, there are plenty of benches, picnic tables, and shade trees if you'd like to settle in to enjoy the views across the river and driftwood-covered coastline. A children's playground allows little ones to burn off energy before or after the hike.

At the 0.2-mile mark, note the flagpole with a plaque dedicated to General Thomas Holcomb, a respected Marine Corps officer and native of New Castle. In a few more steps, a green trail sign marks the 0.25-mile point on the trail. From here, a distance marker pops up every 0.25 mile on the Battery Park Trail until you reach the turnaround point, which is marked by an iron fence (so you absolutely do not miss the end of the trail).

Along this path at Battery Park in New Castle, look for a mileage marker to appear alongside the trail every 0.25 mile.

Continue on, then stop at the 0.5-mile mark to snap a photo of the pastel-colored mural on the small building to the right of the trail owned by the New Castle Sailing Club. This club sails out of Battery Park from the last weekend in April until the last weekend in October. Look left into the Delaware River and you may see a dozen small club-owned sailboats gently floating on the water, tethered to mooring buoys.

As you proceed along the Battery Park Trail, you'll exit Battery Park and pass a few more quiet benches before the trail splits at the 0.9-mile mark. Stay left to continue along the river until you reach Deemers Beach at the 1.4-mile mark. In the 1920s, this was home to amusements like a merry-go-round and a dance hall. Today, there is only a small parking area to the right of the trail and a sandy beach on the left that's popular with fishing enthusiasts eager to drop a line. Note that fishing is prohibited at Battery Park but allowed outside the park's limits, just west of the sailing club mural.

A tidal wetlands area is now to the right of the trail, and as you may note, is rather popular with resident geese disinterested by passing walkers and bikers. The geese may not even move off the trail as you proceed to the end of the path. At the 1.8-mile mark, the Battery Park Trail comes to a clear end, marked by a prominent sign that reads "No Trespassing Beyond Fence." From here, retrace your steps to the parking area. Once at the wharf, several placards allow you to learn about the ferries that once crossed the Delaware River, as well as icebreakers used to keep wooden ships safe. To the left, partake in the delightful views of the Delaware Memorial Bridge.

This easygoing paved path begins at Battery Park in New Castle and follows along the Delaware River.

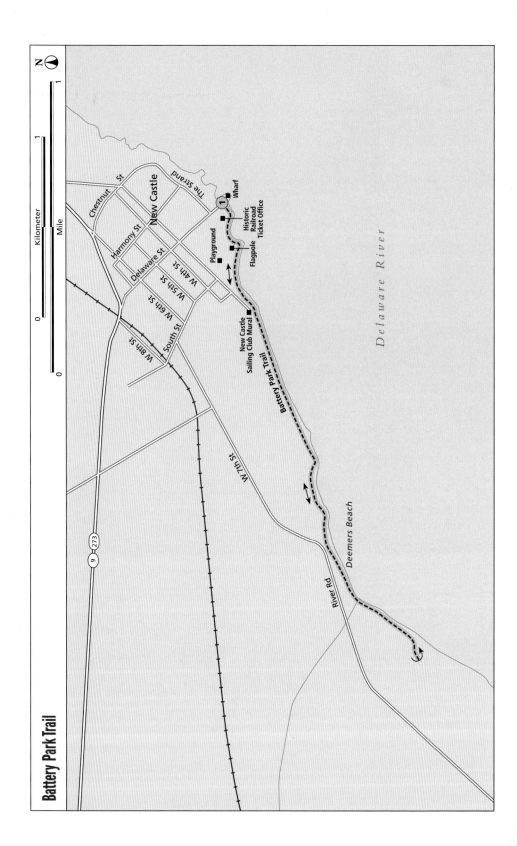

Battery Park Trail

New Castle

Chestnut St

The Strand

Wharf

Historic Railroad Ticket Office

Playground

Flagpole

New Castle Sailing Club Mural

Harmony St

Delaware St

W 4th St

W 5th St

W 6th St

South St

W 8th St

W 7th St

Battery Park Trail

River Rd

Deemers Beach

Delaware River

9 273

1

N

Kilometer

Mile

0 1

0 1

A colorful mural next to the trail touts the New Castle Sailing Club, which moors a fleet of club-owned boats on the Delaware River.

MILES AND DIRECTIONS

0.0   Begin this hike to the right of the wharf at the end of Delaware Street.

0.2   Arrive at a flagpole with a plaque and dedication to New Castle native General Thomas Holcomb.

0.5   Reach the pastel-colored mural for the New Castle Sailing Club.

0.9   The trail splits. Stay left to continue on the Battery Park Trail.

1.4   Reach a parking area and Deemers Beach, a popular spot with local fishermen.

1.8   Arrive at the end of the trail. Retrace your steps to return to the wharf.

3.7   Arrive back at the wharf. Your hike is complete.

2 BOARDWALK AND DIKE TRAILS

This scenic hike wows with views across freshwater wetlands, as well as plenty of wildlife watching at this stopover for migratory birds on the Atlantic Flyway that runs from Canada to South America.

Start: Prime Hook National Wildlife Refuge visitor center
Elevation gain: 10 feet
Maximum grade: 1%
Distance: 1.5-mile lollipop
Difficulty: Easy
Hiking time: About 1 hour
Best seasons: Year-round
Fees and permits: Free
Trail contact: Prime Hook National Wildlife Refuge, 11978 Turkle Pond Rd., Milton, DE; (302) 684-8419; fws .gov/refuge/Prime_Hook
Dogs: Yes, on a leash no longer than 6 feet

Trail surface: A mix of gravel and short sections of boardwalk
Land status: National wildlife refuge
Nearest town: Milton
Maps: National Geographic Trails Illustrated Topographic Map 772 (Delmarva Peninsula). Trail maps are also available at the large trail kiosk in front of the restrooms and online at fws.gov/refuge/Prime_Hook/map .html.
Amenities: Restrooms, picnic tables
Cell service: Reliable

FINDING THE TRAILHEAD

The trailhead is located across from a large trail kiosk toward the front of the visitor center parking area. GPS: N38°49'49.4" / W75°14'53.6"

THE HIKE

Established in 1963, Prime Hook National Wildlife Refuge is a 10,144-acre refuge located on the marshes of the Delaware Bay's west shores. The refuge is a key stopover for migratory birds traveling the Atlantic Flyway, which follows Canada's Atlantic coast all the way to the Caribbean and on to South America. The wildlife refuge features a mix of freshwater and saltwater wetlands attractive to migratory waterfowl like wood ducks and sandpipers, as well as native species like the Delmarva Peninsula fox squirrel. At Prime Hook, you'll find six easy hiking trails, as well as a 7-mile water trail along Prime Hook Creek for canoes, kayaks, and small motorboats.

The hiking trails at this wildlife refuge are all quite short, ranging from 0.3 mile to 1.6 miles in length. For this coastal hike, cobble together the Boardwalk Trail and Dike Trail to create an enjoyable and fully accessible trail with scenic overlooks, stretches of boardwalk, and a wooden observation tower with far-reaching views across the marsh.

This hike begins directly across the parking area from the restrooms and a large trail kiosk. A partially obscured sign on the left side of a flat path marks the Boardwalk Trail. From here, stroll along mild gravel terrain to reach the Morris family cemetery on the left-hand side of the trail at the 0.1-mile mark. There are eight tombstones with deceased dates that range from 1818 to 1864. Family members lived on the property in the Morris Mansion, which could not be preserved and was torn down in 1968.

Continue on to the first stretch of wooden boardwalk trail that winds across freshwater marsh at the 0.2-mile mark. Along the way, placards educate on wildlife you may see,

At the start of the Dike Trail, a wooden fishing pier allows for views across the verdant wetlands.

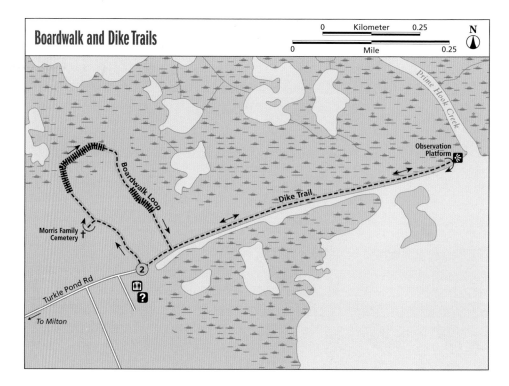

like bald eagles, muskrats, and dowitchers, as well as the role wetlands play in our ecosystem. Notably, wetlands filter out pollutants and help lessen damage caused by destructive floods and storms. Once you step off this section of boardwalk, walk across a stretch of gravel trail to approach a second stretch of wooden boardwalk. Here, you'll learn about the role marshes play as homes for wood ducks before you reach the end of the Boardwalk Trail.

At the 0.5-mile mark, turn left onto the Dike Trail, which is marked by a yellow arrow. As you walk along this sun-splashed trail, the wetlands are on your left and a water-filled dike is on the right. It's a short walk to a two-story platform for views across the marsh. Climb nine steps to the upper level to enhance your views with a metal viewfinder. A ramp allows for access to the lower level that wows with equally impressive vistas. From here, retrace your steps on the Dike Trail, which ends at the start of the Boardwalk Trail. Fishing enthusiasts may appreciate the small fishing pier to the left of the trail just before the end of this hike.

MILES AND DIRECTIONS

0.0   The Boardwalk Trail begins across the main parking lot from the large trail kiosk, restrooms, and visitor center.

0.1   Arrive at the Morris family cemetery on the left-hand side of the trail.

0.2   Reach the first section of wooden boardwalk.

0.4   Arrive at the second section of wooden boardwalk.

0.5   Turn left onto the Dike Trail.

This hike begins on the Boardwalk Trail with scenic views across the wetlands from a wooden boardwalk.

1.0   Reach the accessible observation platform for views across the marsh. Retrace your steps to return along the Dike Trail.

1.5   Arrive at the end of the Dike Trail. Your hike is complete.

3 BOB TRAIL

A scenic loop around Trap Pond State Park in Laurel wows with views of 90-acre Trap Pond and plenty of curious bald cypress trees that appear to sprout right out of the pond.

Start: Baldcypress Nature Center
Elevation gain: 39 feet
Maximum grade: 2%
Distance: 4.9-mile loop
Difficulty: Easy
Hiking time: 2 to 3 hours
Best seasons: Year-round
Fees and permits: $-$$
Trail contact: Trap Pond State Park, 33587 Baldcypress Ln., Laurel, DE; (302) 875-5153; destateparks.com/TrapPond
Dogs: Yes, on a leash no longer than 6 feet

Trail surface: A mix of gravel, dirt, paved, and boardwalk trails
Land status: State park
Nearest town: Laurel
Maps: National Geographic Trails Illustrated Topographic Map 772 (Delmarva Peninsula). A trail map is also available online at destateparks .com/TrapPond.
Amenities: Restrooms, picnic tables, playground
Cell service: Reliable

FINDING THE TRAILHEAD

There is no dedicated trailhead, but the trail can be picked up behind the Baldcypress Nature Center, which is to the right of the primary parking area. GPS: N38°31'32.2" / W75°28'46.6"

THE HIKE

The 3,653-acre Trap Pond State Park in Laurel is one of the largest surviving expanses of what was once an extensive wetland in Sussex County. From the parking area, you can see a small group of bald cypress trees in Trap Pond. It's as if they are growing out of the lake. They can be wildly mesmerizing.

Begin this hike behind the Baldcypress Nature Center in what appears to be a sea of picnic tables, all angling for the wide-open views across the park's 90-acre Trap Pond. There is no designated trailhead, but the nature center is a great place to start. Keep your eyes open for a placard dedicated to Senator Robert "Bob" Venables, an outdoor enthusiast and resolute supporter of Delaware's state parks. In 2015, the Loblolly Trail was renamed the Bob Trail in recognition of Venables's support and love for the parks—in particular, Trap Pond State Park. The Bob Trail circumnavigates nearly the entire state park, including Trap Pond.

Start by walking southeast along the gravelly Bob Trail. At the 0.1-mile mark, the trail splits in two. You can either stay right to continue on the wide, gravel Bob Trail or take a quick detour to hike along the Island Trail, which will shortly reconnect with the Bob Trail. The Island Trail is more narrow, but meanders along the shoreline. Stay to the left and you will catch your first glimpses of a bald cypress swamp on the left at the 0.3-mile mark. Then, at the 0.4-mile mark and 0.5-mile mark, you can walk right out to the edge of Trap Pond for even more views of the curiously intriguing bald cypress

An easygoing bridge guides visitors across a sensitive stretch of swamp along the Bob Trail.

trees. These are less stumpy and in fact look simply like evergreen trees blithely sitting on top of the water.

The Island Trail reconnects with the forested Bob Trail at the 0.6-mile mark. Turn left to continue on the wide, gravel path. Settle in on a bench at the 1.0-mile mark for views across Trap Pond from the southeast end of the pond. At the 1.7-mile mark, the trail ends at Wootten Road, but signage directs you left to return to the trail after crossing a bridge over lily pad–strewn Raccoon Pond. Pick the trail back up on the other side of the bridge for a shaded, woodsy walk.

At the 2.2-mile mark, you will arrive at a T-intersection. You can either turn left to continue on the Bob Trail or make a short detour with a stop at Bethesda Church, a historic landmark that was erected in 1879 to replace an older chapel in the same location. This style of rural church was once very common in Delaware. Regular church services were held at this chapel until the 1970s. A short time later, the church fell into disrepair.

Bethesda Church was purchased by the Delaware Division of Parks and Recreation in 2000. It was completely restored by 2008 and is now used for special events and park programs. Take a few minutes to check out the church, as well as the small cemetery behind the chapel. Here you'll also find restrooms, as well as a dedicated parking area if you wish to explore the church at a later point during your visit.

From the church, retrace your steps to the trail, then forge straight ahead at the intersection. The path meanders through the woods until you arrive at a wooden footbridge over a sensitive area at the 3.2-mile mark. Continue on to reach the parking area for the

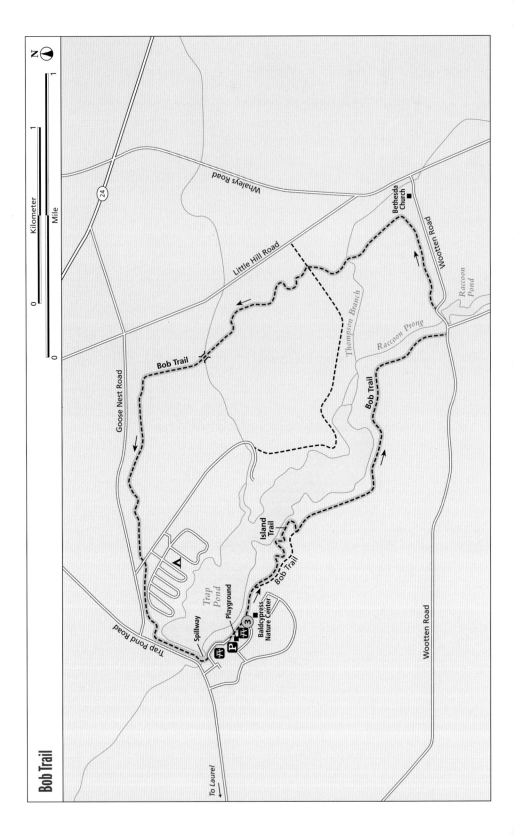

Bob Trail

N

0 1 Kilometer

0 1 Mile

Goose Nest Road

24

Whaleys Road

Little Hill Road

Bob Trail

Thompson Branch

Raccoon Prong

Raccoon Pond

Bethesda Church

Wootten Road

Bob Trail

Bob Trail

Island Trail

Trap Pond Road

Spillway

Trap Pond

Playground

Baldcypress Nature Center

P

3

To Laurel

Wootten Road

Take in the views from a bridge overlooking the mill spillway toward the end of the hike on the Bob Trail.

boat launch at the 4.4-mile mark. Walk through the lot, but keep your eyes to the left to see more bald cypress trees sprouting out of Trap Pond. Turn left to walk on a paved trail adjacent to Trap Pond Road with views across Trap Pond.

Stay left again at the 4.7-mile mark to cross a pedestrian footbridge alongside a scenic mill spillway. Once you pass the spillway, you will be at the far west end of the sea of picnic tables. You will also pass the boat rentals shack. Boats, including rowboats, pedal boats, canoes, and kayaks, can be rented from May to mid-October. In a few more steps, you will see the nature center. Your hike is complete at the 4.9-mile mark.

MILES AND DIRECTIONS

0.0 Pick up the Bob Trail behind the Baldcypress Nature Center. Begin walking southeast along the Bob Trail.

0.1 Veer left to pick up the Island Trail for views across Trap Pond, including curious bald cypress trees.

0.6 Turn left to reconnect with the Bob Trail.

1.7 Turn left on Wootten Road to cross over Raccoon Pond. On the other side, reconnect with the shaded trail.

2.2 Arrive at a T-intersection. If you choose, turn right to visit Bethesda Church, a restored, historic rural chapel. Otherwise, turn left to stay on the Bob Trail.

On the Island Trail, enjoy unmatched views of the bald cypress trees that just seem to grow right out of Trap Pond.

3.2 Cross over a wooden footbridge.

4.4 Arrive at a boat launch parking area. Cut across the lot to reach Trap Pond Road, then turn left to walk on a paved path adjacent to the park road.

4.7 Turn left to cross a pedestrian footbridge and enjoy views of a scenic mill spillway.

4.9 Arrive back at the Baldcypress Nature Center. Your hike is complete.

4 BURTON ISLAND NATURE PRESERVE

An easygoing hike around Burton Island Nature Preserve leads to scenic views across verdant wetlands and salt marsh grasses.

Start: Indian River Marina
Elevation gain: 13 feet
Maximum grade: 1%
Distance: 1.3-mile lollipop
Difficulty: Easy
Hiking time: About 1 hour
Best seasons: Fall through spring
Fees and permits: Free
Trail contact: Delaware Seashore State Park, 25039 Coastal Hwy., Rehoboth Beach, DE; (302) 227-2800; destateparks.com/Beaches/DelawareSeashore
Dogs: Yes, on a leash no longer than 6 feet
Trail surface: A mix of sand, dirt, and grass trails, as well as boardwalk

Land status: State park
Nearest town: Dewey Beach
Maps: National Geographic Trails Illustrated Topographic Map 772 (Delmarva Peninsula). You can also scan a QR code at the trailhead to access a digital trail guide on your smartphone with marked points of interest.
Amenities: None
Cell service: Reliable
Special considerations: There is a fee to enter Delaware Seashore State Park, but no fee station for Burton Island Nature Preserve, which is located behind the Indian River Marina.

FINDING THE TRAILHEAD

This hike begins to the left of a large trail kiosk behind the Indian River Marina at Delaware Seashore State Park. GPS: N38°36'57.0" / W75°04'18.9"

THE HIKE

The trailhead to reach Burton Island Nature Preserve is not a cinch to find, but it will be well worth your efforts to seek out this coastal trail tucked behind the Indian River Marina at Delaware Seashore State Park near Dewey Beach. Burton Island feels much like an annex, situated on its own on the south end of the state park. A small parking area for the trail is located at the north end of the marina. You will see a large trail kiosk to the right of the gravelly walkway that leads across the gently lapping Indian River Inlet.

Once you cross over to Burton Island, the wildly scenic views across the verdant wetlands are immediate. Depending on the season, you may also spy more than a few dead horseshoe crabs in a very small pond adjacent to the trail. The Delaware Bay region is home to the largest population of horseshoe crabs in the United States. It's also home to the world's largest concentration of spawning horseshoe crabs when they come ashore by the thousands in May and June.

As you proceed along, the Burton Island Trail will split at the 0.3-mile mark. It's a loop so you can go either way, but for the purposes of this hike, stay to the right for a counterclockwise hike. In a few more steps, cross over a boardwalk with views across the tidal wetlands. Near the 0.5-mile mark, you will notice two separate spur trails on the right—both very short—that lead off to the edge of the wooded area for views across the salt marsh grasses. Continue along and you'll reach another, more scenic spur trail

Walk through a grove of enchanting coastal pines as you hike across Burton Island Nature Preserve.

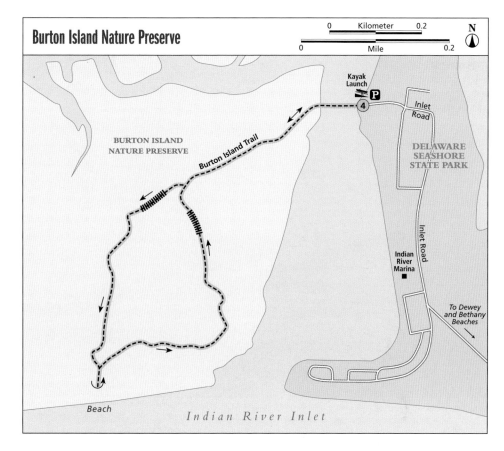

Burton Island Nature Preserve

0   Kilometer   0.2

0   Mile   0.2

N

Kayak Launch

4

Inlet Road

BURTON ISLAND NATURE PRESERVE

Burton Island Trail

DELAWARE SEASHORE STATE PARK

Inlet Road

Indian River Marina

To Dewey and Bethany Beaches

Beach

Indian River Inlet

on the right that guides to a small, driftwood-covered sandy beach with incredible views of the Indian River Inlet Bridge (officially the Charles W. Cullen Bridge). Here you can also see across the Indian River Bay to South Shore Marina, a privately owned housing community on the South Inlet. Waterfowl frequent the area, so look out for such birds as ospreys and silvery Forster's terns.

Retrace your steps to the Burton Island Trail, then turn right to continue on the loop. Keep your eyes open for the deep purple berries of the hackberry tree, a tree with cork-like bark that can be found across the state. Known to tolerate poor, sandy soils, it's not uncommon to find hackberry trees along coastal paths throughout Delaware. The small berries are not poisonous, but are best saved as sustenance for native birds and mammals. You'll also notice an abundance of loblolly pines on this side of the trail, with dead pine needles scattered about the sandy path.

At the 1.0-mile mark, cross a second boardwalk trail over a sensitive wetlands area before closing the loop at the 1.1-mile mark. Stay to the right, then retrace your steps to the trailhead. You will complete your hike at the 1.3-mile mark when you return to the parking area. Be wary that this hike is best done in any season but summer. Or at the very least, avoid hot, humid summer days when the bugs can be especially aggressive in the moist marshes along the Burton Island Trail.

For paddlers, there is a kayak launch to the right of the Burton Island Trail. Here you can drop in a kayak to paddle a 2.8-mile loop along the Cedar Island Water Trail, which circumnavigates Big Cedar Island and Little Cedar Island, which are north of Burton Island Nature Preserve.

MILES AND DIRECTIONS

0.0   Begin this hike to the left of the trail kiosk located behind the Indian River Marina.

0.3   The trail splits; stay to the right. Then, cross over a short section of boardwalk.

0.5   Reach two short spur trails on the right with views across the salt marsh grasses. In a few more steps, another spur trail appears on the right that leads to a small sandy beach.

1.0   Cross over a short section of boardwalk.

1.1   Close the loop, then stay right to retrace your steps to the parking area.

1.3   Arrive back at the parking area. Your hike is complete.

5 FORT DUPONT STATE PARK

Take in far-reaching views across the Delaware River, as well as historic military remains at this riverfront park in Delaware City.

Start: Fort DuPont State Park parking area
Elevation gain: 10 feet
Maximum grade: 1%
Distance: 1.3-mile lollipop
Difficulty: Easy
Hiking time: About 1 hour
Best seasons: Year-round
Fees and permits: $–$$
Trail contact: Fort DuPont State Park, Wilmington Avenue, Delaware City, DE; (302) 834-7941; destateparks.com/History/FortDupont
Dogs: Yes, on a leash no longer than 6 feet

Trail surface: A mix of dirt, grass, and gravel
Land status: State park
Nearest town: Delaware City
Maps: National Geographic Trails Illustrated Topographic Map 772 (Delmarva Peninsula). A printed park map is also available on the large trail kiosk adjacent to the parking area.
Amenities: Picnic tables, porta-potty
Cell service: Reliable
Special considerations: There is a fee to enter Fort DuPont State Park from March 1 to November 30, but no on-site fee station in the parking lot.

FINDING THE TRAILHEAD

The trailhead is located to the right of the large trail kiosk at the back of the parking area. GPS: N39°34'23.6" / W75°34'49.8"

THE HIKE

Fort DuPont State Park in Delaware City is a relatively small park that sits on the Delaware River, but it's steeped in military history that extends from the Civil War to World War II. The riverfront state park was named for Rear Admiral Samuel Francis DuPont, an esteemed US Navy officer and respected member of Delaware's prominent DuPont family. Fort DuPont was built as a coastal defense to shield key port cities, like Philadelphia and Wilmington, from enemy vessels navigating the Delaware River. Today, the River View Trail guides visitors across the land where this fort once stood, sidling past crumbling rapid-fire military batteries that remain standing today.

The trail begins just past the large trail kiosk that provides an overview of Fort DuPont State Park. Follow the yellow arrow to the right to begin walking alongside the Delaware River on a service road that affords wide-open views across the river. Take time to look across to Pea Patch Island, home to Fort Delaware, a Union fortification made of granite and brick that dates to 1859 and was once used to house Confederate prisoners during the Civil War. If you have time, board the small ferry at Battery Park that takes visitors on the 0.5-mile journey across the Delaware River to Pea Patch Island, home to Fort Delaware State Park, to explore the small island or walk the Prison Camp Trail (a separate fee applies).

Once you've taken in the views of Pea Patch Island, note that the River View Trail bends at the 0.3-mile mark and you will arrive at the remains of two historic structures.

Once a coastal defense, visitors can see both Battery Elder and Batteries Read and Gibson along this hiking trail.

On the left you'll see a standing chimney, as well as a ramp leading to a small observation tower for views across the river. On the right are the remains of Battery Elder, which was completed in 1910 and at one time had two 3-inch guns on pedestal mounts. Unfortunately, there are no placards or signage of any kind to educate visitors on the history of the remains.

Continue on and you will arrive at a yellow gate. Turn left here to proceed along a grass path. At the 0.6-mile mark, you will reach a much larger concrete military battery, a combined battery of Battery Read and Battery Gibson, which at one time had two 12-inch guns and two 8-inch guns. Walk to the end, then turn left when you see the yellow trail marker. Continue on this mostly shaded path until the 1.0-mile mark. At this point, you will reach the standing chimney once more and close the loop. Turn right past the chimney and retrace your steps to the parking area, once more savoring the views across the Delaware River. You will reach the trail kiosk at the 1.2-mile mark.

Post-hike, walk out to the point that's just past the trail kiosk. You'll find benches and a picnic table to enjoy the riverfront views. As you exit the park, note additional historic military buildings on the right and left that were once part of the larger military complex. Originally established as a military fort in 1863, Fort DuPont was dedicated as a state park in 1992.

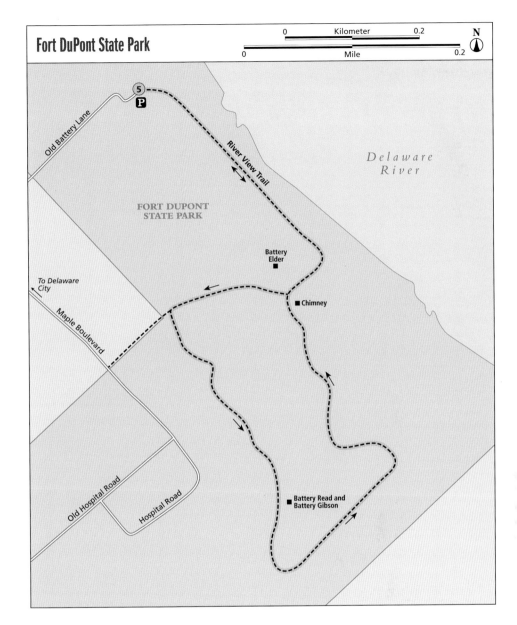

Delaware River

FORT DUPONT STATE PARK

Battery Elder

Chimney

To Delaware City

Battery Read and Battery Gibson

Old Battery Lane

River View Trail

Maple Boulevard

Old Hospital Road

Hospital Road

MILES AND DIRECTIONS

0.0 The trail begins to the right of the large trail kiosk in the parking area.

0.3 Arrive at a chimney, observation platform, and the remains of Battery Elder.

0.5 Reach a yellow gate. Turn left here to stay on the River View Trail.

0.6 Arrive at the remains of Battery Read and Battery Gibson.

The River View Trail at Fort DuPont State Park begins with a breezy stroll alongside the Delaware River.

1.0   Close the loop when you arrive at the chimney. Retrace your steps to the parking area.

1.3   Arrive back at the parking area. Your hike is complete.

6 GORDONS POND TRAIL

As one of the crown jewels in the Delaware State Parks system, a breezy hike at Cape Henlopen State Park in Lewes leads to overlooks across Gordons Pond, a scenic section of wooden boardwalk, and a sandy stroll on the beach with refreshing views across the Delaware Bay.

Start: Gordons Pond main parking lot
Elevation gain: 52 feet
Maximum grade: 3%
Distance: 4.7-mile loop
Difficulty: Easy
Hiking time: 2 to 3 hours
Best seasons: Year-round
Fees and permits: $-$$
Trail contact: Cape Henlopen State Park, 15099 Cape Henlopen Dr., Lewes, DE; (302) 645-8983; destateparks.com/Beaches/CapeHenlopen
Dogs: Yes, on a leash no longer than 6 feet

Trail surface: A mix of gravel and sand, as well as stretches of wooden boardwalk
Land status: State park
Nearest town: Lewes
Maps: National Geographic Trails Illustrated Topographic Map 772 (Delmarva Peninsula). A trail map is also available online at destateparks .com/Beaches/CapeHenlopen.
Other trail users: Cyclists
Amenities: Picnic tables, porta-potties, water bottle filling stations, picnic pavilion
Cell service: Reliable

FINDING THE TRAILHEAD

The trailhead is located in the northwest corner of the main parking lot for Gordons Pond. GPS: N38°44'31.8" / W75°04'55.8"

THE HIKE

Cape Henlopen State Park in Lewes is well-established as one of the crown jewels in the Delaware State Parks system. Set on the Delaware Bay and a stone's throw from the popular Cape May–Lewes Ferry, this state park is deserving of a spot on anyone's go list. The 7,000-acre park is one tract of land, but to go from south to north, you will need to exit the park, then reenter, so be sure to hold on to your day pass to re-present it at the entrance station.

Gordons Pond is located in the south section of Cape Henlopen State Park and can be accessed by way of the Gordons Pond Trail, a mostly gravel trail that's popular with pedestrians and cyclists. The trail sets off from the northwest corner of the parking lot and to the left of a service road. It enjoys alternating stretches of full sun and shade thanks to a smattering of coastal pines alongside the flat path that follows along the pond. There are benches scattered along the trail, too, when you want to take a break and savor the views across Gordons Pond.

At the 0.7-mile mark, you will arrive at a popular two-story overlook for bird's-eye views of the freshwater pond. As you continue along, you may spy various migratory birds, like ibis, egrets, and herons, wading in the shallow waters. More than 280 species of birds can be seen at Cape Henlopen State Park at various times during the year. A second overlook turns up on the right at the 2.2-mile mark with views across the verdant

wetlands before you step foot onto a wooden boardwalk at the 2.4-mile mark. This takes you across sensitive sand dunes and has an overlook on the left near the end of the stretch of boardwalk.

You will arrive at a large trail kiosk at the 2.6-mile mark. This marks the end of the Gordons Pond Trail, but there's more to come on this coastal walk. From here, turn right and then left to walk around a large parking area. On the other side of the lot is a small road that leads up to Herring Point, which is home to a former military bunker and a beach access point. In-season, a shaved ice truck is known to park at the top of the parking area. What a nice surprise on a warm, sunny day. At the top of Herring Point, which overlooks the public beach, several benches and picnic tables welcome park visitors.

Walk along the short trail that leads to the public beach, then turn right once you reach the beach to proceed south. After a few steps you'll notice a quiet section of shoreline—as in, no children frolicking in the surf or building sand castles. This 1.5-mile stretch of beach is set aside for surf fishing. You may see four-wheel-drive vehicles parked on the beach with fishing poles out, lines well into the water, hoping to reel in the big catch.

Take your shoes off if you like to enjoy the ocean waves lapping against your feet as you walk along this stretch of coastline. If nothing else, it can be a lot easier to walk on sand in bare feet than with shoes on, even sandals or flip-flops. At the 4.1-mile mark, you will arrive at the first of two observation towers. The second is just 0.2 mile past the first one. They are not for public use, but instead are called fire towers and were used as watch towers by the US Army during World War II. There are eleven 75–foot–tall watch towers in Delaware and southern New Jersey. In the north section of the park, you'll find Fort Miles, which is home to Tower #7, which can be climbed by visitors for panoramic views of the park. On a clear day, it's said that you can see across more than 14 miles of coastline. During World War II, soldiers manned the towers to watch for approaching enemy ships and submarines.

Continue on and you will see the next beach access point at the 4.6-mile mark. Turn right here and once off the beach, you will arrive at the Gordons Pond parking area. Your hike is complete at the 4.7-mile mark.

MILES AND DIRECTIONS

0.0   The trail begins in the northwest corner of the main parking lot for Gordons Pond.

0.7   Arrive at a two-story overlook for views across Gordons Pond.

2.2   Reach a second overlook for views across the tidal wetlands area.

2.4   Cross over a wooden boardwalk and stop at the overlook for views across the dunes.

A large trail kiosk guides visitors across multiple hiking trails at Cape Henlopen State Park.

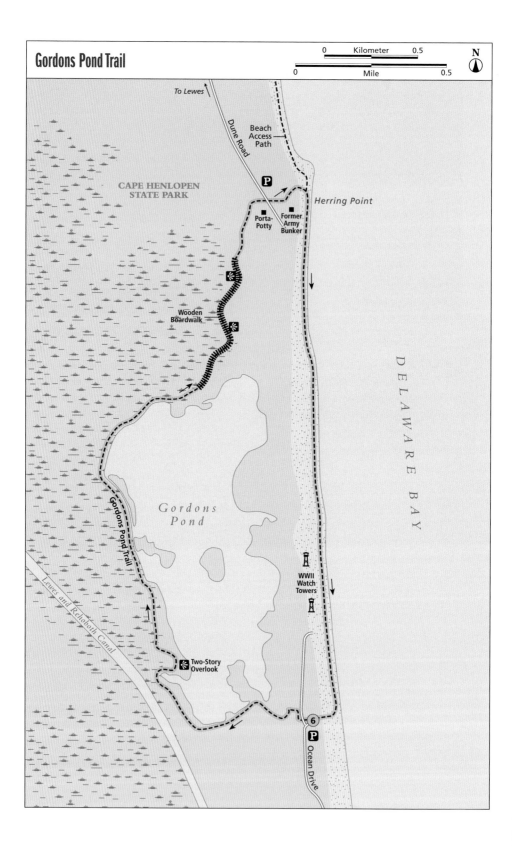

Gordons Pond Trail

0   Kilometer   0.5

0   Mile   0.5

N

To Lewes

Dune Road

Beach
Access
Path

**CAPE HENLOPEN
STATE PARK**

P

Porta-
Potty

Former
Army
Bunker

Herring Point

Wooden
Boardwalk

D E L A W A R E   B A Y

*Gordons
Pond*

Gordons Pond Trail

Lewes and Rehoboth Canal

WWII
Watch
Towers

Two-Story
Overlook

6

P

Ocean Drive

2.6 Reach a large trail kiosk. Turn right here, then left, to walk around the large parking area to reach Herring Point, home to public beach access and a former military bunker. Exit to the beach, then continue south along the shore.

4.1 Arrive at the first of two World War II fire towers on the beach.

4.3 Reach the second World War II fire tower.

4.6 Turn right to exit the beach at the public beach access point.

4.7 Arrive back at the parking area. Your hike is complete.

7 JAMES FARM ECOLOGICAL PRESERVE

The land of a longtime family farm is today an ecological preserve dedicated to protecting wildlife, restoring habitats, fostering environmental education, and allowing for joy through outdoor recreation on its sandy beach, hiking trails, tidal wetlands, and observation platforms.

Start: James Farm Ecological Preserve parking area
Elevation gain: 30 feet
Maximum grade: 2%
Distance: 1.7-mile loop
Difficulty: Easy
Hiking time: About 1 hour
Best seasons: Year-round
Fees and permits: Free
Trail contact: James Farm Ecological Preserve, 30048 Cedar Neck Rd., Ocean View, DE; (302) 226-8105; inlandbays.org/projects-and-issues/all/james-farm-preserve

Dogs: Yes, on a leash no longer than 6 feet
Trail surface: A mix of sand, gravel, dirt, and grass, as well as short boardwalk sections
Land status: County park
Nearest town: Bethany Beach
Maps: National Geographic Trails Illustrated Topographic Map 772 (Delmarva Peninsula). Park maps are also available at the trail kiosk in the parking area.
Amenities: Porta-potties
Cell service: Reliable

FINDING THE TRAILHEAD

The trailhead is located next to a large trail kiosk toward the front of the parking area. GPS: N38°34'29.9" / W75°04'46.2"

THE HIKE

The 150-acre James Farm property was gifted to Sussex County, Delaware, in 1992 by longtime resident Mary Lighthipe, the last direct descendant of the James family. After many years as a family farm, and many generations of family working on the farm, Lighthipe donated the property on the condition that the farm be used as a source of recreation and environmental education. In 1998, Sussex County tapped the Delaware Center for the Inland Bays to manage the property, thereby transforming this working farm into an ecological preserve for all to enjoy free of charge.

Today, visitors come to the James Farm Ecological Preserve for 3 miles of hiking trails, wooden lookout platforms, wildflower gardens, and a sandy beach at Pasture Point Cove. More than 4,000 trees have also been planted across the preserve as part of a reforestation project to benefit local wildlife, including migratory birds like the great egret and snowy egret. For paddlers, a local outfitter arranges kayak and stand-up paddleboard rentals, classes, and tours of the Indian River Bay from the preserve (fee applies).

One look at the trail map and you may note that every color of the rainbow is represented on the list of hiking trails. It's true, and what's more, this loop hike around the preserve touches five of the six colors. Only the short and simple Yellow Trail is not included in this perimeter hike. From the trail kiosk, walk straight back along the Red Trail on a path made of crushed oyster shells. At the 0.1-mile mark, jog left, then right, to

The Red Trail leads to a sandy beach on Pasture Point Cove at James Farm Ecological Preserve.

Migratory waterfowl, like snowy egrets and great egrets, frequent the shoreline at James Farm Ecological Preserve.

stay on this easy trail. In a few more steps, you'll catch a glimpse of the Bayshore Mobile Home Park on the left. A short spur trail allows nature-loving residents quick and easy access to James Farm Ecological Preserve.

Continue on, then stay left to connect with the Blue Trail at the 0.3-mile mark to reach a wooden observation platform. A dozen steps lead up to a small platform that wows with scenic views across the wetlands, even as far as the Indian River Bay. From here, keep walking on the Blue Trail, which guides visitors through a delightful grove of fragrant loblolly pines that are so tall they seem to touch the sky.

At the 0.5-mile mark, stay left to reconnect with the Red Trail, which leads visitors on a wooden boardwalk across marsh grasses to reach the sandy beach at Pasture Point Cove on Indian River Bay. The north-facing views are especially spectacular. On the west end, keep your eyes open for migratory birds, like egrets, hunting for treasures in the gently lapping waters. This is a great spot to enjoy a picnic lunch. Retrace your steps to the Red Trail, then turn left to continue on the loop. At the 0.6-mile mark, turn left for the Orange Trail and traverse a short section of boardwalk through the coastal forest.

Enjoy this shady, easygoing section of trail but stay alert, as you'll reach a fork at the 0.8-mile mark. Turn left here to connect with the Green Trail. If you're keeping track, you've now stepped foot on four different colors of trails. Just one more to go, but first, a two-story observation blind turns up at the 0.9-mile mark. Step up to the top for views across the marsh, and perhaps a sighting of a heron or hawk.

Continue past the observation blind to connect with the Purple Trail, which crosses over Cedar Neck Road at the 1.1-mile mark to reach the east section of the ecological

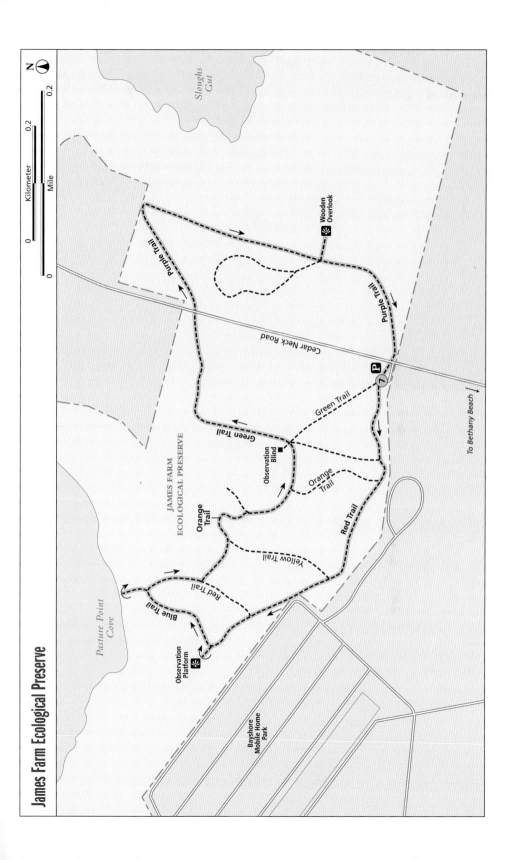

James Farm Ecological Preserve

Observation Platform

Blue Trail

Pasture Point Cove

Red Trail

Yellow Trail

Orange Trail

Bayshore Mobile Home Park

JAMES FARM ECOLOGICAL PRESERVE

Orange Trail

Observation Blind

Green Trail

Green Trail

Red Trail

Cedar Neck Road

To Bethany Beach

Purple Trail

Purple Trail

Wooden Overlook

Sloughs Gut

N

Kilometer

0   0.2   0.2

0   0.2

Mile

preserve. This section is largely a reforestation area, though you can take in views of Sloughs Gut from a wooden overlook that's just off the trail at the 1.5-mile mark. This is the site of a significant habitat enhancement project to return naturally flowing water into the marsh. Proceed on the Purple Trail and you will once again reach Cedar Neck Road. Cross at the crosswalk to return to the parking area and trail kiosk. Your hike is complete at the 1.7-mile mark.

MILES AND DIRECTIONS

- **0.0** The Red Trail begins next to a large trail kiosk toward the front of the parking area.
- **0.3** Stay left to connect with the Blue Trail, then climb a dozen steps to reach the top of a wooden observation platform for views across the wetlands.
- **0.5** Stay left to reconnect with the Red Trail. Then, walk across a wooden boardwalk to a sandy beach at Pasture Point Cove. Retrace your steps, then stay left for the Red Trail.
- **0.6** Turn left to connect with the Orange Trail.
- **0.8** Arrive at a fork on a section of wooden boardwalk. Stay left for the Green Trail.
- **0.9** Reach a two-story observation blind. Continue past the blind to connect with the Purple Trail.
- **1.1** Cross over Cedar Neck Road. Note, there is no crosswalk.
- **1.5** Arrive at a wooden overlook for views across Sloughs Gut.
- **1.7** Cross Cedar Neck Road at the crosswalk, and arrive back at the parking area and trail kiosk. Your hike is complete.

8 PORT PENN WETLANDS TRAIL

Revel in the views across two stretches of tidal wetlands, as well as far-reaching panoramas across the Delaware River, on this relaxing hike in the historic village of Port Penn.

Start: Across the road from the Port Penn Interpretive Center
Elevation gain: 46 feet
Maximum grade: 2%
Distance: 2.8 miles out and back
Difficulty: Easy
Hiking time: 1.5 to 2 hours
Best seasons: Year-round
Fees and permits: Free
Trail contact: Port Penn Interpretive Center, 5 Port Penn Rd., Middletown, DE; (302) 834-7941; destateparks .com/PortPenn

Dogs: Yes, on a leash no longer than 6 feet
Trail surface: A mix of paved, gravel, and grass trails, as well as sections of wooden boardwalk
Land status: State park
Nearest town: Middletown
Maps: National Geographic Trails Illustrated Topographic Map 772 (Delmarva Peninsula)
Amenities: Porta-potty
Cell service: Reliable

FINDING THE TRAILHEAD

The trailhead is located across Port Penn Road from the Port Penn Interpretive Center. GPS: N39°31'05.7" / W75°34'43.6"

THE HIKE

The Port Penn Wetlands Trail begins across Port Penn Road from the Port Penn Interpretive Center in Middletown. This easy hiking trail affords spectacular views across tidal marshes and the Delaware River. But first, visitors receive an education on the life and times of those who once made a living from the natural resources of the Delaware River, including fishermen and fur trappers. A floating fishing cabin sits to the left of the trail with a placard describing how floating cabins and muskrat-skinning shacks were once symbols of the marsh. Nineteenth-century outdoorsmen made their livings in the marsh trapping muskrats to sell their pelts and fishing for sturgeon to sell their roe (as caviar).

In a few steps, you will reach the start of a stretch of wooden boardwalk that crosses the marsh. Settle in for a few minutes on the bench in the middle for views of wading birds. You may even see an egret or two land on the hand railing. The boardwalk ends at the 0.1-mile mark and the path changes to mowed grass. You will arrive at a small wooden observation platform at the 0.3-mile mark for views across the marsh. This overlook is at a T-intersection. You must turn right or left, but there is no signage to indicate which way is the right way to go. Turn right here and you will shortly reach North Congress Street.

At North Congress Street, turn left to walk alongside the paved road. On the right, you can see across a tidal wetlands area, maybe all the way to the Delaware River. At this point, you may not be sure you are still on a trail, but continue north on this paved road. You will wind around a building complex for the Delaware Division of Fish and Wildlife. At the 0.5-mile mark, the road ends at a porta-potty and a gate across this road.

The Port Penn Wetlands Trail begins across the street from the Port Penn Interpretive Center, which features a historic schoolhouse.

Settle in on a wooden bench for views across the wetlands on the Port Penn Wetlands Trail.

Walk around the gate and you'll note that the trail picks back up and turns into a mostly gravel path, guiding you alongside a scenic wetlands area on the left that is frequented by migratory birds. The Delaware River is on the right as you walk along a narrow strip of land. At the 1.1-mile mark, this full-sun gravel path turns west away from the Delaware River and comes to an end at the 1.4-mile mark. From here, retrace your steps to the trailhead for the Port Penn Wetlands Trail.

From time to time, the Port Penn Interpretive Center hosts free, guided Wetlands Walk programs to educate visitors on the importance of the wetlands to the Port Penn community. Check in with the center for dates and times. For further views across the wetlands, there are two overlooks within the neighboring Augustine Wildlife Area. One is in the Penn Tract, just north of the Port Penn Interpretive Center on Port Penn Road. The second overlook is in the Ashton Tract. To reach this overlook, drive north on Port Penn Road, then turn left onto Thorntown Road. Turn right at the sign for the Ashton Tract and drive to the parking area at the end of the gravel road. A short spur trail leads to the overlook.

MILES AND DIRECTIONS

0.0 Begin at the trailhead across Port Penn Road from the Port Penn Interpretive Center. In a few steps, arrive at the floating cabin on the left and wooden boardwalk over the marsh.

0.3 Turn right at the wooden observation platform. Then, turn left onto paved North Congress Street, which winds around a building complex for the Delaware Division of Fish and Wildlife.

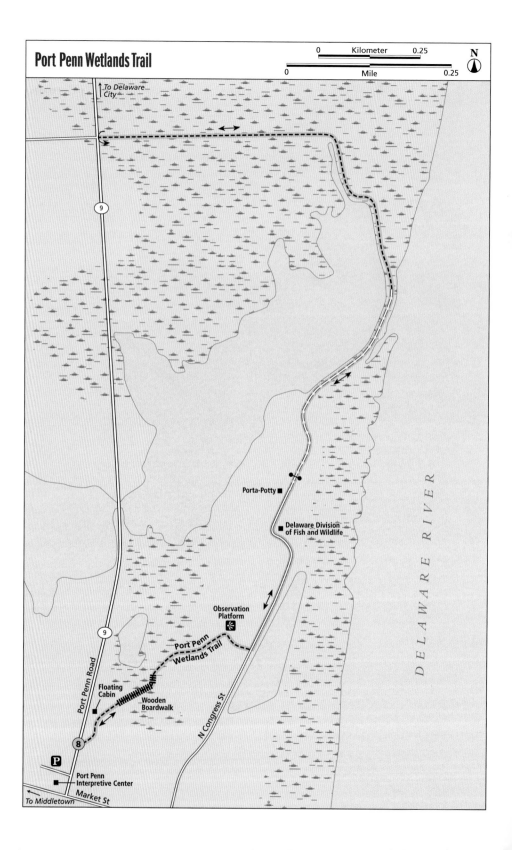

Port Penn Wetlands Trail

0   Kilometer   0.25

0   Mile   0.25

N

↑ To Delaware City

9

DELAWARE RIVER

Porta-Potty ■

■ Delaware Division of Fish and Wildlife

Observation Platform

9

Port Penn Road

Port Penn Wetlands Trail

N Congress St.

Floating Cabin

Wooden Boardwalk

8

P

■ Port Penn Interpretive Center

Market St

← To Middletown

Keep your eyes open for waterfowl, like the great blue heron, that spend time in the wetlands at the Augustine Wildlife Area.

0.5 The road ends at a gate. Walk around the gate and continue on the gravel path. The wetlands will soon come into view on the left side of the trail.

1.4 The trail comes to an end. Retrace your steps to the trailhead.

2.8 Arrive back at the trailhead. Your hike is complete.

9 SEAHAWK TRAIL

The easygoing Seahawk Trail at Holts Landing State Park in Southern Delaware charms with a vibrant mix of freshwater ponds, tidal marshes, sandy beaches, and maritime forest.

Start: Holts Landing State Park main parking area
Elevation gain: 16 feet
Maximum grade: 1%
Distance: 1.5-mile loop
Difficulty: Easy
Hiking time: About 1 hour
Best seasons: Year-round
Fees and permits: $-$$
Trail contact: Holts Landing State Park, 27046 Holts Landing Rd., Dagsboro, DE; (302) 227-2800; destateparks.com/HoltsLanding
Dogs: Yes, on a leash no longer than 6 feet

Trail surface: A mix of sand, gravel, and dirt, as well as boardwalk sections
Land status: State park
Nearest town: Bethany Beach
Maps: National Geographic Trails Illustrated Topographic Map 772 (Delmarva Peninsula). A trail map is also available online at destateparks.com/HoltsLanding.
Amenities: Restrooms, picnic tables, playground, horseshoe pits, soccer field, fishing pier
Cell service: Reliable

FINDING THE TRAILHEAD

The trailhead is located to the left of a large trail kiosk on the south side of the parking area. GPS: N38°35'24.4" / W75°07'41.9"

THE HIKE

At 203-acre Holts Landing State Park on the Indian River Bay in Southern Delaware, enjoy a variety of landscapes, including sandy beaches, hardwood forest, and tidal grasses, along an easy and accessible 1.5-mile hike. The trailhead is a cinch to find, though little ones may have their eyes trained on the children's playground just to the left of the start of the trail. Thankfully, this is a short and sweet hike, leaving time for slides and climbing structures.

The hike begins to the left of the large trail kiosk next to the parking area. From here, the path winds into the forest, quickly leading to a placard in front of a hackberry grove. While the park is home to trees common to Southern Delaware, like loblolly pines, holly, and cedars, it's also home to the native hackberry tree, which produces deep purple berries in September and October.

Continue on and you'll cross a short section of boardwalk trail at the 0.1-mile mark. Keep moving through the shaded forest and you will come upon several small ponds. These are referred to as "borrow pits," per a placard alongside the trail. The park land was purchased from the Holt family, and in 1957 the State Highway Department excavated some of the soil for use in other area projects. The "borrow pits" left behind collected rainwater and became freshwater ponds that are today a comfortable habitat for painted turtles and wood ducks. Some fish species also call these ponds home, including the eastern mosquitofish and the inland silverside. Several well-placed benches alongside the ponds allow for rest, relaxation, and reflection as you stroll this coastal path.

Continue following the signs for the yellow Seahawk Trail. At the 0.9-mile mark, turn right to continue on this gravel trail. In a few more steps, at the 1.1-mile mark, you will reach a fork in the trail. Stay to the left to walk out to the beach on the Indian River. Look left to see an elevated nesting platform created for migratory birds, like ospreys and herons. Revel in the views across the riverfront, then retrace your steps to the Seahawk Trail. Turn left to continue on. You'll reach a short section of boardwalk across a tidal marsh at the 1.5-mile mark. At the other end is the west end of the parking area to complete your hike.

MILES AND DIRECTIONS

- **0.0** Begin this hike to the left of the trail kiosk located on the south side of the main parking area.
- **0.1** Cross a short section of boardwalk trail.
- **0.2** Arrive at one or more "borrow pits," which today are small freshwater ponds.
- **0.9** Turn right to stay on the Seahawk Trail.

Holts Landing State Park sits along the Indian River, affording gorgeous coastal views from several small sandy beaches.

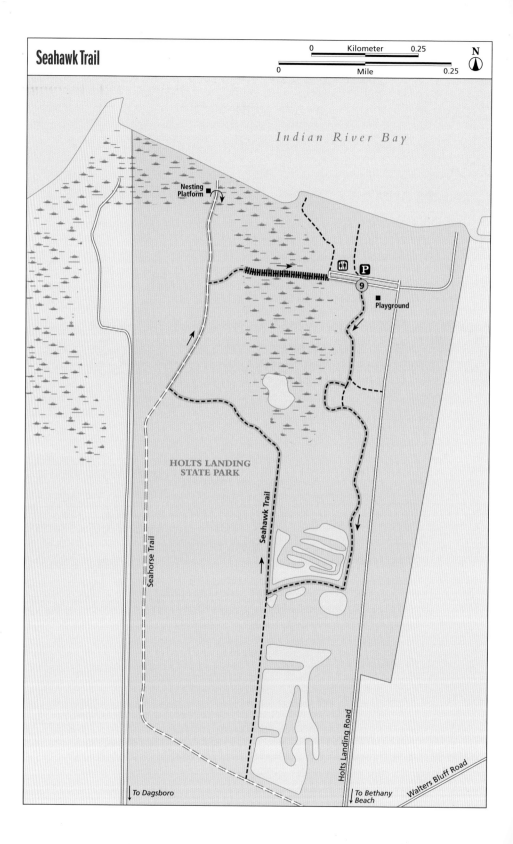

Seahawk Trail

0   Kilometer   0.25

0   Mile   0.25

N

Indian River Bay

Nesting
Platform

Playground

9

HOLTS LANDING
STATE PARK

Seahorse Trail

Seahawk Trail

Holts Landing Road

Walters Bluff Road

To Dagsboro

To Bethany
Beach

As you look out onto the pond along the Seahawk Trail, keep your eyes open for wood ducks and painted turtles.

1.1   Reach a fork in the trail. Stay left to walk out to the sandy beach. Retrace your steps, then turn left when you reach the main trail.

1.4   Cross a short section of boardwalk over a tidal marsh to reach the west end of the parking area.

1.5   Walk east across the parking lot to arrive back and the trailhead and complete your hike.

10 THOMPSON ISLAND NATURE PRESERVE

A short hike leads to far-reaching views across verdant tidal wetlands on a parcel of land with spiritual significance to local Native American tribespeople.

Start: Parking area at the end of Bay Road
Elevation gain: 26 feet
Maximum grade: 2%
Distance: 1.4 miles out and back
Difficulty: Easy
Hiking time: About 1 hour
Best seasons: Year-round
Fees and permits: Free
Trail contact: Delaware Seashore State Park, 39415 Inlet Rd., Rehoboth Beach, DE; (302) 227-2800; destateparks.com/Beaches/DelawareSeashore
Dogs: Yes, on a leash no longer than 6 feet
Trail surface: Mostly gravel trail, some wooden boardwalk

Land status: State park
Nearest town: Dewey Beach
Maps: National Geographic Trails Illustrated Topographic Map 772 (Delmarva Peninsula). A trail map is also available online at destateparks .com/Beaches/DelawareSeashore.
Amenities: None
Cell service: Reliable
Special considerations: There is a fee to enter Delaware Seashore State Park, but no fee station for Thompon Island Nature Preserve, which is located on a separate tract of land 15 minutes north of the coastal state park.

FINDING THE TRAILHEAD

Begin this hike from the trail at the back of the small parking area at the end of Bay Road at Thompson Island Nature Preserve. GPS: N38°42'15.9" / W75°05'24.1"

THE HIKE

One look at the map and you'll notice that the 68-acre Thompson Island Nature Preserve isn't actually on an island, but rather a scenic peninsula that juts out into the Rehoboth Bay. It's got history, too. The peninsula is known as *Tawundeunk*—or "the place where we bury our dead"—in the native Algonquin language spoken by the Nanticoke tribespeople whose lands are located in the Chesapeake Bay and coastal Delaware regions. In May 2000, Thompson Island Nature Preserve was dedicated and a formal agreement was put in place to ensure the sacred land is preserved and protected for the Nanticoke people. Today, visitors can freely and respectfully stroll the well-shaded conifer forest. A crushed gravel trail leads to views across tidal wetlands alongside the Lewes and Rehoboth Canal, even as far as the Rehoboth Bay.

The hike along the Thompson Island Trail begins from a parking area at the end of Bay Road in a small neighborhood between Rehoboth Beach and Dewey Beach. It's a small lot, with room for no more than six cars. As you begin the drive down the gravel road to the parking area, you'll see a small brown sign on the right for Thompson Island Nature Preserve, but otherwise, you may have no idea it's there. Once you park your car, you'll note that there is still no signage of any kind. You'll see a trail for pedestrians only

A two-level wooden overlook offers views across the verdant wetlands, a favorite destination among migratory birds.

that leads off to the south, as if an extension of the gravel road, but nothing else to indicate you're in the right place. Not to worry, this is the place.

Begin walking along this peaceful shaded path. The early part of the trail runs adjacent to Spring Lake Drive, so you'll see a few peeks of homes through the trees, but it's still very quiet. At the 0.2-mile mark, you'll reach a large trail kiosk with a colorful trail map, your first proof positive that you are on the correct path. Continue right around the bend and you'll reach a short stretch of boardwalk across a sensitive wetlands area at the 0.4-mile mark. On the other side is a wooden bench for those eager for a quick break to take in the coastal views.

At the 0.7-mile mark, arrive at a two-level wooden observation deck with two benches that are just right for viewing migratory birds, like egrets and herons, in the wide-open marshes. From here, retrace your steps to the parking area to complete your hike.

As a part of Delaware Seashore State Park, park interpreters periodically offer 90-minute guided hikes across the Thompson Island Nature Preserve. Park staff educate visitors on the preserve's Native American significance, as well as wildlife that call this peninsula home.

MILES AND DIRECTIONS

0.0   Begin this hike from the parking area at the end of Bay Drive.

0.2   Arrive at a large trail kiosk with a trail map.

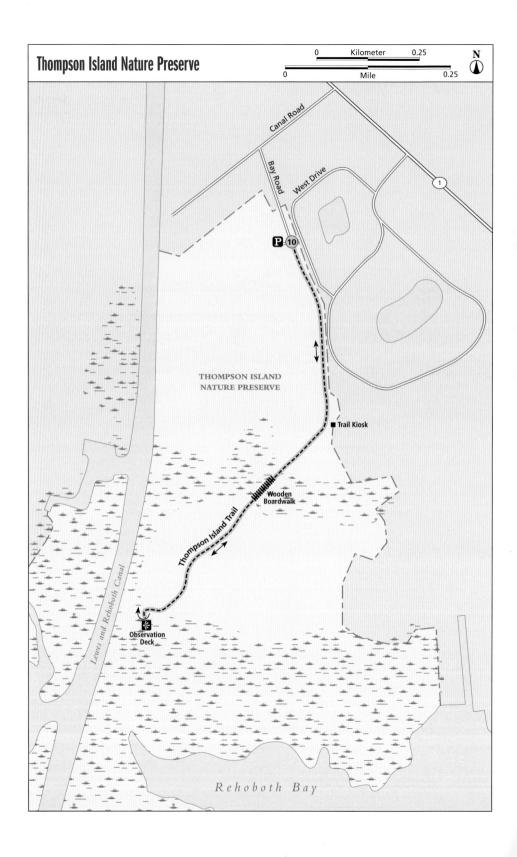

Thompson Island Nature Preserve

0   Kilometer   0.25

0   Mile   0.25

N

Canal Road

Bay Road

West Drive

1

P 10

THOMPSON ISLAND
NATURE PRESERVE

Trail Kiosk

Wooden
Boardwalk

Thompson Island Trail

Lewes and Rehoboth Canal

Observation
Deck

Rehoboth Bay

Take a seat on the wooden bench at the end of the boardwalk to enjoy the views before continuing on to the overlook at the end of the trail.

0.4 Cross a wooden boardwalk over a sensitive wetlands area.

0.7 Reach the two-story observation deck for views across the verdant marsh. Retrace your steps to the parking area.

1.4 Arrive back at the parking area. Your hike is complete.

11 BEVERLY TRITON NATURE PARK

The former site of one of the most popular beach resorts on the Chesapeake Bay is today home to a woodland area with a fishing pond, tidal wetlands, and a natural shoreline.

Start: Parking area on Triton Beach Road
Elevation gain: 46 feet
Maximum grade: 2%
Distance: 2.8-mile loop
Difficulty: Easy
Hiking time: 1.5 to 2 hours
Best seasons: Year-round
Fees and permits: Free
Trail contact: Beverly Triton Nature Park, 1202 Triton Beach Rd., Edgewater, MD; (410) 222-7317; aacounty.org/departments/

recreation-parks/parks/beverly-triton
Dogs: Yes, on a leash no longer than 6 feet
Trail surface: Mostly dirt and sand trails, some boardwalk sections
Land status: County park
Nearest town: Annapolis
Maps: National Geographic Trails Illustrated Topographic Map 772 (Delmarva Peninsula)
Amenities: Porta-potty
Cell service: Reliable

FINDING THE TRAILHEAD

The trailhead for the Trident Trail is on the right once you enter from the parking area on Triton Beach Road. GPS: N38°53'05.3" / W76°29'43.7"

THE HIKE

At Beverly Triton Nature Park in Anne Arundel County, Maryland, a loop hike around the park guides visitors through a shady forest, around a pond, and alongside a sandy beach on the Chesapeake Bay. Quietly tucked away on the Mayo Peninsula, many have no idea that this parcel of land was once the site of the most popular private resort on the Chesapeake Bay, complete with bustling cabanas, sunbathers, big bands, and slot machines. The resort closed in 1968 when the owner lost a federal court battle to keep the resort as whites-only.

This stunning 340-acre stretch of undeveloped bayfront is now part of a county park and is hardly visited for its white sand beach. There are fewer than a dozen parking spaces, none of which are close to the sand and shore. For those able to snatch a space, a calming woodland awaits where the cherry on top is the small yet pristine white sand beach. For clarity, it's a natural shoreline, as it is not a swimming beach. You will, however, find more than 5 miles of nature trails.

From the small parking area on Triton Beach Road, this hike begins on the yellow-blazed Trident Trail, which is on the right once you enter from the parking area. Your first steps are on a wide, shaded path, which looks more like a service road than a hiking trail. At the 0.1-mile mark is a directional sign of sorts. No trails are noted. You see only colored arrows: red, brown, and yellow. At this point, turn right (brown arrow) onto an unnamed service road. At the 0.2-mile mark, turn right onto the orange-blazed Pond Trail, which circumnavigates Deep Pond. It's a relaxing walk, but one also known for sensitive and unstable terrain, as you'll note a two-slat-wide wooden boardwalk that guides you across select sections, which can get quite muddy after a good rain.

Keep your eyes open for the wooden teepee on the pristine white sandy beach at the end of this hike.

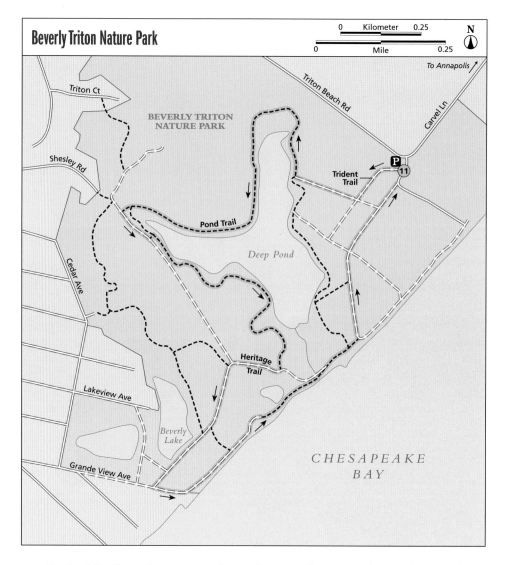

Beverly Triton Nature Park

0   Kilometer   0.25

0   Mile   0.25

N

To Annapolis

Triton Ct

BEVERLY TRITON
NATURE PARK

Triton Beach Rd

Carvel Ln

Shesley Rd

Trident
Trail

P

11

Pond Trail

Cedar Ave

Deep Pond

Heritage
Trail

Lakeview Ave

Beverly
Lake

CHESAPEAKE
BAY

Grande View Ave

By the 0.6-mile mark, you come close to Deep Pond. Step out close to the water for gorgeous waterside views. As you continue along, you'll reach a junction at the 0.9-mile mark. Turn left to stay on the Pond Trail. In a few more steps, turn left at the orange arrow to step closer to the pond. From here on, the pond views are fantastic, especially on a clear blue-sky day.

At the 1.5-mile mark, there is another arrow–oriented trail sign. Turn right for the red-blazed Heritage Trail, which traverses a forest to reach a fishing pond and a sandy beach. The trail continues to the far south end of the park before looping back for a walk mostly along the beach. Note the closed section of trail at the 1.6-mile mark. In spring, the section on the right transforms into a vernal pool that provides a nutrient-rich breeding habitat for frogs, toads, and salamanders.

Beverly Lake is a popular spot with anglers eager to catch a fish or two at Beverly Triton Nature Park.

At the 1.8-mile mark, Beverly Lake comes into view on the right. This is a popular spot with anglers. At the 1.9-mile mark, turn left to continue the walk, first parallel to the sandy beach, then closer, on the beach. At the 2.3-mile mark, a wooden teepee makes a nice photo op. In a few more steps, at the 2.4-mile mark, turn left to take this trail all the way back to the parking area. Your hike is complete at the 2.8-mile mark.

MILES AND DIRECTIONS

0.0 Begin on the Trident Trail. You will see a yellow trail sign on the right once you enter the park from the small parking area.

0.1 Turn right at the directional arrow sign. Follow the brown arrow onto a service road.

0.2 Turn right at the orange arrow onto the Pond Trail.

0.9 At a trail junction, turn left to stay on the Pond Trail.

1.5 Turn right for the red-blazed Heritage Trail.

1.6 Reach a closed section that is home to a vernal pool in spring.

1.8 Beverly Lake turns up on the right. This is a popular fishing spot with anglers.

1.9 Turn left to loop around and walk parallel to, then alongside, the natural shoreline.

2.4 Turn left to take the trail back to the parking area.

2.8 Arrive back at the parking area. Your hike is complete.

12 BLACK MARSH LOOP

This hike wows with spectacular wetlands views, as well as historic relics from the Bay Shore Amusement Park, a popular summer destination that drew in visitors with bumper cars, carnival games, and a merry-go-round from 1906 to 1947.

Start: Parking area on the left, just past the entrance to North Point State Park
Elevation gain: 30 feet
Maximum grade: 1%
Distance: 2.4-mile loop
Difficulty: Easy
Hiking time: 1 to 1.5 hours
Best seasons: Year-round
Fees and permits: $-$$
Trail contact: North Point State Park, 8400 North Point Rd., Edgemere, MD; (410) 477-0757; dnr.maryland.gov/publiclands/Pages/central/northpoint.aspx
Dogs: Yes, on a leash no longer than 6 feet

Trail surface: Mostly dirt and gravel trails
Land status: State park
Nearest town: Baltimore
Maps: National Geographic Trails Illustrated Topographic Map 772 (Delmarva Peninsula). A park map can also be found in a box marked Trail Maps in the parking area.
Other trail users: Cyclists (only on the Hiker-Biker Trail and Wetlands Trail sections of this hike)
Amenities: Porta-potty, picnic tables, swimming beach, fishing pier
Cell service: Reliable

FINDING THE TRAILHEAD

The trailhead is located in the northeast corner of the parking area that's on the left, just past the entrance to North Point State Park. GPS: N39°13'14.3" / W76°25'48.7"

THE HIKE

Situated on the Chesapeake Bay, North Point State Park in Edgemere is a stone's throw from Baltimore. Uniquely, this 1,310-acre state park was once home to Bay Shore Amusement Park, a popular waterside destination frequented by summer visitors from 1906 to 1947. Here you'll find relics of the 20-acre amusement destination, including the old trolley station (now a covered picnic area) and an ornamental water fountain.

This hike begins from the parking area just past the entrance station. You'll see a marker noting the white-blazed Black Marsh Trail and a gravel path leading into the leafy forest and ultimately to the Black Marsh Natural Area, a protected state wildlands area. Before you begin, look for a mailbox in the lot that holds trail maps to help guide you across the park.

As you proceed along the shaded trail, you will spy small placards here and there educating on wildlife found across the park, including green herons, pileated woodpeckers, and muskrats. At the 0.3-mile mark, you will reach Black Marsh. Walk along a delicate strip of land no more than 10 feet wide that cuts across the marsh for 0.1 mile. The views on either side across the wetlands are spectacular. There are many spots along this thin strip where visitors can pop out to get very close to the marsh for first-rate photos.

The loop hike at North Point State Park begins with a scenic walk across the wetlands of the Black Marsh Natural Area.

A short spur trail leads out to a cliff overlooking a rocky beach on the Chesapeake Bay.

At the 0.4-mile mark, you will reach a trail marker for the light blue–blazed Observation Trail. From the trail name, you may be naturally moved to venture down this forested path to see what there is to observe. However, it's worth skipping. If you do opt to check it out, you will reach a red wooden platform tucked into an overgrown section of 10-foot-tall wetland reeds that block all views across the marsh. Tacking on this short trail adds an extra 0.7 mile to the overall hike.

Bypassing the Observation Trail, you will continue along the marsh with views primarily on the right-hand side across the wetlands. At the 0.7-mile mark, an old graffiti-laden concrete powerhouse comes into view. It's both curious and curiously out of place. The generators here once supplied voltage to amusement park rides, as well as to city streetcars in nearby Baltimore. There is a No Trespassing sign, but it's clear that many visitors cut through the old powerhouse to see what it's about, then quickly reconnect with the Black Marsh Trail on the other side.

At the 0.8-mile mark, a short trail on the left leads to a cliff overlooking a rocky beach on the Chesapeake Bay. It's a nice view, but note that there is no railing and it's at least 10 to 15 feet above the beach, so there is no way to access the water from this overlook. There are two more similar viewpoints within the next few steps on this scenic trail.

Turn left at the 1.0-mile mark onto the blue-blazed Ferry Grove Trail. This short forested trail leads to a crumbling concrete pier that was once part of Bay Shore Amusement Park. At one time, visitors could reach the park by steamboat from Baltimore, which dropped them off at the Ferry Grove Pier. Today, a metal fence keeps visitors from proceeding past the end of the trail and onto the deteriorating pier. It's fun to imagine

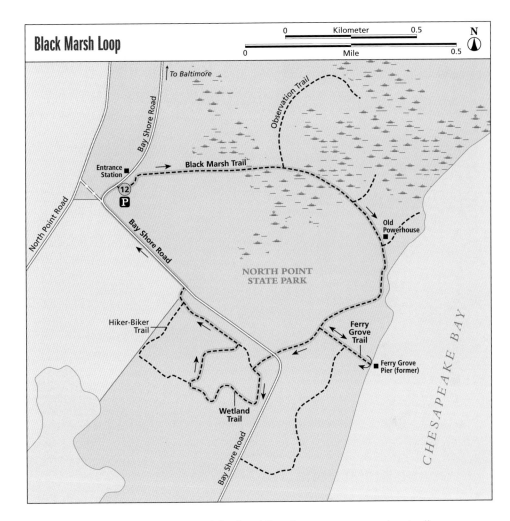

Black Marsh Loop

0 — Kilometer — 0.5
0 — Mile — 0.5

N

To Baltimore

Observation Trail

Bay Shore Road

Entrance Station

Black Marsh Trail

12
P

North Point Road

Bay Shore Road

Old Powerhouse

NORTH POINT
STATE PARK

Hiker-Biker
Trail

Ferry
Grove
Trail

Ferry Grove
Pier (former)

CHESAPEAKE BAY

Wetland
Trail

Bay Shore Road

park-goers arriving, eager to spend the day riding the merry-go-round and roller coaster, even playing classic carnival games like ring toss.

From here, retrace your steps to the Black Marsh Trail, then turn left to continue on this path. At the 1.4-mile mark, cross over Bay Shore Road by way of the crosswalk to connect with the white-blazed Wetland Trail. At the 1.5-mile mark, you will reach a wooden overlook that may have at one time served to showcase views of the wetlands, but those views are gone. The wooden overlook is in good shape, but there is nothing to see. Turn left to continue looping along the Wetland Trail. There are no real wetland views, but it's quite a relaxing walk.

At the 1.9-mile mark, turn left onto an unnamed connector trail. At the 2.1-mile mark, the trail opens back up at a farm field where you'll turn right onto the Hiker-Biker Trail, then quickly turn left onto Bay Shore Road. You'll walk along this road (in full sun) for 0.4 mile until you reach the parking area. Your hike is complete at the 2.4-mile mark.

Before you leave North Point State Park, take Bay Shore Road to the parking area at the very end of the road. Here you'll find a visitor center, an old trolley station, an

Just off the trail, keep your eyes open for a graffiti-laden concrete powerhouse that once supplied voltage to amusement park rides.

ornamental fountain, and a bayfront gazebo. There are also plenty of picnic tables, a swimming beach, and a bench–lined fishing pier that wows with scenic views across the bay.

MILES AND DIRECTIONS

0.0 The trailhead is located in the northeast corner of the parking area that's on the left, just past the entrance to North Point State Park.

0.3 Arrive at Black Marsh. Revel in the scenic views of wetlands on both sides of the trail.

0.4 Reach the Observation Trail. Skip this, and continue on the Black Marsh Trail.

0.7 Arrive at an old powerhouse from the early to mid 1900s.

0.8 Reach a spur trail that affords scenic bay views from atop the cliffs.

1.0 Turn left onto the Ferry Grove Trail to see the crumbling amusement park pier. Retrace your steps, then turn left to reconnect with the Black Marsh Trail.

1.4 Cross over Bay Shore Road to connect with the Wetland Trail.

1.5 Arrive at a wooden overlook that once provided visitors with scenic wetland views. Turn left to continue on the Wetland Trail.

1.9 Turn left onto an unnamed connector trail.

2.1 Turn right on the Hiker-Biker Trail, then turn left onto Bay Shore Road. Walk along this road until you reach the parking area.

2.4 Arrive back at the parking area. Your hike is complete.

13 BLUE TRAIL, GREENWELL STATE PARK

Enjoy a quiet forested hike that boasts peeks of Hog Neck Creek and the Patuxent River along this figure-eight-style hiking trail. Tackle this hike once the leaves have fallen for dramatic water views at this state park in Southern Maryland.

Start: Seasonal hunters' parking lot on Steer Horn Neck Road
Elevation gain: 85 feet
Maximum grade: 7%
Distance: 2.9-mile figure eight
Difficulty: Easy
Hiking time: 1.5 to 2 hours
Best seasons: Late fall to early spring
Fees and permits: $
Trail contact: Greenwell State Park, 25420 Rosedale Manor Ln., Hollywood, MD; (301) 872-5688; dnr.maryland.gov/publiclands/pages/southern/greenwell.aspx

Dogs: Yes, on a leash no longer than 6 feet
Trail surface: Mostly grass and dirt trails
Land status: State park
Nearest town: Lexington Park
Maps: National Geographic Trails Illustrated Topographic Map 772 (Delmarva Peninsula). Paper maps are also available at the trail kiosk at the trailhead.
Amenities: Picnic tables, restrooms
Cell service: Reliable

FINDING THE TRAILHEAD

This hike begins on the Yellow Trail, which is located at the large trail kiosk at the back of the seasonal hunters' parking lot west of the main park entrance on Steer Horn Neck Road. GPS: N38°21'53.0" / W76°32'01.4"

THE HIKE

At 596-acre Greenwell State Park in Hollywood, you'll find more than 10 miles of marked hiking trails, including the Blue Trail. Set on the Patuxent River in St. Mary's County, this state park was once farmland, as you'll note early in this hike when you pass an old tobacco barn. John Phillip Greenwell Jr. and his sister, Mary Wallace Greenwell, donated their farm for use by all as a public park more than fifty years ago.

The main entrance to Greenwell State Park is located on Rosedale Manor Lane. However, the Blue Trail, as well as the Red, White, and Yellow Trails, can be accessed from a small hunters' parking lot a short drive west on Steer Horn Neck Road. When you arrive at the parking area, note the large trail kiosk. Your first steps will be on the Yellow Trail as you walk north past the sign. From the full-sun parking lot, the trail quickly enters the substantial shade of the forest.

At the 0.1-mile mark, you will reach a trail marker at a T-intersection indicating which way to go for five different trails. It can be easy to feel overwhelmed, but turn right for the Red Trail, which leads to a historic tobacco barn at the 0.2-mile mark. At first, you may think this is just an old dilapidated barn best served with No Trespassing signs. However, you would be wrong.

Post-hike, take in the views across the Patuxent River from a sandy beach just steps from the Brown Trail.

Safely stepping inside, notice the old farming tools marked with placards to educate visitors on tools once used on the farm, including Oliver plows, pull plows, a hay rake, and a cultivator. On one of the walls is a field guide to tobacco barns, which provides an overview of different styles of tobacco barns, like gambrel-roofed barns and bonnet barns. It's worth exploring the barn to take in the history of the farmland, which even today has crop fields alongside the trails.

From the barn, retrace your steps to return to the trail, then turn right to continue on the Red Trail. At the 0.4-mile mark, you will reach an intersection. At this point, the Red Trail turns into the Blue Trail as you continue walking ahead on the wide path through the forest. Turn left at the 0.6-mile mark to continue on the Blue Trail. In a few steps, you may catch your first glimpses of Hog Neck Creek on the left, though dense foliage in summer will preclude you from the best views. You'll reach another intersection at the 0.9-mile mark. Turn left here to continue on the Blue Trail. Note that this trail is essentially shaped like a figure eight.

As you continue walking along this forested trail, the Patuxent River comes into view through the trees. There are a few spots where you can get better views, particularly at the 1.7-mile mark where you can nearly descend all the way to the water's edge. Once the leaves have fallen, the views are more dramatic through the leafless trees, enabling you to see across the main section of park that's accessed by way of Rosedale Manor Lane.

At the 2.0-mile mark, close the top part of the figure eight, then turn left to stay on the Blue Trail and close the bottom part of the figure eight at the 2.6-mile mark. Retrace

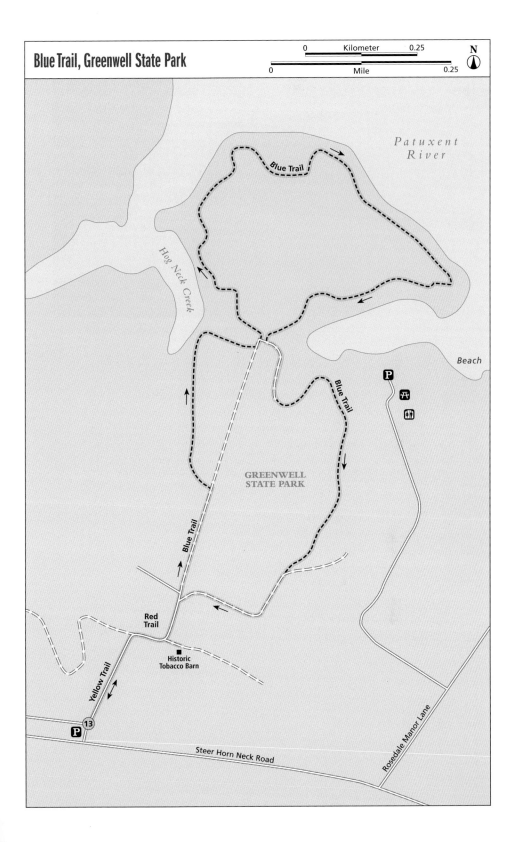

Blue Trail, Greenwell State Park

Patuxent River

Blue Trail

Hog Neck Creek

Beach

P

Blue Trail

GREENWELL STATE PARK

Blue Trail

Red Trail

Historic Tobacco Barn

Yellow Trail

P 13

Steer Horn Neck Road

Rosedale Manor Lane

Early in this hike, a historic tobacco barn turns up. Old farming tools are on display to educate visitors on life on the farm.

your steps along the Red Trail and Yellow Trail to reach the parking area. Your hike is complete at the 2.9-mile mark.

Post-hike, make the short drive to enter Greenwell State Park by way of the main entrance. When you do, note the honor system pay station. Make the first left to drive to the parking lot at the end of the road. From here, follow the Brown Trail to a short spur trail that guides you to a delightful sandy beach on the Patuxent River. Heaven. Have a picnic lunch here or at one of the picnic tables adjacent to the parking area. There are also flush toilets at this parking area.

MILES AND DIRECTIONS

0.0 Begin this hike on the Yellow Trail, which is located at the large trail kiosk at the back of the seasonal hunters' parking lot west of the main park entrance on Steer Horn Neck Road. Proceed north on the Yellow Trail.

0.1 Turn right for the Red Trail.

0.2 Arrive at a former tobacco barn. Explore, then retrace your steps to the trail and turn right to continue on the Red Trail.

0.4 Reach an intersection. Continue straight ahead. The Red Trail turns into the Blue Trail.

0.6 Turn left to remain on the Blue Trail.

0.9 Turn left to remain on the Blue Trail.

2.0 Turn left to remain on the Blue Trail.

2.6 Turn left onto the Red Trail.

2.7 Turn right onto the Red Trail.

2.8 Turn left onto the Yellow Trail.

2.9 Arrive back at the parking area. Your hike is complete.

14 CHAPMAN STATE PARK

Chapman State Park may be a small park on the Potomac River, but this relaxing hike has a lot to offer, including Mount Aventine, a restored pre–Civil War tidewater plantation home, as well as a family cemetery, tobacco farms, tidal wetlands, swamp habitat, and old-growth forest.

Start: Chapman State Park parking area
Elevation gain: 180 feet
Maximum grade: 9%
Distance: 4.0-mile lollipop with spur
Difficulty: Easy
Hiking time: 2 to 3 hours
Best seasons: Year-round
Fees and permits: Free
Trail contact: Chapman State Park, 3452 Ferry Place, Indian Head, MD; (301) 743-7613; dnr.maryland .gov/publiclands/pages/southern/ chapman.aspx
Dogs: Yes, on a leash no longer than 6 feet
Trail surface: Mostly sand and dirt trails, some grass
Land status: State park
Nearest town: Indian Head
Maps: A trail map is available online at dnr.maryland.gov/publiclands/ pages/southern/chapman.aspx.
Amenities: None
Cell service: Reliable

FINDING THE TRAILHEAD

The trailhead is located at the back of the small parking area for Chapman State Park, to the left of a large trail kiosk. GPS: N38°36'44.6" / W77°07'03.2"

THE HIKE

Take a step back in time as you traverse Chapman State Park, home to Mount Aventine, the restored home of the well-to-do Chapman family, who had ties to the families of George Washington and George Mason. Yes, our founding fathers. Alongside this pre–Civil War plantation home, you'll see family burial plots, an old barn, tidal wetlands, a flowing river, and mature old-growth forest.

From the parking area, the hike begins along a wide gravel road, likely the private drive that once led to Mount Aventine. At the 0.3-mile mark, a colorful placard introduces the Coastal Woodland Trail. Turn right to follow white blazes as you enter an upland terrace-gravel forest with gravelly soils that support hickory, oak, beech, and tulip trees.

At the 0.7-mile mark, you will have the option to turn left to return to the entrance road or turn right to continue on the Coastal Woodland Trail. Turn right and you will see yellow blazes, as well as the ruins of an early twentieth-century wooden home that was likely the former residence of Robert Chapman, the last family member to live on the estate. Peer inside to get a peek at the remains, including an old stove and a broken-down refrigerator on its side.

By the 0.9-mile mark, you will descend into a coastal woodland forest and floodplain largely populated by red oaks and loblolly pines. In summer, keep your eyes open for the banana-like fruits of the native pawpaw trees that line the trail. At the 1.3-mile mark, a short spur trail on the left leads to the Chapman Family Cemetery, where at least five

This easygoing hike at Chapman State Park has a lot to offer, including Mount Aventine, a restored pre–Civil War tidewater plantation home.

family members are buried. Each is marked with a headstone. Nearly a dozen other family members are also buried here.

In a few more steps, at the 1.5-mile mark, walk out to the driftwood-littered shore of the Potomac River. Retrace your steps, then turn right to reconnect with the Coastal Woodland Trail. In a few more steps, turn right onto the Potomac River Trail to walk out to a second access point for the Potomac River, this one marked with a placard educating on the former Chapman Point Fishery and Chapman's Landing, which ferried local people between Potomac plantations and the port cities of Alexandria, Annapolis, and Baltimore, as well as the Northern Neck of Virginia.

Retrace your steps from the Potomac River, then continue straight ahead along the Potomac River Trail. Turn right at the 1.9-mile mark onto the Marsh Trail. You will enter a river bottom habitat with rich, moist soil that supports large oak trees and poplars, as well as sweet gum and sycamore trees. Shortly, you will reach a scenic "scrub-shrub" freshwater marsh on the right, which sadly is threatened by westerly winds and tides that push trash and debris from the river into the marsh. Note that the Marsh Trail is just 0.7 mile (one-way), but there is no defined endpoint. You will see a ramshackle home on the Potomac River. This essentially serves as the endpoint, though the path does continue on if you turn left here.

From the dilapidated home, retrace your steps to the start of the Marsh Trail at the 3.3-mile mark. Stay right to reconnect with the Potomac River Trail, a historic roadway that led from Mount Aventine to the Potomac River. You will soon see a large barn on your left. At the 3.6-mile mark, you can turn left to walk to Mount Aventine for a self-guided

Just off the trail, walk out to the driftwood-littered shore of the Potomac River at Chapman State Park in Maryland.

Chapman State Park

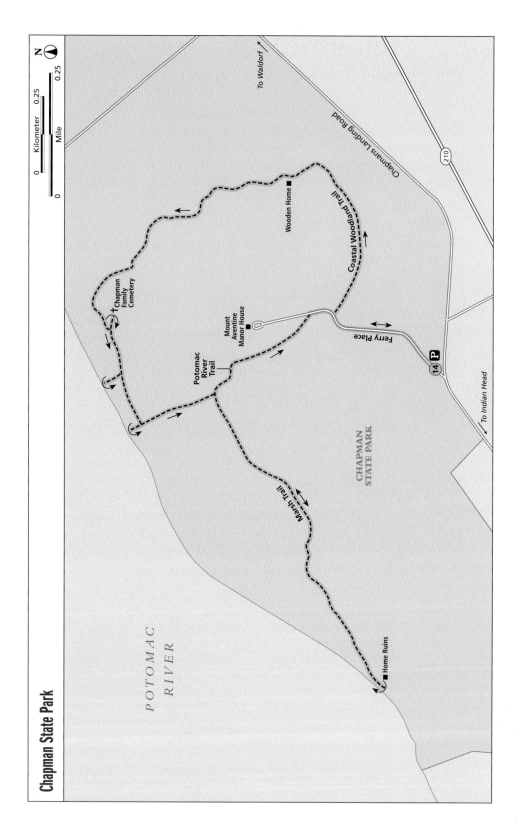

N

0   Kilometer   0.25

0   Mile   0.25

POTOMAC RIVER

To Waldorf

Chapmans Landing Road

210

Wooden Home

Coastal Woodland Trail

Chapman Family Cemetery

Mount Aventine Manor House

Potomac River Trail

Ferry Place

CHAPMAN STATE PARK

Marsh Trail

Home Ruins

14 P

To Indian Head

Early in the hike, visitors pass the ruins of an early twentieth-century wooden home.

tour. Alternatively, you can turn right to retrace your steps on the gravel road to reach the trailhead at the 4.0-mile mark.

MILES AND DIRECTIONS

0.0   Begin to the left of the large trail kiosk that is located at the back of the small parking area for Chapman State Park.

0.3   Turn right onto the Coastal Woodland Trail.

0.7   Turn right to stay on the Coastal Woodland Trail. A dilapidated early twentieth-century home is on the left side of the trail.

1.3 Turn left onto a short spur trail leading to the Chapman Family Cemetery. Retrace your steps to the Coastal Woodland Trail.

1.5 Turn right to walk to the driftwood-littered shore of the Potomac River. Retrace your steps, then turn right onto the Coastal Woodland Trail.

1.7 Turn right at a placard to walk out to the Potomac River by way of the Potomac River Trail. Retrace your steps, then walk straight ahead.

1.9 Turn right onto the Marsh Trail.

2.6 Reach a ramshackle house. Retrace your steps to the start of the Marsh Trail, then stay to the right to reconnect with the Potomac River Trail.

3.6 Reach the road to Mount Aventine. You have the option to turn left to walk to the former plantation home. Or, turn right for the final steps to the trailhead.

4.0 Arrive back at the trailhead. Your hike is complete.

15 DISCOVERY AND JAVA HISTORY TRAILS

The forested hike on the grounds of the Smithsonian Environmental Research Center guides visitors on a shady hike across land that has been reclaimed by nature, but also preserved for visitors with boardwalks and overlooks with views across the Rhode River and Muddy Creek.

Start: Reed Education Center
Elevation gain: 128 feet
Maximum grade: 6%
Distance: 2.6 miles out and back
Difficulty: Easy
Hiking time: 1 to 1.5 hours
Best seasons: Fall through spring
Fees and permits: Free
Trail contact: Smithsonian Environmental Research Center, 647

Contees Wharf Rd., Edgewater, MD; (443) 482-2200; serc.si.edu
Dogs: No
Trail surface: Mostly dirt trails
Land status: Private property
Nearest town: Edgewater
Maps: National Geographic Trails Illustrated Topographic Map 772 (Delmarva Peninsula)
Amenities: Picnic tables
Cell service: Reliable

FINDING THE TRAILHEAD

The trailhead is located behind the Reed Education Center at the Smithsonian Environmental Research Center. GPS: N38°53'12.7" / W76°32'34.3"

THE HIKE

It's interesting that at a private research institution—the Smithsonian Environmental Research Center, to be exact—you'll find four forested hiking trails. In fact, the research campus is open Monday through Saturday from 8:30 a.m. to 4:30 p.m. for hiking, biking, and paddling. When you arrive, you'll reach a security station and receive a paper slip to place on your dashboard, but then you're in.

The three primary trails include the Java History Trail (1.3 miles, loop), the Discovery Trail (1.3 miles, out and back), and the Contee Farm Trail network (1.6-2.5 miles, loop). All three wow in their own ways. The Java History Trail educates on how Native Americans, scientists, and farmers have used the land over time. Meanwhile, the Contee Farm Trails (Contee Watershed Trail and Squirrel Neck Loop) begin with a look at the ruins of the Contee Mansion followed by scenic views from an overlook on the Rhode River. This hike, which is a variation of the Discovery Trail, allows you to enjoy plenty of waterside views, while taking in the quiet beauty of the marshes.

From the parking area, walk behind the Reed Education Center. You'll see a wide gravel path with a large tool shed on the left. You can also sneak a peek at what looks like the back of a trail sign. Yes, this is the trail. Actually, this is the Java History Trail, but it leads to the Discovery Trail. On the front of the placard, you'll learn what to expect on the Java History Trail, including a dive into the lives of the Mattaponi, the Piscataway, and the Choptank native peoples who shared this area, hunting and fishing in the Rhode River. The land was later transformed into a tobacco plantation, then a dairy farm, before

it was allowed to return to nature. This loop trail begins just to the right, but for this hike, stay to the left for the Java History Trail.

As you begin walking on the Java History Trail, you'll see a living classroom on the right, then a small wooden footbridge and a spot to walk out to the Rhode River. Shaded benches allow you to savor the views across the water, maybe even spot a family of geese. This is a good spot to settle in and enjoy a bag lunch. As you continue on, you'll reach a placard at the 0.2-mile mark with an overview of the area's return to nature, including the ill impact of plant and animal species that were at times inadvertently introduced, like blackflies, cockroaches, and gray rats. Other species, like the kudzu vine, were introduced to solve erosion problems, but have now become a pest. Introduced species have come to compete with, even replace, native species. A positive example, however, is Japanese honeysuckle, which was introduced from Asia but is not parasitic, and has therefore not been destructive to other species in the forest.

In a few more steps, you'll reach an open marsh with a wooden boardwalk, including an octagonal overlook in the center with wooden benches. There is also an elevated overlook, which provides far-reaching views from a vantage point of four to five steps above the boardwalk. Once you reach the end of the boardwalk, you'll see a trail sign on the left. Stay to the left for the 0.3-mile connector trail that leads to the Discovery Trail. From here, you'll walk up a dozen steps.

At the 0.6-mile mark, you'll arrive at a four-way intersection. Turn left for gravelly Fox Point Road (more a trail than a road). Take this to the end, at the 0.9-mile mark, where you'll reach Fox Point. Wooden steps go down to an overlook with stunning views

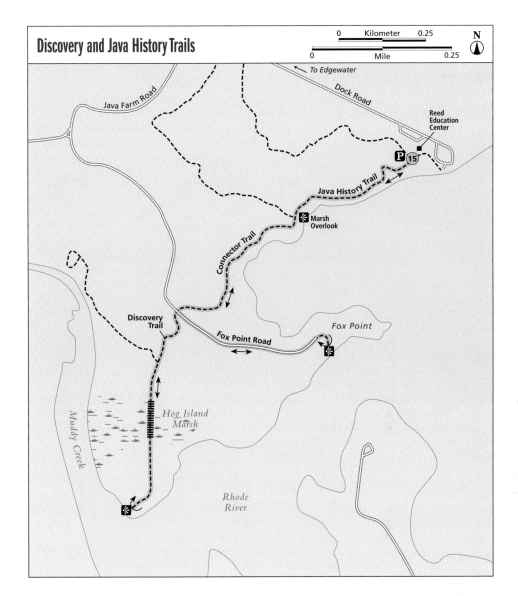

across the Rhode River. Once you've savored the views, retrace your steps to the four-way intersection, then turn left at the 1.2-mile mark. You are now on the Discovery Trail. By the 1.4-mile mark, you will reach a boardwalk to cross Hog Island Marsh. Benches on the boardwalk allow for a brief rest.

At the 1.6-mile mark, you will reach a bench at an overlook looking out over Muddy Creek and the Rhode River. Retrace your steps to the four-way intersection at the 2.0-mile mark. Continue straight ahead, then proceed on to the parking area. Your hike is complete at the 2.6-mile mark.

A bridge leads visitors across Hog Island Marsh along the Discovery Trail.

MILES AND DIRECTIONS

0.0 Begin on the gravel trail behind the Reed Education Center. Stay left for the Java History Trail.

0.2 Reach a wooden boardwalk and an open marsh overlook. At the end of the boardwalk, stay left for the connector trail to the Discovery Trail.

0.6 At the four-way intersection, turn left onto Fox Point Road.

0.9 Arrive at the overlook. Retrace your steps to the four-way intersection.

1.2 Turn left onto the Discovery Trail.

1.6 Reach a second overlook with a bench. From here, retrace your steps to the four-way intersection.

2.0 Arrive at the four-way intersection. Proceed straight ahead. Retrace your steps to the Reed Education Center and parking area.

2.6 Arrive back at the Reed Education Center. Your hike is complete.

16 DOWNS PARK

Enjoy a scenic loop around Downs Park on a mostly paved trail, making stops for a dog beach, kayak launch, and fitness stations before settling in on one of a half-dozen benches overlooking the Chesapeake Bay at the end of this hike.

Start: Parking area on the east side of Downs Park
Elevation gain: 197 feet
Maximum grade: 5%
Distance: 3.8-mile loop
Difficulty: Easy
Hiking time: 1.5 to 2 hours
Best seasons: Year-round
Fees and permits: $$
Trail contact: Downs Park, 8311 John Downs Loop, Pasadena, MD; (410) 222-6230; aacounty.org/departments/recreation-parks/parks/downs

Dogs: Yes, on a leash no longer than 6 feet
Trail surface: Mostly paved
Land status: County park
Nearest town: Pasadena
Maps: National Geographic Trails Illustrated Topographic Map 772 (Delmarva Peninsula)
Other trail users: Cyclists
Amenities: Flush toilets, picnic tables, visitor center, playground, dog beach
Cell service: Reliable

FINDING THE TRAILHEAD

Pick up the trail to the right of the "Welcome to Downs Park" sign in front of the large parking area on the east side of the park. GPS: N39°06'38.8" / W76°26'03.1"

THE HIKE

Anne Arundel County's Downs Park has something for everyone, even the furriest family members thanks to a dedicated dog beach. At this 236-acre park you'll find picnic pavilions, basketball courts, a children's playground, and sensational views across the Chesapeake Bay. You'll also find more than 5 miles of paved and natural trails, including this 3.8-mile loop around the entire park.

Make your way to the large parking area on the far east side of the park. Here you're steps from the bench-lined bay for terrific views. Adjacent to the parking area there's a Victorian-style garden and a visitor center that's open every day except Tuesday. You will see a sign that reads "Welcome to Downs Park." Here your hike begins on a paved path that leads down to the water and to the loop that encircles this delightful county park. At the water's edge, turn left onto the unnamed paved trail for a counterclockwise loop around the park.

In a few steps, you'll reach a spot where you can step out onto a sandy beach that's popular with local fishing enthusiasts. You can also see one of the fishing piers not far off in the distance. Hop back onto the trail and you'll reach a sign guiding you to Dog Beach at the 0.2-mile mark. A metal gate turns up on the right at the 0.4-mile mark, where you'll descend a half-dozen steps to Dog Beach. If you're lucky, you'll spy two or three furry pups living their best lives, freely splashing in the refreshing bay water. Retrace your steps and turn right on the paved path.

Settle in on a bench at Downs Park to enjoy the views across the Chesapeake Bay.

Turn right in a few steps to stroll down a wooden ramp to a platform overlooking a small pond. A couple of benches allow you to sit and savor the views, while a photo-filled placard educates on wildlife you may see at the pond, like box turtles and monarch butterflies. Leave your fishing poles—no fishing is allowed at this pond.

At the 0.5-mile mark, you'll pass restrooms on your right, then arrive at a fork in the trail. Turn right to proceed on the paved path. As you continue along, notice picnic tables set off the trail here and there. Cross over busy Pinehurst Road by way of a pedestrian bridge, then arrive at a kayak launch with several waterfront picnic tables at the 1.1-mile mark. Located on Locust Cove, a tributary of Bodkin Creek, this is one of two kayak launch points at Downs Park. The other is situated on the park's choppy bay side, left of the visitor center.

At the 1.6-mile mark, you will reach a bench situated on the opposite side of Locust Cove from the kayak launch. It's the perfect place to sit and watch water-lovers set off on human-powered canoes, kayaks, and stand-up paddleboards. As you continue on, enjoy the shade of the forest as you loop around the park. Cross back over Pinehurst Road at the 2.4-mile mark, then make your second right to reconnect with the trail (the first right simply parallels Pinehurst Road). You will see fitness stations along the trail for exercises like beam jumps, ladder crosses, and inclined body curls.

You'll get close to the bay again at the 3.7-mile mark when you arrive at a wooden overlook with a viewfinder for savoring the views across the Chesapeake Bay. Your final steps are alongside the bay, where at least a half-dozen benches implore you to sit and

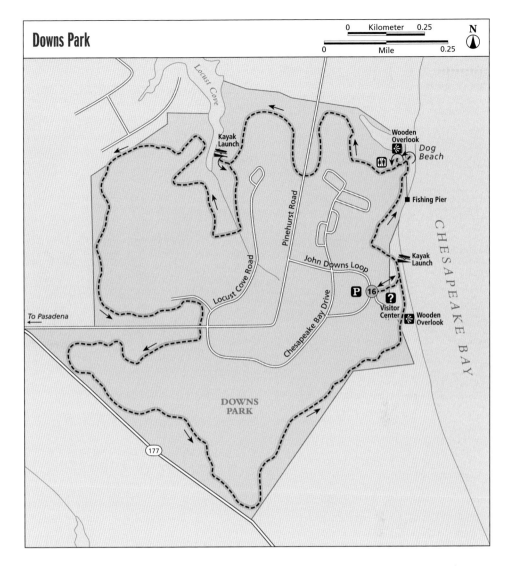

0   Kilometer   0.25

N

0   Mile   0.25

Locust Cove

Kayak
Launch

Wooden
Overlook

Dog
Beach

Pinehurst Road

Fishing Pier

CHESAPEAKE BAY

Kayak
Launch

Locust Cove Road

John Downs Loop

P   16

To Pasadena

Chesapeake Bay Drive

Visitor
Center

Wooden
Overlook

DOWNS
PARK

177

soak in the water views. At the 3.8-mile mark, turn left for the final steps to the parking area. Your hike is complete.

MILES AND DIRECTIONS

0.0   Pick up the trail to the right of the "Welcome to Downs Park" sign in front of the large parking area on the east side of the park.

0.4   Arrive at Dog Beach.

0.5   Reach restrooms, then turn right at the fork in the path.

0.8   Cross over Pinehurst Road by way of a pedestrian bridge.

1.1   Arrive at the kayak launch at Locust Cove.

1.6   Reach a bench with views across Locust Cove.

2.4   Cross back over Pinehurst Road at a crosswalk.

3.7   Arrive at a wooden bay overlook on the right.

3.8   Turn left to arrive back at the parking area. Your hike is complete.

17 DUNCAN'S POND AND NORTH RIDGE TRAILS

This short loop hike guides visitors through forested heights and along boardwalk trails over ponds teeming with native wildlife and waterfowl, like ospreys and red-bellied turtles.

Start: Flag Ponds Nature Park parking lot 2 or 3
Elevation gain: 121 feet
Maximum grade: 8%
Distance: 1.7-mile loop
Difficulty: Easy
Hiking time: 1 to 1.5 hours
Best seasons: Year-round
Fees and permits: $-$$ (cash or check only; no credit cards)
Trail contact: Flag Ponds Nature Park, 1525 Flag Ponds Pkwy., Lusby, MD; (410) 586-1477; calvertparks .org/fpp.html
Dogs: Yes, on a leash no longer than 6 feet

Trail surface: Mostly sand and dirt trails, some grass and boardwalk
Land status: County park
Nearest town: Lusby
Maps: National Geographic Trails Illustrated Topographic Map 772 (Delmarva Peninsula). Park maps are also available at the entrance station.
Amenities: Restrooms, picnic tables, visitor center
Cell service: Reliable
Special considerations: The last visitor is allowed in one hour before the park closes. The beach closes one hour before the park closes.

FINDING THE TRAILHEAD

Begin this hike along the blue-blazed North Ridge Trail from the back of parking lot 2 or parking lot 3. GPS: N38°26'47.1" / W76°27'39.4"

THE HIKE

In Calvert County, you'll find a delightful 545-acre nature park that wows with a sandy beach, forested trails, tidal wetlands, and three scenic ponds. Flag Ponds Nature Park in Lusby is a former fishery turned true gem situated on the Chesapeake Bay.

There are three parking areas at this coastal park, but for this hike your best bet is to park in lot 2. This is the second lot you will encounter after you pass through the entrance station. Lot 2 is mostly gravel, while lot 3 is mostly grass. Farther into the park, the primary lot is lot 1 and is entirely paved with restrooms and picnic tables.

From the entrance to parking lot 2 (or lot 3), look to the back of the lot for blue blazes that mark the North Ridge Trail. You can access this forested trail from both lots. Shortly after stepping foot on this blue-blazed trail, you will encounter a fork in the trail. From lot 2, stay to the right to meet up with the trail, but from lot 3, you'll want to stay right, then left, for the trail (or you'll end up walking into lot 2).

The trail begins with a minimal incline, guiding hikers through a cool, shady forest. It's a refreshing break after time spent on the park's sun-drenched beach that leans out into the Chesapeake Bay. At the 0.6-mile mark, a dozen or so steps usher hikers down 50 feet to a lower level of the forest on the way to Richardson's Pond and Duncan's Pond.

Continue on the North Ridge Trail, then turn left at the 0.8-mile mark onto the yellow-blazed Duncan's Pond Trail. Walk across a delightful stretch of wooden boardwalk

Over several decades, the beach moved out to the bay, leaving behind ponds and later swamps at Flag Ponds Nature Park.

that crosses a verdant wetlands area of grasses and reeds at Richardson's Pond. This is one of three small ponds at the park that were once part of the beach. They came to be over several decades as the beach moved out into the bay, leaving behind a pond and later a swamp, like what you see today, which is covered with floating green algae with trees growing up out of the murky waters.

At the 1.0-mile mark, turn left onto a spur trail to quietly walk out to a wooden observation blind that you will reach in less than 0.1 mile. Look out at Duncan's Pond (also called Flag Pond) to catch views of native wildlife and waterfowl—without them getting scared off by visitors. Inside the observation blind, a colorful poster educates visitors on what can be seen at Duncan's Pond, including ospreys, great blue herons, diamondback terrapins, belted kingfishers, and red-bellied cooters. Retrace your steps to the start of the spur trail, then turn left to follow the yellow blazes along the Duncan's Pond Trail.

At the 1.3-mile mark, look to the left and walk out onto a wooden overlook for scenic views across the small pond. You'll also see a placard outlining the changing species that call the pond home as the area has transformed from sandy shoreline to forested pond. Keep your eyes open for river otters, green tree frogs, and red-bellied turtles.

You'll reach the end of the Duncan's Pond Trail at the 1.4-mile mark. From here, turn right onto a paved beach path that becomes Flag Ponds Parkway, the park road that runs the length of the nature park. At the 1.7-mile mark, you will reach parking lot 2 (or 3) to complete your hike.

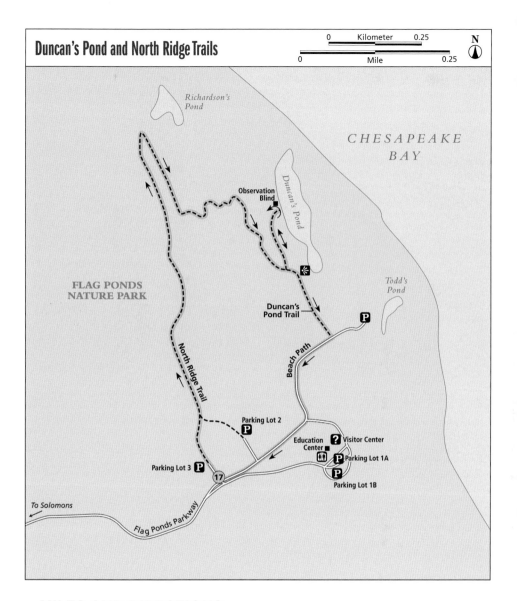

Duncan's Pond and North Ridge Trails

Kilometer 0 — 0.25
Mile 0 — 0.25

N

Richardson's Pond

CHESAPEAKE BAY

Observation Blind

Duncan's Pond

FLAG PONDS NATURE PARK

Todd's Pond

Duncan's Pond Trail

North Ridge Trail

Beach Path

Parking Lot 2

Education Center

Visitor Center

Parking Lot 1A

Parking Lot 3

17

Parking Lot 1B

To Solomons

Flag Ponds Parkway

MILES AND DIRECTIONS

0.0 Begin this hike along the blue-blazed North Ridge Trail from the back of parking lot 2 or parking lot 3.

0.1 Turn right to continue following the blue blazes into the forest.

0.6 Walk down a dozen steps to a lower level of the forest.

0.8 Turn left onto the yellow-blazed Duncan's Pond Trail. Cross over Richardson's Pond on a wooden boardwalk trail.

1.0 Turn left onto a spur trail to an observation blind with views across Duncan's Pond. Retrace your steps to the Duncan's Pond Trail, then turn left to continue following the yellow blazes.

Descend the steps on the blue-blazed North Ridge Trail on your way to Richardson's Pond and Duncan's Pond at Flag Ponds Nature Park.

1.3   Walk out onto a wooden overlook, then retrace your steps. Turn left to continue on the yellow-blazed hiking trail.

1.4   Reach the end of the Duncan's Pond Trail. Turn right to ascend the paved beach path, which turns into Flag Ponds Parkway, the park road.

1.7   Arrive back at parking lot 2 or 3. Your hike is complete.

18 FERRY POINT LANDING TRAIL

This shaded hike to the sandy beach at Drum Point by way of the Ferry Point Landing Trail at Wye Island Natural Resources Management Area is a popular one with families, as well as those eager to cool off under a canopy of trees and in the gently lapping waves of the Wye River.

Start: Ferry Point Landing Trail parking area
Elevation gain: 20 feet
Maximum grade: 1%
Distance: 1.5-mile lollipop
Difficulty: Easy
Hiking time: 45 minutes to 1 hour
Best seasons: Year-round
Fees and permits: Free
Trail contact: Wye Island Natural Resources Management Area, 632 Wye Island Rd., Queenstown, MD; (410) 827-7577; dnr.maryland .gov/publiclands/pages/eastern/ wyeisland.aspx

Dogs: Yes, on a leash no longer than 6 feet
Trail surface: Mostly dirt trails
Land status: Natural resources management area
Nearest town: Stevensville
Maps: National Geographic Trails Illustrated Topographic Map 772 (Delmarva Peninsula)
Other trail users: Cyclists, equestrians
Amenities: Porta-potties, picnic table
Cell service: Reliable

FINDING THE TRAILHEAD

The trailhead is located at the opening in the wooden fence, adjacent to the Ferry Point Landing Trail sign. GPS: N38°52'42.5" / W76°10'45.4"

THE HIKE

Wye Island Natural Resources Management Area is located in the tidal recesses of the Chesapeake Bay between the Wye River and the Wye East River. It may not feel like an island, but if you zoom out on an online map, you'll see that it is in fact an island. It's as if it broke off from the mainland. Of the island's 2,800 acres, 2,450 are carefully managed by the Maryland Park Service, largely to provide a safe and suitable habitat for wintering waterfowl populations and other native wildlife, like white-tailed deer, bald eagles, and Delmarva fox squirrels. One of the agency's primary objectives is to stabilize the 30 miles of rapidly eroding shoreline.

On Wye Island, you'll find 6 miles of trails, including the Schoolhouse Woods Nature Trail and the Holly Tree Trail. These hiking trails turn up on the left and right as you motor along Wye Island Road all the way to the southwest end of the natural area. Once you've driven about as far as you can go, you'll reach the parking area for the Ferry Point Landing Trail, a popular path among those eager to spend the day on the small sandy beach at Drum Point.

At the parking area, there is enough room for at least a dozen or so cars, as well as a porta-potty. An opening in a slatted wooden fence ushers you onto the Ferry Point Landing Trail. A small trail sign and a trail kiosk ensure you are in the right place. From here, it's an easy walk on a wide dirt trail that guides you beneath a lush canopy of Osage

A casual hike along the Ferry Point Landing Trail at Wye Island Natural Resources Management Area leads to Drum Point.

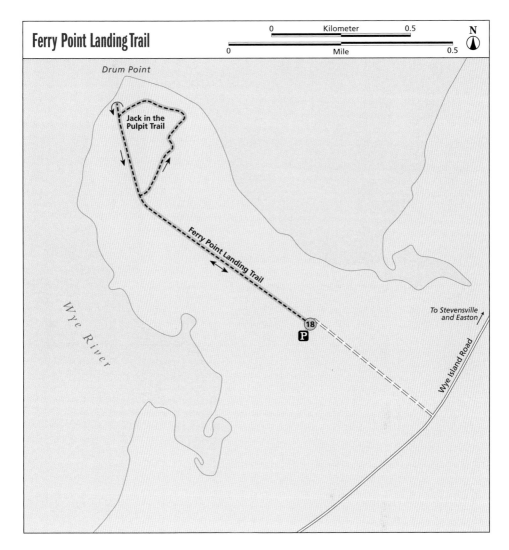

Ferry Point Landing Trail

Drum Point

Jack in the Pulpit Trail

Ferry Point Landing Trail

Wye River

To Stevensville and Easton

Wye Island Road

18

orange trees, which flower between May and July. Oddly, the flowers—or fruit rather—are green, not orange, in color.

On this easygoing hike, you can take the direct route to the sandy beach by staying on the Ferry Point Landing Trail all the way to the shoreline. Or, at the 0.4-mile mark, you can turn right onto the Jack in the Pulpit Trail, which loops into a more dense forest before reconnecting with the Ferry Point Landing Trail at the 0.8-mile mark. From here, turn right and you're steps from Drum Point and the sandy shore. Wade in the gently lapping waters of the Wye River. There is also a wooden picnic table for a relaxing lunch by the water. Tidal grasses on the beach make this an oasis-like destination to laze away the afternoon.

When it's time for the fun to end, walk the Ferry Point Landing Trail all the way back to the parking area, bypassing the Jack in the Pulpit Trail. As you walk along the Ferry

The forested Ferry Point Landing Trail guides visitors to a sandy beach to enjoy the gently lapping waves of the Wye River.

Point Landing Trail, you'll see a large porta-potty on the right, which serves as a more than adequate changing room. You will reach the parking area at the 1.5-mile mark.

MILES AND DIRECTIONS

0.0   Begin at the opening in the wooden fence, at the sign for the Ferry Point Landing Trail.

0.4   Turn right onto the Jack in the Pulpit Trail.

0.8   Turn right to reconnect with the Ferry Point Landing Trail. In a few more steps, arrive at the soft sand beach at Drum Point. Retrace your steps on the Ferry Point Landing Trail to the parking area.

1.5   Arrive back at the parking area. Your hike is complete.

19 GENERAL'S WALK FOOT TRAIL

The short hike on the General's Walk Foot Trail at Smallwood State Park weaves visitors in and out of forest, though the campground, onto a wooden bridge over scenic wetlands, and over to the former home of Revolutionary War General William Smallwood.

Start: Smallwood State Park office
Elevation gain: 171 feet
Maximum grade: 12%
Distance: 2.2-mile loop
Difficulty: Easy
Hiking time: 1 to 1.5 hours
Best seasons: Year-round
Fees and permits: $
Trail contact: Smallwood State Park, 2750 Sweden Point Rd., Marbury, MD; (301) 743-7613; dnr.maryland .gov/publiclands/pages/southern/ smallwood.aspx

Dogs: Yes, on a leash no longer than 6 feet
Trail surface: Mostly sand and dirt trails, some grass
Land status: State park
Nearest town: Indian Head
Maps: A trail map is available online at dnr.maryland.gov/publiclands/ pages/southern/smallwood.aspx.
Amenities: Flush toilets, picnic tables, benches
Cell service: Reliable

FINDING THE TRAILHEAD

The trailhead is located next to the park office. GPS: N38°33'10.9" / W77°11'03.6"

THE HIKE

The short hike on the General's Walk Foot Trail at Smallwood State Park guides visitors through the forest, across the park campground, onto a pedestrian footbridge over scenic wetlands, and onto the property of Revolutionary War General William Smallwood. This trail starts and stops, often ending on a park road only to be picked back up a few steps away, so keep your eyes wide open on the trail.

You can access the nature trail in several spots across the park, but your best bet is to park in the small lot at the park office. You'll see a sign for the General's Walk Foot Trail just past the office and parking area, on the same side of the road (though do note you'll also see a sign for the trail on the other side of the park road).

Once you enter the hardwood forest, you'll see a couple of dilapidated and crumbled wooden houses on the left before you reach the 0.1-mile mark on this white-blazed nature trail. It's relaxing and delightfully shaded—a huge win on a warm summer day. The trail seems to end at the 0.4-mile mark when you reach the campground. At this point, turn right onto Smallwood Road. Turn right again at the 0.5-mile mark to cross a wooden bridge that leads to the boat launch area. You'll see several cabins on the left, as well as a small outdoor amphitheater. The bridge over the tidal wetlands area is especially scenic. Simply cross over, then cross back.

Continue along Smallwood Road. You will see restrooms on your left, then a sign on your right to reconnect with the forested General's Walk Foot Trail. At the 1.0-mile mark, the habitat changes from mature forest to coastal wetland. In spring, mountain laurel flourishes on both sides of the nature trail. In a few steps you will see a trail sign.

Cross over a wooden footbridge for especially scenic views across the tidal wetlands.

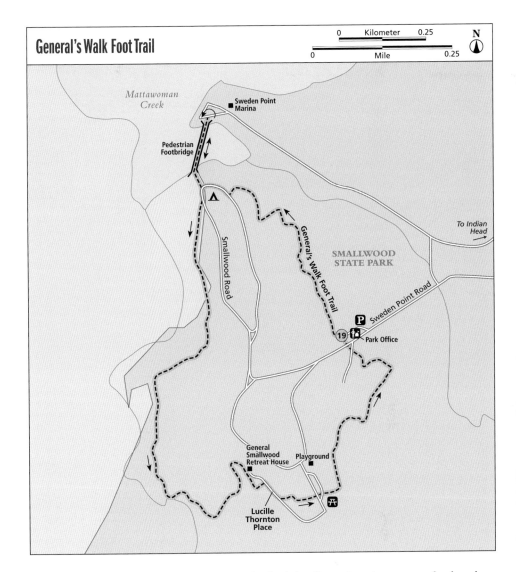

Stay right to proceed to the historic area. At the 1.4-mile mark, a pleasant wooden bench encourages you to take a break before continuing on. Take advantage of the bench, since the next stretch of trail takes you uphill on your way to the General Smallwood Retreat House.

About midway up the hill, you will reach another bench that's just right for a break, then a set of stairs as you continue ascending the trail. At the 1.5-mile mark, you will arrive at a clearing. You have reached the historic area, which includes benches, picnic tables, a historic home, a delightful garden, a grave site, and several outbuildings. As you cut across the area, note the brick trail that leads off to the left (a service road is on the right). This brick path goes to restrooms and an old wooden barn.

At the 1.8-mile mark, cross over Lucille Thornton Place. You will see a parking area, as well as a picnic pavilion on the right and a recycled tire playground on the left. Straight

Midway along the General's Walk Foot Trail you will pass the former home of General William Smallwood, a native of Charles County, Maryland, who served in the Revolutionary War.

ahead you will see a sign for the General's Walk Foot Trail. Follow this sign to reenter the mature hardwood forest. From here, you will step down into the forest and enjoy a shaded walk to end the hike at the 2.2-mile mark.

MILES AND DIRECTIONS

0.0 Begin at the General's Walk Foot Trail sign located on the same side of the road as the park office. Descend several steps into the hardwood forest.

0.1 A couple of small dilapidated wooden homes are on the left side of the trail.

0.4 Turn right onto Smallwood Road, which leads through the campground.

0.5 Turn right to cross a wooden bridge over tidal wetlands. Once on the other side of the bridge at the boat launch, retrace your steps to return across the bridge. Stay to the right.

0.6 Reconnect with the General's Walk Foot Trail and reenter the hardwood forest.

1.4 Arrive at a wooden bench in a new habitat, a coastal wetland.

1.5 Reach the General William Smallwood historic area. Explore the area, then cut across to reconnect with a brick trail, which leads to restrooms and a wooden barn.

1.8 Cross over Lucille Thornton Place. You will see a picnic pavilion on the right and a recycled tire playground on the left. The trail picks up straight ahead at the trail sign.

2.2 Arrive back at the park office. Your hike is complete.

20 KATIE AND WIL'S TRAIL

This easygoing hike guides visitors over Dundee Creek and into the forest for overlooks and wetland views aplenty at this gem in Baltimore County.

Start: Marshy Point Nature Center
Elevation gain: 20 feet
Maximum grade: 2%
Distance: 1.4-mile lollipop
Difficulty: Easy
Hiking time: About 1 hour
Best seasons: Year-round
Fees and permits: Free
Trail contact: Marshy Point Nature Center, 7130 Marshy Point Rd., Middle River, MD; (410) 887-2817; marshypoint.org

Dogs: Yes, on a leash no longer than 6 feet
Trail surface: Mostly paved
Land status: Private nature center
Nearest town: Baltimore
Maps: National Geographic Trails Illustrated Topographic Map 772 (Delmarva Peninsula). A trail map can also be accessed online at marshypoint.org.
Amenities: Restrooms, picnic tables, nature center
Cell service: Reliable

FINDING THE TRAILHEAD

Pick up the orange-blazed Katie and Wil's Trail to the left of the Marshy Point Nature Center. GPS: N39°20'56.0" / W76°22'14.5"

THE HIKE

The Marshy Point Nature Center in Baltimore County is a true gem, boasting ten named hiking trails, as well as accessible viewpoints, a self-guided paddling trail, a butterfly garden, a cartop boat launch, a community garden, and children's programs. A waddling resident duck keeps watch inside the nature center, while owls, turkeys, and a domestic chicken named Henrietta are eager to greet visitors from their outdoor enclosures adjacent to the center.

This hike that begins on the orange-blazed Katie and Wil's Trail sets off steps from the nature center. Shortly before the 0.1-mile mark, you will be tempted to stroll along a spur trail on the right, presumably for views across Dundee Creek from the overlook. Unfortunately, the reeds top 10 feet tall, making it impossible to see much of anything, though there is a nice bench for a quick rest. There are views, however, and they are just around the corner.

Bypassing the walk to the overlook, continue on Katie and Wil's Trail and you will arrive at a wooden bridge across Dundee Creek at the 0.1-mile mark. These are the money views, and they are spectacular. Cross the bridge and continue on the paved path until you reach a bench at the 0.2-mile mark. At the 0.4-mile mark, turn right onto the purple-blazed Brinkmans Trail. The path is no longer paved, but is a gravel service road. Turn right again at the 0.5-mile mark onto the wooded Vernal Pond Trail.

Down this path you'll find a group camping site with picnic tables, rustic log benches, and a privy, as well as a short spur trail that leads to an overlook with views across the wetlands. It's a fairly narrow walk to the overlook, with tall reeds on either side, but you will find worthwhile views from the water's edge. Retrace your steps to the group

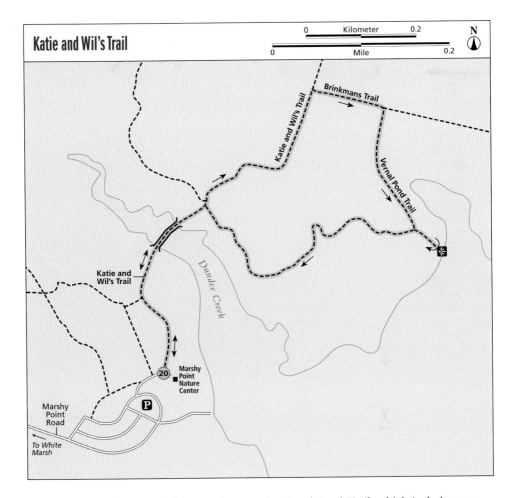

Katie and Wil's Trail

camping site, then turn left to continue on the Vernal Pond Trail, which includes steps on a three-slat-wide boardwalk path.

At the 1.2-mile mark, turn left to reconnect with Katie and Wil's Trail. Retrace your steps to the trailhead. Your hike is complete at the 1.4-mile mark.

MILES AND DIRECTIONS

0.0 Pick up the orange-blazed Katie and Wil's Trail to the left of the Marshy Point Nature Center.

0.1 Bypass the walk to the overlook. Instead, continue on to cross the bridge over Dundee Creek.

0.4 Turn right on the Brinkmans Trail.

0.5 Turn right on the Vernal Pond Trail.

1.2 Turn left on Katie and Wil's Trail.

1.4 Arrive back at the trailhead. Your hike is complete.

21 LIFE OF THE DUNES, FOREST, AND MARSH TRAILS

You can't go to Assateague Island National Seashore and not see free-roaming wild ponies. Thankfully, between three short must-hike trails—Life of the Dunes, Life of the Forest, and Life of the Marsh—you are nearly guaranteed to see them. You may even see ponies wandering the bike trail or grazing in the parking area, even carousing at the campground.

Start: Last parking area at the end of Bayberry Road
Elevation gain: 5 feet
Distance: 1.8 miles (total)
Difficulty: Easy
Hiking time: 2 to 2.5 hours
Best seasons: Fall through spring
Fees and permits: $$$$ for vehicles (good for 7 days); no entry fee for cyclists or pedestrians
Trail contact: Assateague Island National Seashore, 7206 National

Seashore Ln., Berlin, MD; (410) 641-1441; nps.gov/asis
Dogs: No
Trail surface: Mostly sand and dirt trails, some grass
Land status: National seashore
Nearest town: Ocean City
Maps: National Geographic Trails Illustrated Topographic Map 772 (Delmarva Peninsula). Park maps are also available at the Assateague Island Visitor Center.

FINDING THE TRAILHEAD

The Life of the Dunes trailhead is located at the back of the last parking area at the end of Bayberry Road. GPS: N38°11'25.0" / W75°09'33.7"

THE HIKE

Three coastal hiking trails are located along Bayberry Drive at Assateague Island National Seashore: the Life of the Dunes Trail (0.8 mile), Life of the Forest Trail (0.5 mile), and Life of the Marsh Trail (0.5 mile). Each of the three trails allows visitors to explore a unique aspect of the national seashore, and given the short length of each one, they're well worth the time, even though you will need to make a short drive or bicycle ride to reach each trailhead.

LIFE OF THE DUNES TRAIL

Begin at the south end of the national seashore with the Life of the Dunes Trail and work your way forward. The terrain of the Life of the Dunes Trail is almost entirely soft sand. It's not the easiest terrain for walking, but there's much to this short trail beyond beach sand, namely the remains of a 15-mile road called Baltimore Boulevard that once extended to the Maryland-Virginia state line.

Within the first few steps on this trail, you'll notice a number 1 on a sign. A self-guided trail guide interprets numbered posts and is available for purchase at the visitor center. However, there are plenty of trail signs that educate visitors on dune formation, native wildlife, even poison ivy you may encounter along the sandy trail.

The sunny Life of the Dunes Trail provides shade every once in a while thanks to a smattering of coastal pines.

At the 0.1-mile mark, stay to the left on this lollipop trail to reach a placard on Baltimore Boulevard, as well as asphalt slab remains of this road, which was built in the 1950s but then destroyed by a storm in March 1962, never to be rebuilt. The broken slabs are now used by gulls that drop and crack open clams on the hard surface. Developers cleared land for more than 130 side streets along Baltimore Boulevard. Thankfully, nature has largely retaken the area since the destructive storm. Some say that this great nor'easter was the single most important event that led to the creation of the Assateague Island National Seashore in 1965.

Continue looping around and you will reach a wooden overlook at the 0.4-mile mark. There is a nice bench for a respite, as well as a placard educating on native flora like dune grasses, beach heather, and bayberries. Step down from the overlook and proceed on. You'll approach a sign on the different types of poison ivy you may see along the trail, including clinging vine, ground vine, and upright shrubs. Who knew there were so many varieties of poison ivy?

In a few more steps, the sand dune flattens out as you enter a section with some shade thanks to a few coastal pines. At the 0.5-mile mark, there is a live oak tree. It's the only one on the trail, with its long octopus-like branches reaching out to passersby. At the 0.7-mile mark, you will close the loop. Stay left until you return to the trailhead. At the 0.8-mile mark, your sandy hike is complete.

LIFE OF THE FOREST TRAIL

For the Life of the Forest Trail, backtrack along Bayberry Road less than 2 miles until you reach the parking area with room for nearly a dozen vehicles on the left side of the road. The trailhead is located on the southeast side of the parking area. As you proceed, note that no pets are allowed on this trail, and that it is only accessible to pedestrians—as in, no cyclists. There is a bike rack to the right of the trail.

As you proceed along a crushed oyster shell trail, you will be enveloped by coastal pines, which thankfully provide some semblance of shade. By the 0.1-mile mark, you will reach a naturally occurring freshwater pond, one of several scattered throughout the national seashore's forested area. These small ponds can form in shallow depressions between old dunes or in low-lying areas, and they serve as an oasis for thirsty island dwellers, like white-tailed deer and wild ponies. Freshwater pockets float atop more-dense salt water and are replenished by rainfall.

In a few more steps, you will arrive at a short section of boardwalk trail that leads to an over-water wooden walkway for views across the scattered tidal wetlands. Continue straight ahead, then veer left to walk out to the end of the boardwalk. Here you'll also learn more about Assateague's maritime forests, which are ruled by tall loblolly pines that block wind and sun, creating sheltered habitats for plants and animal life, like ponies and deer that seek refuge in the pine forest during storms. Retrace your steps, then turn left at the 0.3-mile mark for more views of coastal grasses and pines. Retrace your steps again, then turn left to continue on to the trailhead to complete your hike at the 0.5-mile mark.

LIFE OF THE MARSH TRAIL

The third hike, the Life of the Marsh Trail, is less than 1 mile from the Life of the Forest Trail, tucked away on Bayside Drive, across from the Bayside Campground. There is a dedicated parking area on the left side of Bayside Drive. The loop hike begins at a large trail kiosk on the east side of the parking area. From here, proceed along the elevated

An elevated boardwalk trail showcases the tidal marshes on Assateague Island on the Life of the Marsh Trail.

boardwalk trail until you reach an over-water boardwalk that showcases the tidal marshes of Assateague Island. Keep your eyes open for kayakers paddling among the marsh grasses.

At the 0.2-mile mark, turn left on this boardwalk path. In a few steps, you will reach a placard focusing on the waterbirds of the tidal marsh, including the greater snow goose, snowy egret, and black skimmer. In any given year, more than a hundred species of birds may be spotted in and around the freshwater and tidal marshes of Assateague Island. Depending on the season, they may be migrating, nesting, or breeding. Often, they are in search of food.

In a few more steps, a colorful placard educates on bay ecology. Bays serve as vast nurseries and feeding grounds for fish, mollusks, crustaceans, and various other marine life. Vital nutrients produced by tidal marshes and seagrass communities enrich bay waters, which in turn enrich all marine life. Step down a few wooden steps and walk out onto the sandy beach. Notice that the waters are rather shallow, so you can walk out quite a distance. Retrace your steps to the fork at the 0.4-mile mark, and stay left to return to the parking area. At the 0.5-mile mark, your hike is complete.

MILES AND DIRECTIONS

LIFE OF THE DUNES TRAIL

0.0   Begin to the right of the large trail kiosk at the back of the parking area.

0.1   Stay left on this lollipop trail to reach a placard on Baltimore Boulevard. From here, explore and walk across asphalt slab remains of this road.

0.4   Arrive at a wooden overlook, which includes a relaxing bench.

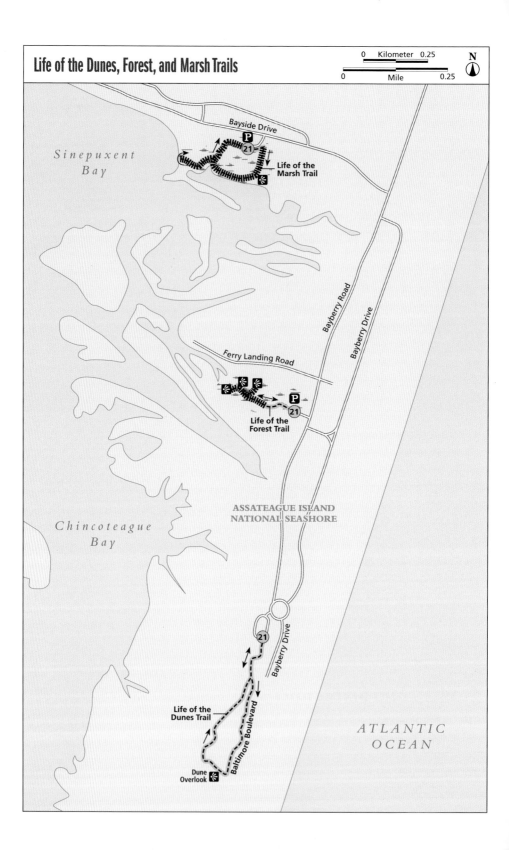

Life of the Dunes, Forest, and Marsh Trails

Sinepuxent Bay

Bayside Drive

P

21

Life of the
Marsh Trail

Bayberry Road

Bayberry Drive

Ferry Landing Road

P

21

Life of the
Forest Trail

ASSATEAGUE ISLAND
NATIONAL SEASHORE

Chincoteague
Bay

21

Bayberry Drive

Life of the
Dunes Trail

Baltimore Boulevard

Dune
Overlook

ATLANTIC
OCEAN

0   Kilometer   0.25

0   Mile   0.25

N

0.7 Close the loop, then turn left for the final steps of the trail.

0.8 Arrive back at the trailhead. Your hike is complete.

LIFE OF THE FOREST TRAIL

0.0 Begin from the trailhead on the southeast side of the parking area.

0.1 Reach a naturally occurring freshwater pond. Then, walk along a section of boardwalk trail before strolling along an over-water wooden boardwalk for views across the wetlands. Stay left to walk to the end.

0.2 Reach the end of the wooden boardwalk, then retrace your steps.

0.3 Arrive at a fork, then turn left for more views of coastal grasses and pines. Retrace your steps again, then turn left at the fork to continue on to the trailhead.

0.5 Arrive back at the trailhead. Your hike is complete.

LIFE OF THE MARSH TRAIL

0.0 Begin at the large trail kiosk on the east side of the parking area. Proceed along an elevated boardwalk, then move across an over-water section of wooden boardwalk.

0.2 Turn left until you reach an overlook, then placards on waterbirds and bay ecology. Step down, then walk out onto the beach. Retrace your steps.

0.4 Reach a fork, then stay to the left to return to the parking area.

0.5 Arrive back at the trailhead. Your hike is complete.

22 MALLOWS BAY PARK HIKING TRAIL

Mallows Bay is home to more than 185 documented shipwrecks, including nearly 100 wooden-hulled steamships that date back to World War I. Some historic vessels date all the way back to the Revolutionary War. This forested hike guides visitors across the park and alongside Mallows Bay for glimpses of the submerged vessels, as well as mature forest and marsh habitats.

Start: Mallows Bay Park parking area
Elevation gain: 125 feet
Maximum grade: 7%
Distance: 2.0-mile loop
Difficulty: Easy
Hiking time: 1 to 1.5 hours
Best seasons: Fall through spring
Fees and permits: Free
Trail contact: Mallows Bay–Potomac River National Marine Sanctuary, 1440 Wilson Landing Rd., Nanjemoy, MD; (301) 932-3470; sanctuaries .noaa.gov/mallows-potomac/
Dogs: Yes, on a leash no longer than 6 feet

Trail surface: Mostly sand and dirt trails, some grass
Land status: National marine sanctuary
Nearest town: Indian Head
Maps: A trail map is available online at nmssanctuaries.blob.core.windows .net/sanctuaries-prod/media/ docs/20200427-mallows-bay-hiking -guide.pdf.
Amenities: Porta-potties, picnic tables
Cell service: Reliable
Special considerations: For best viewing of the ghost fleet of submerged ships, visit at low tide.

FINDING THE TRAILHEAD

The trailhead for the Mallows Bay Park Hiking Trail is located on the south side of the parking area, adjacent to the scenic overlook. GPS: N38°28'06.7" / W77°15'45.3"

THE HIKE

A short drive from Washington, DC, lies the largest ship graveyard in the Western Hemisphere, extending across 14 square miles in Mallows Bay. More than 185 documented shipwrecks are underwater. Many are visible at low tide. In 2020, the National Oceanic and Atmospheric Administration (NOAA) named Mallows Bay the first national marine sanctuary in the state of Maryland and the Chesapeake Bay watershed in order to protect what remains of the abandoned steamships and vessels.

Today, a hike around Mallows Bay–Potomac River National Marine Sanctuary guides visitors across floodplains, alongside ponds, through a sweetgum forest, and adjacent to wetlands, allowing for views of the historic vessels on the way. Before you take your first steps, make time for the scenic overlook with an all-weather telescope that enables better viewing of some of the more prominent, close-in ships, like "Gateway to Bethlehem" and "The Barge Wreck."

Left of the overlook is a large trail kiosk that marks the Mallows Bay Park Hiking Trail, which in reality is an aggregation of three park trails: the Nature Loop, Beaver Trail, and

Mallows Bay is home to more than 185 documented shipwrecks, including nearly 100 wooden-hulled steamships that date back to World War I.

Ridge Trail. Walk around the brown iron gate, then stay right until you see a sign that reads "Start Nature Loop." Turn left to walk alongside Mallows Bay for a counterclockwise loop hike. You'll soon pass a picnic table, then a bench at an overlook that looks out at one of the shipwrecks.

From here, the trail descends into the forest. At the 0.1-mile mark, you will reach a marker with a green arrow pointing to the left to mark the continuation of the trail. But wait, what's to the right? Walk down the hill to the right and you will arrive at a marshy habitat with water-level views of one of the ghost ships, as well as a bench. Painted turtles can frequently be seen sunning on exposed logs in the marsh. Brightly colored wildflowers line the trail in spring, while clusters of green pawpaw fruits can be seen overhead in summer courtesy of the abundant pawpaw trees.

Retrace your steps, then turn right to reconnect with the green-blazed Nature Loop. Shortly, you will be well above the beaver pond. An overlook with a bench allows you to rest for a spell and take in the views before arriving at a trail sign at the 0.5-mile mark. Turn right to connect with the Beaver and Ridge Trails. You'll see a "Start Beaver Trail" sign and will soon reach a second bench overlooking the scenic beaver pond.

At the 0.6-mile mark, the Beaver Trail splits in two. An "Easy Route" is straight ahead, but for this hike, turn right for the Beaver Trail. Not to worry, you're not in for a strenuous hike by failing to opt for the easy route. Descend for water-level views of the beaver pond, then cross a small footbridge and arrive at yet another bench. As you proceed, you

Settle in on one of several benches placed along the trail to enjoy views across Mallows Bay.

will enter a sweetgum forest. Note the presence of spiky fruits, also known as burr balls or gum balls, scattered on the forest floor and trail.

The Beaver Trail ends at the 1.0-mile mark, just before Wilson Landing Road, the road that leads into the park. On the other side of the road, the Ridge Trail begins, guiding you through an old-growth forest dominated by pines. At the first overlook, peer down into the creek, tinted red from tannins that have naturally leached from plant matter. At the 1.2-mile mark is an unusual sight in a mature forest, what's left of an old farm truck. Remains from the Wilson family farm can be seen on the trail, including the 1932 Packard pickup truck.

You'll pass a few more benches before the Ridge Trail seems to end at the 1.4-mile mark. Turn right, as if to walk back to the parking area, then jump back onto the trail after a few steps. Stay right to continue on to Mallows Bay. A small peninsula juts out, revealing lush wetlands on the right and a historic vessel on the left, settled in Burning Basin. Burning Basin is where the Bethlehem Steel Corporation drained the water in 1942 to allow the burning and scuttling of World War I ships.

From the peninsula, retrace your steps and turn right to pass a bench and a picnic table before arriving at a launch for nonmotorized watercraft, like kayaks and canoes, at the 1.9-mile mark. Walk up the paved road on the left to reach the scenic overlook adjacent to the trail kiosk. Your hike is complete at the 2.0-mile mark.

Mallows Bay Park Hiking Trail

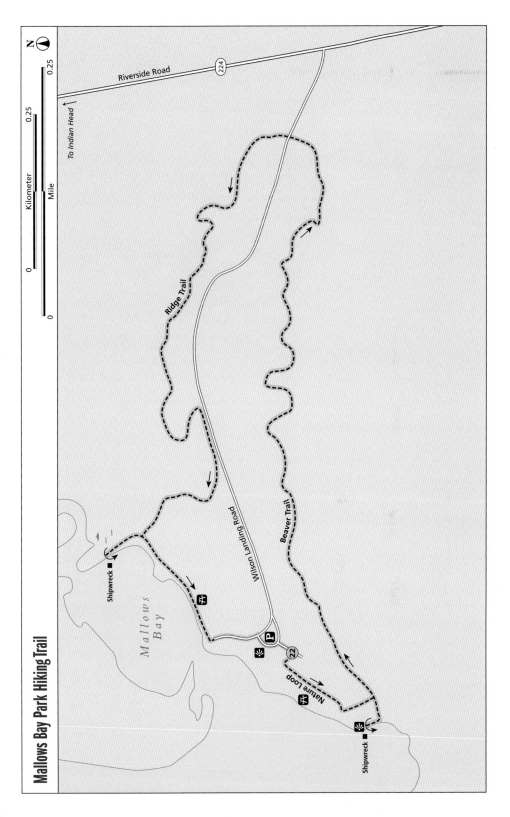

Bring a picnic lunch and make a stop at one of two shaded picnic tables along the hiking trail at Mallows Bay–Potomac River National Marine Sanctuary.

MILES AND DIRECTIONS

0.0 Begin at the large trail kiosk for the Mallows Bay Park Hiking Trail. Here, the Nature Loop begins.

0.1 Stay right to walk out to a marshy habitat with water-level views of one of the ghost ships. Retrace your steps to the Nature Loop, then turn right onto the trail.

0.5 Turn right at the sign for the Beaver and Ridge Trails.

0.6 The Beaver Trail splits into two trails. Continue on the right path.

1.0 The Beaver Trail ends. Cross over Wilson Landing Road to connect with the Ridge Trail.

1.2 Notice the remains of the Wilson family farm, including a 1932 Packard pickup truck.

1.4 The Ridge Trail ends, but stay to the right to continue on to Mallows Bay to walk out onto a small peninsula at Burning Basin. Retrace your steps, then turn right onto the trail.

1.9 Arrive at a paved area and launch for nonmotorized watercraft. Walk up the paved road to the scenic overlook.

2.0 Arrive back at the trailhead. Your hike is complete.

23 MYRTLE POINT PARK

This delightful loop hike in St. Mary's County guides visitors along a stretch of sandy beach, through a grove of coastal pines, and alongside a scenic saltwater pond. Plan to settle in at Ghost Beach and take in the views of the Governor Thomas Johnson Bridge over the Patuxent River.

Start: Myrtle Point Park main parking area
Elevation gain: 75 feet
Maximum grade: 4%
Distance: 2.7-mile loop
Difficulty: Easy
Hiking time: 1.5 to 2 hours
Best seasons: Year-round
Fees and permits: $–$$$$ (cash only)
Trail contact: Myrtle Point Park, 24050 Patuxent Blvd., California, MD; (301) 475-4200; myrtlepoint.org
Dogs: Yes, on a leash no longer than 6 feet
Trail surface: Mostly sand, grass, and dirt trails
Land status: Private park
Nearest town: Lexington Park

Maps: National Geographic Trails Illustrated Topographic Map 772 (Delmarva Peninsula). A trail map is also available online at myrtlepoint .org/hikingmap.html.
Amenities: Picnic tables, porta-potties
Cell service: Reliable
Special considerations: A per-vehicle entry fee is only charged on weekends and holidays from the first Saturday in May through Labor Day. The park is closed to vehicles from December 1 to March 31. Like many parks in Maryland, the fee for those who live outside the state or county (in this case, St. Mary's County) is higher than the state or county resident fee.

FINDING THE TRAILHEAD

The start of Mill Creek Lane (hiking trail) is just past the back of the main parking area. GPS: N38°19'48.3" / W76°29'47.2"

THE HIKE

It's not hard to see why Myrtle Point Park in St. Mary's County is a special recreation area and a favorite among county residents and those who come from farther away in the mid-Atlantic region to experience the joy of this relaxing park on the water. Set on a peninsula that juts out into the Patuxent River, the 192-acre park wows with scenic water frontage, saltwater ponds, and native wildlife like the belted kingfisher and the eastern box turtle.

There is more than one spot where you can begin the yellow-blazed perimeter hike that loops around Myrtle Point Park, but it's most straightforward to begin from the main gravel parking area. Take a few steps past the wooden fence at the back of the parking area. You'll see a picnic area to the right, as well as a large trail kiosk that makes clear in no uncertain terms that dogs must be leashed at all times. A trail map illustrates the five blazed trails at Myrtle Point Park, including the yellow-blazed park loop. A few steps to the left is a large sign for Mill Creek Lane guiding hikers along a wide grassy trail. If you were to take this 0.5-mile trail to the end, you would reach a small picnic area that overlooks Mill Creek.

Walk alongside the water and take in the views of the Governor Thomas Johnson Bridge from the Wet Sox Trail.

A stretch of the Kingfisher Trail wows with coastal pines that warmly welcome visitors along the hiking trail.

Begin walking along this partly shaded trail, but instead of walking to the end, turn right at the 0.2-mile mark to proceed into the dense forest at the sign for the Deep Woods Trail. Along this wooded trail, you'll meander alongside oak, holly, and tulip trees. You will also pass twisted cherry trees and fern-like running cedar plants. From the trail, you can peek out at Mill Creek, and even catch glimpses of the homes across the creek in the Scotch Point neighborhood.

At the 1.2-mile mark, you may begin to see Kingfisher Pond, as well as a serene sandy beach situated in front of the saltwater pond. Then, the trail cuts back inland, but don't worry, you will get your chance to see the pond and step foot on the sandy shore when you turn left onto the Kingfisher Trail at the large trail kiosk at the 1.4-mile mark.

In a few more steps, at the 1.5-mile mark, a spur trail leads off to the left, enabling visitors serene views across Kingfisher Pond. You can also walk along the driftwood-covered beach and take in the views of the Governor Thomas Johnson Bridge that leads to Solomons Island. Retrace your steps to return to the Kingfisher Trail, then turn left to continue encircling the park. You are now walking along the sandstone cliffs that overlook the Patuxent River. Note that this section of trail is replete with coastal pines, as dead pine needles cover the path. At the 1.7-mile mark, a short spur trail on the left enables a second opportunity to descend to the beach for oasis-like water views.

Continue walking and you will reach a wooden bench on the left with views from the cliffs. As you proceed along, follow the signs for waterfront access that leads to an open area with a handful of picnic tables. On the left side of this area, wooden steps lead out to a magnificent stretch of wide sandy beach called Ghost Beach that's just right for building sand castles. Take off your shoes and splash in the refreshing water of the lower

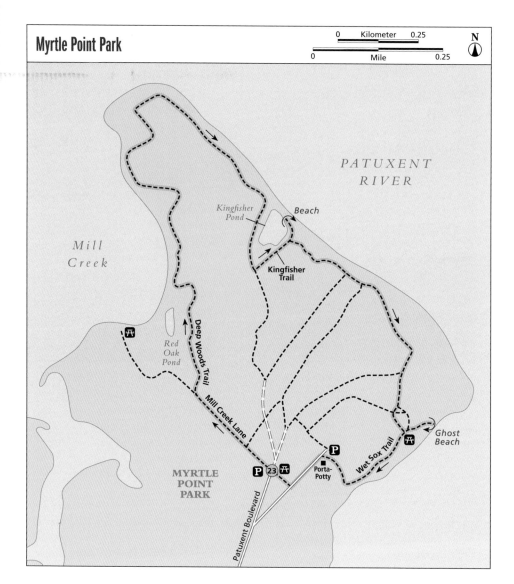

PATUXENT
RIVER

Kingfisher
Pond

Beach

Mill
Creek

Kingfisher
Trail

Red
Oak
Pond

Deep Woods Trail

Mill Creek Lane

Ghost
Beach

P

Wet Sox Trail

P 23

Porta-
Potty

MYRTLE
POINT
PARK

Patuxent Boulevard

Patuxent River while ogling views of the 1.37-mile bridge named for the first governor of Maryland, Thomas Johnson, that joins Calvert County and St. Mary's County.

Once you've enjoyed your time on the beach, retrace your steps up to the picnic area, then cut across to hook up with the Wet Sox Trail. It should come as no surprise that you can wind up with wet socks while walking this trail, especially at high tide or after a heavy rain, as the trail sidles up against the water and reeds on the beach.

At the 2.5-mile mark, a set of steps guides you up to a grassy area and a secondary parking area, one that is closer to Ghost Beach for those who only wish to spend a day digging in sand and splashing in water. From this parking area, turn left onto Patuxent Boulevard, the main road through the park. You will soon see picnic tables on the right. When you do, walk across this grassy section to arrive at the large trail kiosk and main parking area to complete this delightfully scenic loop hike at Myrtle Point Park.

Splash on the driftwood-adorned beach along the Patuxent River at Myrtle Point Park.

MILES AND DIRECTIONS

0.0 Begin on Mill Creek Lane (a 0.5-mile hiking trail), which begins just past the back of the main parking area.

0.2 Turn right onto the Deep Woods Trail.

1.4 Arrive at a large trail kiosk. Turn left onto the Kingfisher Trail.

1.5 Stay left for a spur trail that leads to Kingfisher Pond and a sandy beach. Retrace your steps to the Kingfisher Trail, then turn left.

1.7 Turn left onto a short spur trail that offers a second opportunity to walk out to the beach and savor views across the Patuxent River. Retrace your steps to the Kingfisher Trail, then turn left.

2.1 Arrive at a small picnic area. Walk down wooden steps to walk out to Ghost Beach. Retrace your steps, then walk across the picnic area to connect with the Wet Sox Trail.

2.5 Walk up wooden steps to reach the secondary parking area at Myrtle Point Park. Turn left onto Patuxent Boulevard, the primary park road.

2.7 At the picnic tables, turn right to cut through the area and arrive back at the large trail kiosk and main parking area. Your hike is complete.

Plan to spend a full day at Point Lookout State Park, which sits at the southernmost tip of Southern Maryland. Splash at the swimming beach, explore the historic lighthouse, and brush up on Civil War history at the fortification and prison camp.

Start: Point Lookout Lighthouse
Elevation gain: 20 feet
Maximum grade: 1%
Distance: 2.9-mile loop
Difficulty: Easy
Hiking time: 1.5 to 2 hours
Best seasons: Year-round
Fees and permits: $
Trail contact: Point Lookout State Park, 11175 Point Lookout Rd., Scotland, MD; (301) 872-5688; dnr.maryland.gov/publiclands/pages/southern/pointlookout.aspx
Dogs: Yes, on a leash no longer than 6 feet

Trail surface: Mostly sand, grass, and dirt trails
Land status: State park
Nearest town: Lexington Park
Maps: National Geographic Trails Illustrated Topographic Map 772 (Delmarva Peninsula). A park map is also available at the entrance station or online at dnr.maryland.gov/publiclands/pages/southern/pointlookout.aspx.
Amenities: Picnic tables, restrooms, camp store, nature center, cartop boat launch, fishing pier, museum
Cell service: Reliable

FINDING THE TRAILHEAD

The hike begins at the top of the Point Lookout Road loop, in front of the Point Lookout Lighthouse. GPS: N38°02'20.7" / W76°19'19.9"

THE HIKE

You could easily spend an entire day at Point Lookout State Park, a refreshing coastal park that sits on a peninsula in St. Mary's County. Located at the southernmost tip of Southern Maryland, it's a winner with a historic lighthouse, nature center, swimming beach, and Civil War re-creations, including a prisoner camp. From the marina, you can even take a day cruise on the Chesapeake Bay to Smith Island. There's also a campground with more than a hundred wooded campsites that can accommodate tents and RVs to make it a weekend at this pristine state park.

For this hike, take Point Lookout Road all the way to the Point Lookout Lighthouse, an original structure that once served the shipping community. The lighthouse was in service from 1830 until it was darkened in 1966. After this time, the lighthouse and grounds were used at various points by the US Navy, then handed over to the Maryland Park Service in 2006. Efforts are under way to restore the appearance of the lighthouse to its look in the 1920s.

Just before you reach the lighthouse, you'll see a small parking area, as well as restrooms. From the lighthouse, walk along the west side of Point Lookout Road. You will see a hiking trail to the right of rocks that help protect the peninsula from erosion. Walk north along this sandy trail for a clockwise loop. Take in the views across the Potomac River as you make your way to the unguarded swimming beach at the 0.4-mile mark. Here

Make time for a re-creation of Camp Hoffman, a prisoner camp during the Civil War. Here you'll find prisoner tents and a post office.

you're steps away from a massive shaded picnic area with restrooms that can be hopping on weekends.

By the 0.5-mile mark, the trail on the beach essentially ends and you'll jog right, then left to walk along a gravel service road. As you walk along you'll begin to encounter educational placards that add to the hike, like one on shipwrecks in general and those that surely litter the bottom of the Potomac River and Chesapeake Bay. At the 0.7-mile mark, you will reach Fort Lincoln, a re-creation of a Civil War fortification, which includes barracks and officer quarters. Explore the grounds of Fort Lincoln, then look for the exit sign at the northwest corner of the re-creation. This will guide you out of the fortification and back onto the gravel trail.

At the 0.9-mile mark, stay to the left to continue walking out to a pristine stretch of coastline that's shaded with coastal pines. This is a great spot to stop for a snack or lunch break while taking in the views from the water's edge. If you walk all the way to the end, look to your right to catch a glimpse of the marina on Lake Conoy and the small ship that takes guests to Smith Island. From here, retrace your steps, then turn left at the 1.2-mile mark. The trail is fairly narrow in a few places, but it's not a long walk to reach Point Lookout Road. Walk across the road to watch casual anglers dropping their lines from the fishing pier. There's a parking area, restrooms, and a small slice of beach to the left of the pier that's begging to be explored.

From the pier, retrace your steps to Point Lookout Road, then turn left to continue closing the loop on the return to the lighthouse. At the 2.0-mile mark, you will reach a re-creation of Camp Hoffman, a Civil War prisoner-of-war camp, which includes prisoner tents and a post office. Continue south along Point Lookout Road and it will soon

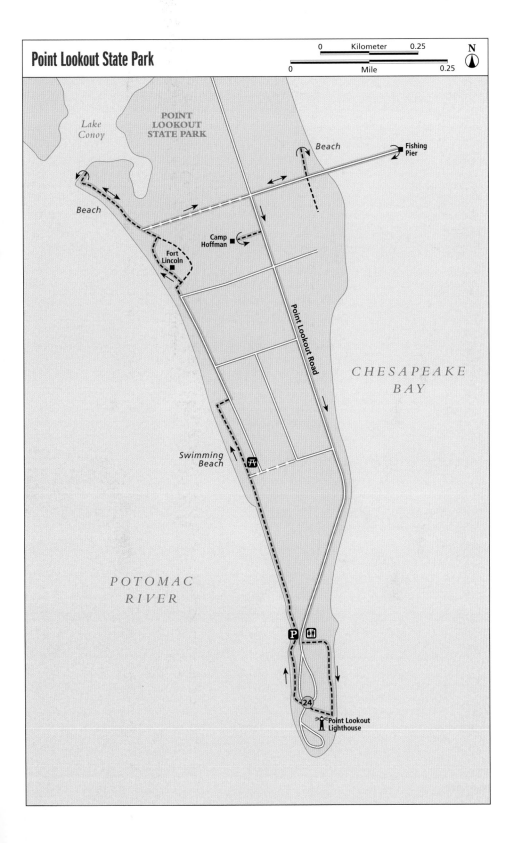

Point Lookout State Park

0   Kilometer   0.25

0   Mile   0.25

N

Lake Conoy

POINT LOOKOUT STATE PARK

Beach

Fishing Pier

Beach

Camp Hoffman

Fort Lincoln

Point Lookout Road

CHESAPEAKE BAY

Swimming Beach

POTOMAC RIVER

P

24

Point Lookout Lighthouse

The loop hike around Point Lookout State Park in Scotland begins on a stretch of trail that looks out across the Potomac River.

open up and expose a hiking trail on the east side along the water. Hop back on the trail and take this all the way to the lighthouse, which you will reach at the 2.9-mile mark to complete your hike.

MILES AND DIRECTIONS

0.0   Begin at the top of the Point Lookout Road loop, in front of the Point Lookout Lighthouse. Look for a narrow northbound trail on the west side of the road.

0.4   Arrive at a swimming beach.

0.5   The beach trail ends. Turn right, then left to access a gravel service road.

0.7   Arrive at Fort Lincoln. Explore the area, then cut across to the exit sign at the north-west corner of the re-creation to reconnect with the trail.

0.9   Stay to the left to walk out onto a pristine stretch of sandy beach with views of Lake Conoy and the marina. Retrace your steps.

1.2   Turn left onto a narrow connector trail that leads to Point Lookout Road. Walk across the park road to reach the fishing pier and small stretch of beach. Retrace your steps to Point Lookout Road, then turn left onto the park road.

2.0   Arrive at a re-creation of Camp Hoffman, a former Civil War prisoner camp. Retrace your steps to the park road, then turn right. Shortly, a sandy hiking trail comes into view on the east side of the park road.

2.9   Arrive back at the Point Lookout Lighthouse. Your hike is complete.

25 QUIET WATERS PARK

This easygoing county park wows with a reflecting pool, a scenic river overlook, a chill dog beach, even formal gardens. A loop hiking trail on the south end of Quiet Waters Park allows you to enjoy all of these features and more on a visit to this recreation area.

Start: Quiet Waters Park butterfly garden
Elevation gain: 151 feet
Maximum grade: 7%
Distance: 2.8-mile loop
Difficulty: Easy
Hiking time: 1 to 2 hours
Best seasons: Year-round
Fees and permits: $$
Trail contact: Quiet Waters Park, 600 Quiet Waters Park Rd., Annapolis, MD; (410) 222-1777; aacounty.org/departments/recreation-parks/parks/quiet-waters

Dogs: Yes, on a leash no longer than 6 feet
Trail surface: Mostly paved trails
Land status: County park
Nearest town: Annapolis
Maps: National Geographic Trails Illustrated Topographic Map 772 (Delmarva Peninsula). A park map is also available at the entrance station.
Amenities: Picnic tables, restrooms, dog park, dog beach, picnic pavilions, visitor center, formal gardens, playground, cartop boat launch
Cell service: Reliable

FINDING THE TRAILHEAD

 The hike begins at the butterfly garden near the northeast corner of the reflecting pool. GPS: N38°56'13.7" / W76°30'04.6"

THE HIKE

At Quiet Waters Park near Annapolis, you'll be almost overwhelmed by the visitor-pleasing features, like a dog park, a dog beach, formal gardens, a playground, picnic pavilions, and a reflecting pool with fountains. That's just to name a few. It's no wonder this quiet park (no pun intended) is such a fan favorite, even despite the entry fee.

As you enter the park, motor along Quiet Waters Park Road until you reach a large parking area on the left that's nearly adjacent to the reflecting pool. This is one of more than a dozen parking areas at this 340-acre park in Anne Arundel County. Set on a peninsula that touches the South River and Harness Creek, this easy hike affords plenty of opportunities to enjoy water views.

From the parking area, walk across the park road to begin the hike at the butterfly garden. Proceed south along a paved path as the fountains in the crystal-clear reflecting pool on your right spray water high up into the air. At the 0.2-mile mark, turn left to cross back over Quiet Waters Park Road. From here, follow along a shaded path, passing an outdoor concert stage on your right, then a dog park on your left.

At the 0.7-mile mark, turn left at the sign for the South River Overlook that guides visitors out to views across the South River. You'll first approach a scenic overlook with two shaded gazebos and two metal viewfinders for seeing far across the water to Old Cedar Point and Cape Loch Haven on the other side of the river. From here, descend a flight of stairs and turn left for the sandy dog beach adjacent to Loden Pond. Retrace

Follow the signs to the South River Overlook to revel in far-reaching views across the South River from under a shaded gazebo.

your steps to the stairs, then proceed along a walkway most often used by fishing enthusiasts eager to drop a line. Retrace your steps again, then turn left onto a pathway that leads up the hill and alongside Harness Creek.

At the 1.4-mile mark, you will once again be at the sign for the South River Overlook. Turn left to walk toward a small picnic area that overlooks the creek. In summer, the views are largely covered up by dense foliage. Continue into the shaded forest to reach an unobscured scenic overlook with two benches and a picnic table steps off the trail on the left. Stay on the paved trail and you'll pass the Holly Pavilion before the path sidles up alongside Quiet Waters Road.

At the 2.3-mile mark, turn left to walk on the park road next to the formal gardens, visitor center, and Blue Heron Center. The path then ducks into the woods on the left. Stay right at the Dogwood Pavilion, then stay right again to keep on this path. At the stop sign, exit to the right to jump into the parking area, then walk alongside the Blue Heron Center, visitor center, and formal gardens, which are now on the right.

At the 2.7-mile mark, you will arrive at the reflecting pool. Turn left to walk along the perimeter, which is lined with benches to enjoy the relaxing views. At the end of the reflecting pool, turn right then continue on to the butterfly garden. Your hike is complete at the 2.8-mile mark.

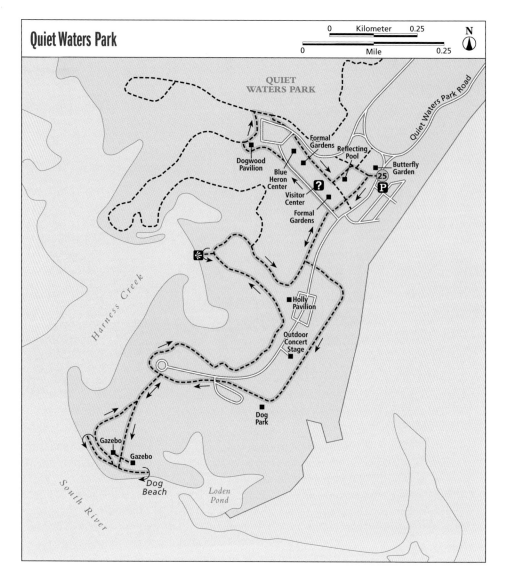

MILES AND DIRECTIONS

0.0 The hike begins at the butterfly garden near the northeast corner of the reflecting pool. Walk south along the paved path. The reflecting pool is on your right.

0.2 Turn left to cross over Quiet Waters Park Road. Follow this path around to pass the outdoor stage and dog park.

0.7 Turn left at the sign for the South River Overlook.

0.9 Arrive at the South River Overlook. Then, walk down the steps and turn left to walk to the dog beach. Retrace your steps and walk past the stairs to the end of the path.

1.1 Reach the end of the fishing wall. Retrace your steps, then turn left onto a path that goes up the hill toward Harness Creek.

The final steps of this hike across Quiet Waters Park near Annapolis follow along floral-filled formal gardens.

1.4   Arrive at the sign for the South River Overlook, then turn left onto the path. You will see a couple of picnic tables on the left side of the path.

1.9   Reach an overlook with two benches and a picnic table.

2.1   Pass the Holly Pavilion, then turn left to walk on the path alongside Quiet Waters Park Road.

2.3   Turn left on the park road to pass the formal gardens, visitor center, and Blue Heron Center.

2.4   Reconnect with the path that leads back into the woods on the left. Stay right at the Dogwood Pavilion, then right again at the T-intersection.

2.6   At the stop sign, step into the parking area, then reconnect with the path. The Blue Heron Center, visitor center, and formal gardens are on your right.

2.7   Turn left at the reflecting pool, then turn right.

2.8   Arrive back at the butterfly garden. Your hike is complete.

26 RED AND ORANGE TRAILS, CALVERT CLIFFS STATE PARK

Dramatic sandstone cliffs and the promise of fossilized keepsake treasures await at the end of the Red Trail at Calvert Cliffs State Park. Create a loop with the Orange Trail, which adds another dimension to this hike by guiding visitors through an old-growth forest.

Start: Parking area closest to the park entrance
Elevation gain: 299 feet
Maximum grade: 9%
Distance: 5.0-mile loop
Difficulty: Easy
Hiking time: 2 to 3 hours
Best seasons: Year-round
Fees and permits: $
Trail contact: Calvert Cliffs State Park, 10540 H. G. Trueman Rd., Lusby, MD; (443) 975-4360; dnr .maryland.gov/publiclands/pages/ southern/calvertcliffs.aspx
Dogs: Yes, on a leash no longer than 6 feet

Trail surface: Mostly dirt, gravel, and sand trails; some paved and wooden boardwalk sections
Land status: State park
Nearest town: Solomons
Maps: National Geographic Trails Illustrated Topographic Map 772 (Delmarva Peninsula). A trail map is also available online at dnr.maryland .gov/publiclands/pages/southern/ calvertcliffs.aspx.
Amenities: Picnic tables, restrooms
Cell service: Reliable
Special considerations: The Orange Trail is located within the hunting area of Calvert Cliffs State Park. The park asks that visitors wear orange if hiking between September and May.

FINDING THE TRAILHEAD

The hike begins at the trail kiosk for the Red Trail to the right of the fishing pond in front of the parking area closest to the park entrance. GPS: N38°23'41.0" / W76°26'06.4"

THE HIKE

More than 13 miles of designated hiking trails crisscross Calvert Cliffs State Park in Lusby, but the trail that sees the lion's share of foot traffic is the Red Trail, which leads directly to dramatic Calvert Cliffs. These stunning sandstone cliffs that dominate the Chesapeake Bay shoreline were formed 10 to 20 million years ago when all of Southern Maryland was essentially underwater. When the sea receded, the sandstone cliffs were exposed, but have slowly eroded over time. In fact, a large section of the cliffs is designated as a "look from a distance, but don't dare touch" area, as noted by the Danger—Do Not Enter sign blocking a section of the sandy beach.

Today, the sand-covered shoreline at Calvert Cliffs is known for 600 species of fossils, like sharks, whales, rays, and seabirds, some as large as small aircraft. Fossil hunting is allowed, even with sieves and shovels, so bring your own tools to gently excavate for prehistoric souvenirs.

From the front parking area, following the sign for the Red Trail past the fishing pond on the left and the trail kiosk on the right. The hiking trail starts out as paved, but transitions to other surfaces including gravel, dirt, wooden boardwalk, and footbridges over the

At Calvert Cliffs State Park, the Red Trail leads directly to the sandy beach framed by dramatic sandstone cliffs.

Once you reach the beach at Calvert Cliffs State Park, heed the Do Not Enter sign to protect the sandstone cliffs from further erosion.

course of this 5-mile hike. At the 0.2-mile mark, the Red Trail sidles up against a service road, but stay to the right to continue on.

You'll reach another service road at the 0.3-mile mark, but stay right again for the Red Trail. Note that bikers and horseback riders are restricted to the service roads in this state park, which is designated as a wildlands area. From here, walk alongside Grays Creek. The trail transitions frequently between sandy surface and wooden boardwalk as you traverse a vast and verdant tidal wetlands area, including ghost trees. These dead, leafless trees were the victims of saltwater intrusion as brackish water moved in from the bay. Well-placed benches along the way allow visitors to sit and take in the views.

At the 1.6-mile mark, the Red Trail meets up with the Orange Trail. You will see a couple of porta-potties on the left side of the trail. Continue on the Red Trail to reach the beach at Calvert Cliffs at the 1.9-mile mark. Take time to walk the beach in search of fossil treasures. However, pay heed to park signage and do not walk on areas that are closed to visitors by the state park.

Once you've finished enjoying the beach, retrace your steps to the start of the Orange Trail at the 2.1-mile mark. Turn right, walk past the porta-potties on the left, and begin a rather steep ascent, which is followed by a steep descent before you cross over a second wetlands area on a wooden footbridge. Much of the Orange Trail is a shady hike through old-growth forest along a path that's quieter and far less-trafficked than the Red Trail.

Red and Orange Trails, Calvert Cliffs State Park

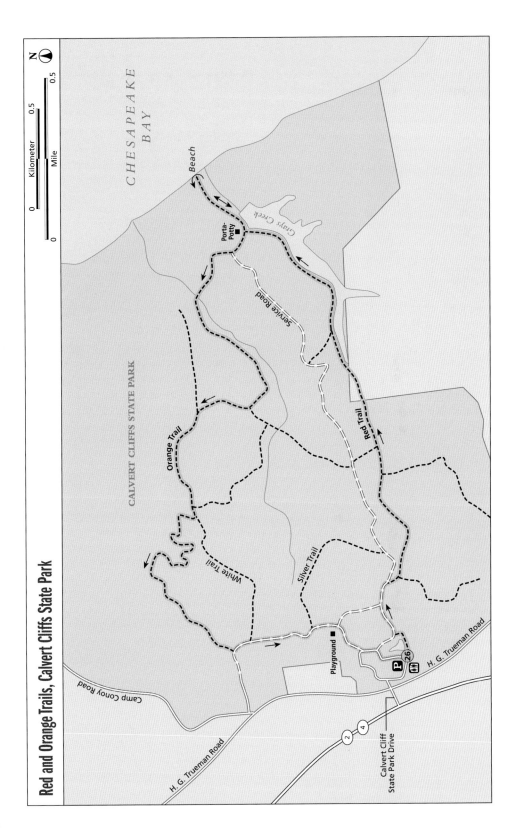

CHESAPEAKE BAY

CALVERT CLIFFS STATE PARK

Grays Creek

Beach

Porta-Potty

Service Road

Orange Trail

Red Trail

White Trail

Silver Trail

Playground

Camp Conoy Road

H. G. Trueman Road

H. G. Trueman Road

Calvert Cliff State Park Drive

N

Kilometer 0 0.5 0.5

Mile 0 0.5

On the Orange Trail, visitors are guided across wooden footbridges and through old-growth forest.

At the 4.4-mile mark, turn left to stay on the Orange Trail. From here, the trail intersects the White Trail, Silver Trail, and another service road (pass by all three) before reaching the park road at the 4.8-mile mark. Follow this road to the parking area. You will pass a recycled tire playground on the right, as well as picnic tables, on the way to your vehicle. Your hike is complete at the 5.0-mile mark.

MILES AND DIRECTIONS

0.0 The hike begins at the trail kiosk for the Red Trail to the right of the fishing pond in front of the parking area closest to the park entrance.

0.2 Stay to the right to continue on the Red Trail.

0.3 Stay to the right to continue on the Red Trail. Walk alongside Grays Creek, then a vast tidal wetlands area.

1.6 The Orange Trail appears on the left, but stay to the right for the Red Trail.

1.9 Arrive at the sandy beach and sandstone cliffs. Retrace your steps to the Orange Trail.

2.1 Turn right on the Orange Trail. The trail continues into an old-growth forest.

4.4 Turn left to stay on the Orange Trail.

4.8 Reach the park road. Continue on this road to the parking area.

5.0 Arrive back at the parking area. Your hike is complete.

27 SANDY POINT STATE PARK

Enjoy a relaxing hike across sandy beach and tidal wetlands at Sandy Point State Park in Annapolis. The vistas of the historic 4.3-mile dual-span bridge are unparalleled. Get schooled on the Sandy Point Shoal Lighthouse before you end your day at this gem of a state park.

Start: Sandy Point State Park main parking lot
Elevation gain: 13 feet
Maximum grade: 1%
Distance: 1.0-mile double loop
Difficulty: Easy
Hiking time: 45 minutes to 1 hour
Best seasons: Year-round
Fees and permits: $
Trail contact: Sandy Point State Park, 1100 East College Pkwy., Annapolis, MD; (410) 974-2149; dnr.maryland.gov/publiclands/pages/southern/sandypoint.aspx
Dogs: Yes, on a leash no longer than 6 feet

Trail surface: Mostly sand and dirt trails, some grass
Land status: State park
Nearest town: Annapolis
Maps: National Geographic Trails Illustrated Topographic Map 772 (Delmarva Peninsula). A park map is also available online at dnr.maryland.gov/publiclands/pages/southern/sandypoint.aspx.
Amenities: Restrooms, picnic tables, volleyball courts, swimming beach
Cell service: Reliable
Special considerations: Go early for more solitude and fewer bugs at this state park that is very popular with families.

FINDING THE TRAILHEAD

The trailhead is located in the southeast corner of the park's primary parking lot. GPS: N39°00'46.0" / W76°23'49.1"

THE HIKE

There's no question that 786-acre Sandy Point State Park in Annapolis is one of the crown jewels of the Maryland Park Service, which includes more than sixty state parks. With sweeping views of the iconic Chesapeake Bay Bridge—which frequently ranks among the most famous bridges in the United States—it can be easy to just sit and watch the cars and trucks cross this 4.3-mile bridge from one of the cozy benches or picnic tables, even the man-made swimming beach. Keep in mind that given this park's immense popularity, the parking lot can fill to capacity very early on summer weekends, often by 10 a.m.

Sandy Point State Park sits on an east-facing peninsula on the Chesapeake Bay, and wows with breathtaking water views all along a scenic 1-mile stretch of beach. Vibrantly colorful sunrises captivate visitors with the dual-span bridge in the foreground. At the time of its opening in 1952, the Chesapeake Bay Bridge was the world's longest continuous over-water steel structure.

There are two short hiking trails at Sandy Point State Park that allow for shade and a break from full-sun water fun, including the Blue Crab Trail, which is closest to the Chesapeake Bay. A few unmarked stretches connect with the Blue Crab Trail to form a double loop across the east side of this state park.

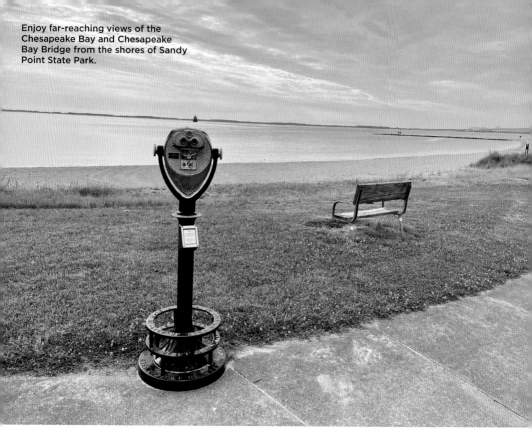

Enjoy far-reaching views of the Chesapeake Bay and Chesapeake Bay Bridge from the shores of Sandy Point State Park.

Begin on the southeast side of the primary parking lot. You will see a wide gravel path, so stay to the right on this path. An Authorized Vehicles Only sign is on the right and a medium-size dumpster is on the left (not to worry, the hike does get better). As you proceed, you'll see at least ten wooden picnic tables tucked away in the well-shaded woods on your left.

At the 0.1-mile mark, you begin to approach the beach. The first of several wooden benches beckons you to come sit for a while, if only to take in the views of the bridge. In a few more steps, you'll be back on a dirt trail, adjacent to picnic tables, but by the 0.2-mile mark, you're back on the beach in earnest. In fact, a short stretch crosses soft sand, so be prepared. Take your shoes off, skip a few stones, put your feet in the water. It can be very relaxing, especially if you go first thing in the morning, before the beachgoers. If you time it right, you may find yourself at the park with only a few anglers and roving treasure hunters with handheld metal detectors.

From the shores of Sandy Point State Park, you can see the Sandy Point Shoal Lighthouse in the distance. A historical placard features then and now photos, key historic dates, and a viewfinder for close-up looks at the redbrick lighthouse that was originally built in 1883 to steer boats away from the dangerous Sandy Point Shoal.

Once you pass the volleyball nets, you'll see a trail pick back up on the left. Stay to your right to continue on a paved trail. Walking on this paved trail, you will pass by picnic pavilions, playgrounds, porta-potties, and a bathhouse. Stay left at the 0.4-mile mark for another bench or two, as well as a second metal viewfinder for close-up views of the bridge.

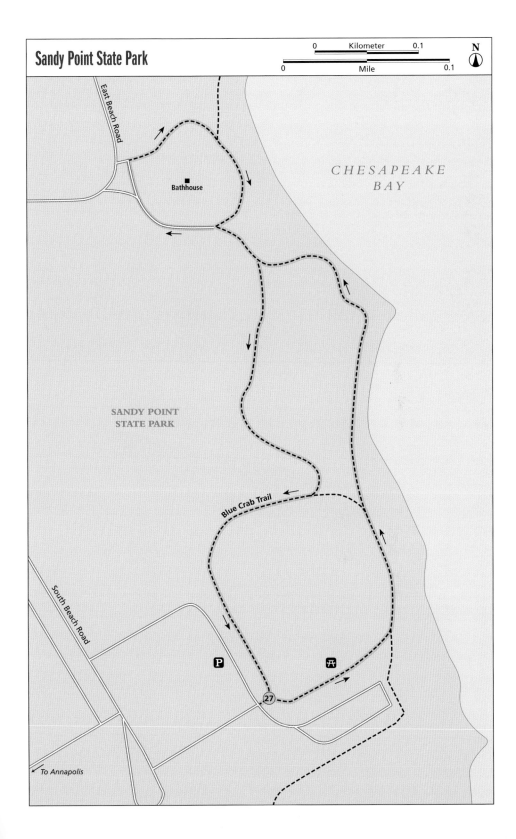

Sandy Point State Park

CHESAPEAKE BAY

Bathhouse

SANDY POINT
STATE PARK

Blue Crab Trail

East Beach Road

South Beach Road

To Annapolis

P

27

Take a seat and savor the views of the historic Chesapeake Bay Bridge from Sandy Point State Park.

At the 0.6-mile mark, you will close the top loop of the double loop. Continue straight ahead, then veer right for the mostly shaded Blue Crab Trail. Cross over a wooden boardwalk and arrive at a small dilapidated building that's worth a quick peek inside, if only to consider why this is here and its purpose at one time. Cross a marsh on a wooden boardwalk before exiting onto a dirt trail. Stay to the right to close the bottom loop, which will guide you through more shaded forest until you return to the trailhead at the 1.0-mile mark to complete your hike.

MILES AND DIRECTIONS

0.0   Begin on the wide gravel path located in the southeast corner of the primary parking lot.

0.1   Pass wooden picnic tables on the left, then approach a wooden bench for bridge views on the right.

0.2   Walk across the soft sand beach. The trail will pick back up on the left, first as grass, then as pavement. Veer right when it turns to a paved path.

0.4   Stay left to walk around the bathhouse and return to waterside.

0.6   Close the top loop. Walk straight ahead, then veer right for the Blue Crab Trail. Cross over a wooden boardwalk and a section of marsh.

0.8   Stay to the right to close the bottom loop.

1.0   Arrive back at the parking area. Your hike is complete.

28 TERRAPIN NATURE PARK

The large, bayfront Terrapin Nature Park is an undeveloped parcel of land on the far west side of Kent County that has been set aside to preserve this environmentally sensitive beach and marsh area. You'll find diverse habitats that range from prairie meadow to tidal marsh, as well as a sought-after sandy beach.

Start: Terrapin Nature Park parking area
Elevation gain: 23 feet
Maximum grade: 3%
Distance: 2.1-mile loop
Difficulty: Easy
Hiking time: 1 to 2 hours
Best seasons: Year-round
Fees and permits: Free
Trail contact: Terrapin Nature Park, 191 Log Canoe Circle, Stevensville, MD; (410) 758-0835; qac.org/Facilities/Facility/Details/Terrapin -Nature-Area-97
Dogs: Yes, on a leash no longer than 6 feet

Trail surface: Mostly sand and dirt trails, some crushed oyster shells
Land status: County park
Nearest town: Stevensville
Maps: National Geographic Trails Illustrated Topographic Map 772 (Delmarva Peninsula)
Amenities: Porta-potty, picnic tables
Cell service: Reliable
Special considerations: The beach at the 0.6-mile mark looks out at the Chesapeake Bay Bridge and is a fantastic place to settle in for a colorful sunset.

FINDING THE TRAILHEAD

The trailhead is located on the north side of the parking area. GPS: N38°59'24.6" / W76°19'17.7"

THE HIKE

The 276-acre Terrapin Nature Park is located on Maryland's Eastern Shore, on the east side of the Chesapeake Bay Bridge. This large, bayfront park is one of a handful of undeveloped parcels on Kent Island that preserve the environmentally sensitive beach and marsh area. It sits quietly between the shores of the Chesapeake Bay and a small, humdrum office park. If you didn't know it was there, you would miss this gem entirely.

The hike begins on the north side of the shady parking area. You'll see a colorful trail kiosk with a park map. This is clearly where to begin. Your first steps are on the Cross Island Trail, a 6.5-mile rail trail that spans east to west across Kent Island. Along this gravel trail, you'll see grills and picnic tables begging you to sit and stay a while, but this hike has only just begun.

At the 0.1-mile mark, you'll reach a fork. While the Cross Island Trail sets off to the right, you'll want to stay to the left. From here, you're walking on the Terrapin Nature Trail. It's not marked with blazes, but it's easy to follow along the loop. But first, a wooden ramp leading to an obscured overlook. Where does it go? In a few short steps, you will reach the top of the overlook with views across a delightful prairie meadow. A placard educates on what to know about this grassy habitat. Retrace your steps, then turn right to continue on the hiking trail. In a few more steps, you'll reach another placard on the importance of leaving the smallest footprint you can on the environment.

A small wooden bridge guides visitors over an inlet then leads to the beach at Terrapin Nature Park.

Kick off your shoes and walk out to the beach for a splash in the Chesapeake Bay at Terrapin Nature Park.

At the 0.2-mile mark, a sign indicates that the beach is to the right. Turn right here to continue on this gravel trail. Proceed ahead, but make time for the wildlife observation blind on the left for a look across the tidal wetlands on your way to the sandy beach. The trail loops around the wetlands, offering up magnificent views on either side. Then, you'll reach a gazebo, a porta-potty, and your first beach access point at the 0.6-mile mark. Prepare to be awed by sensational west-facing views of the Chesapeake Bay Bridge. Spend some time wading or swimming in the Chesapeake Bay, even skipping stones across the gently lapping bay waters.

Walk south along the beach or return to the Terrapin Nature Trail, which now runs parallel to the shoreline. At the 0.8-mile mark, cross a small wooden bridge over an inlet before you return to the nature trail along the beach. On this trail made of sand and crushed oyster shells, you'll pass several benches and beach access points. At the 1.0-mile mark, your time with sandy beach views comes to an end. Continue on the Terrapin Nature Trail by turning left, or add on an extra 1.2-mile loop by turning right for the South Meadow Loop.

For this hike, stay left for the Terrapin Nature Trail. You will enter a forested section and will do so in earnest when you veer left at the 1.3-mile mark. Continue along this mostly shaded section of trail until you reach the 1.9-mile mark. Stay to the right to proceed toward the parking area. Your hike is complete at the 2.1-mile mark.

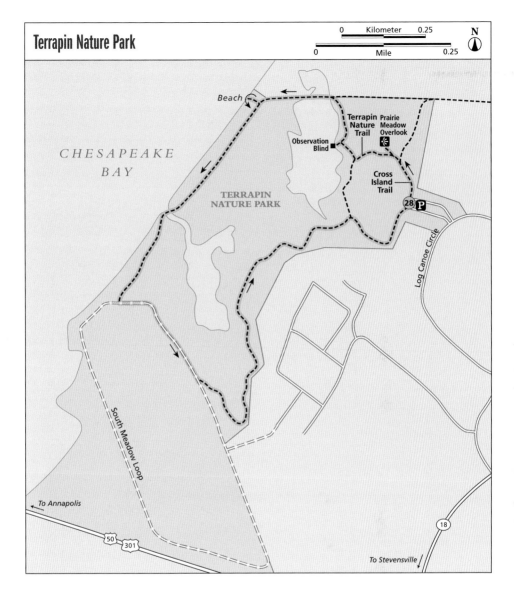

Terrapin Nature Park

CHESAPEAKE
BAY

Beach

Terrapin Prairie
Nature Meadow
Trail Overlook

Observation
Blind

TERRAPIN
NATURE PARK

Cross
Island
Trail

Log Canoe Circle

South Meadow Loop

To Annapolis

50 301

18

To Stevensville

0   Kilometer   0.25
0   Mile   0.25

N

MILES AND DIRECTIONS

0.0   Begin at the trailhead at the north side of the parking area.

0.1   Reach a fork. Stay to the left for the Terrapin Nature Trail. In a few more steps, arrive at a wooden overlook with views across a prairie meadow.

0.2   Turn right at the beach sign. Stop for the wildlife observation blind on the left.

0.6   Arrive at the first beach access point.

0.8   Cross a wooden bridge over an inlet.

1.0   Turn left to proceed on the Terrapin Nature Trail.

1.3   Veer left to continue into the forest.

From the sandy beach at Terrapin Nature Park, take in west-facing views of the iconic Chesapeake Bay Bridge.

1.9 Turn right to proceed to the parking area.

2.1 Arrive back at the parking area. Your hike is complete.

29 TIDAL POND LOOP TRAIL

This coastal hike at the Sassafras Natural Resources Management Area in Kennedyville cuts across various terrains, including old dirt roads, farmlands, and young-growth forest, even a sandy beach at the Sassafras River. Cliffside views wow on the Old Lodge Trail, the best-kept secret in Kent County, Maryland.

Start: Sassafras Natural Resources Management Area parking area
Elevation gain: 151 feet
Maximum grade: 10%
Distance: 3.5-mile lollipop
Difficulty: Easy
Hiking time: 1.5 to 2 hours
Best seasons: Fall through spring
Fees and permits: Free
Trail contact: Sassafras Natural Resources Management Area, 13761 Turners Creek Rd., Kennedyville, MD; (410) 820-1668; dnr.maryland .gov/publiclands/Pages/parkinfo .aspx?parkname=Sassafras%20 NRMA

Dogs: Yes, on a leash no longer than 6 feet
Trail surface: Mostly dirt and grass trails
Land status: Natural resources management area
Nearest town: Chestertown
Maps: National Geographic Trails Illustrated Topographic Map 772 (Delmarva Peninsula)
Other trail users: Cyclists, equestrians
Amenities: Picnic tables
Cell service: Reliable

FINDING THE TRAILHEAD

The trailhead is located on the north end of the parking area. GPS: N39°21'25.9" / W76°00'04.7"

THE HIKE

At the Sassafras Natural Resources Management Area in Kennedyville, more than 9 miles of hiking trails are open to hikers, cyclists, and equestrians. These trails extend across a variety of terrain, including old dirt roads, edges of agricultural fields, sandy beaches and cliffs, and paths that guide visitors through young forest. Plentiful wildlife, like deer, rabbits, turkeys, and songbirds, enliven wonder and curiosity across the scenic trails.

This hike begins at a gravel parking lot along a farm field. A short walk down a trail stemming from the lot leads to a pleasant picnic area. For this hike, however, you'll want to walk past the large trail kiosk and yellow gate at the north end of the parking area. Your first steps on the Tidal Pond Loop Trail begin on a wide dirt path with acres of farmland on the left.

At the 0.3-mile mark, you'll reach a four-way trail junction. Continue straight ahead to remain on the Tidal Pond Loop Trail. At the 0.6-mile mark, stay to the right (you'll see the Old Lodge Trail cutoff to the left). Then, stay to the left as you enter a shaded, young-growth forest and begin the loop section of this hike. In a few more steps, at the 0.8-mile mark, stay to the left to proceed to the sandy beach with far-reaching views across the Sassafras River. Walk up and down the sandy beach that has plenty of stones for skipping and shells for treasure hunting. You may even find pieces of sea glass here and there. Savor the views, maybe even toss down a picnic blanket.

On the Tidal Pond Loop, be sure to savor the views of the tidal wetlands and lily pad-strewn pond.

Once you've enjoyed the vistas, retrace your steps. At the 1.5-mile mark, turn left to reenter the loop trail. You'll now be walking parallel to the beach with lush greenery in between. Note that you will see a trail lead uphill on the right, alongside a farm field, at the 1.6-mile mark. This is not the Tidal Pond Loop Trail. Instead, walk past this to proceed deeper into forest to reach an observation blind overlooking Gilchrest Pond at the 1.8-mile mark. The lily pad–covered pond was named for and dedicated to former congressman Wayne T. Gilchrest in 2008 for his contributions to the stewardship of Maryland's natural resources.

As you continue along, the trail loses its shade and reenters the farmland, with rows of corn on the right as you ascend the hill to close the loop at the 2.3-mile mark. In a few more steps, turn right onto the Old Lodge Trail. You'll quickly see a couple of cement benches on either side of the trail, which appears to have been a road for cars at one point. At the 2.5-mile mark, you'll see a small wooden home that has largely been retaken by nature. It looks as though it could have been a caretaker's home, though there is no "old lodge" to speak of along the trail.

You'll reach a fork in the trail. You can go either way, as the two trails reconnect in only a few steps. Then a slight right turn guides you farther into the woods. At the 2.7-mile mark, you will be rewarded with spectacular views across the Sassafras River from high atop 60-foot-tall bluffs. These cliffs dramatically overlook the shoreline and are surely one of the best-kept secrets in Kent County, Maryland. The cliffs are eroding, so take care

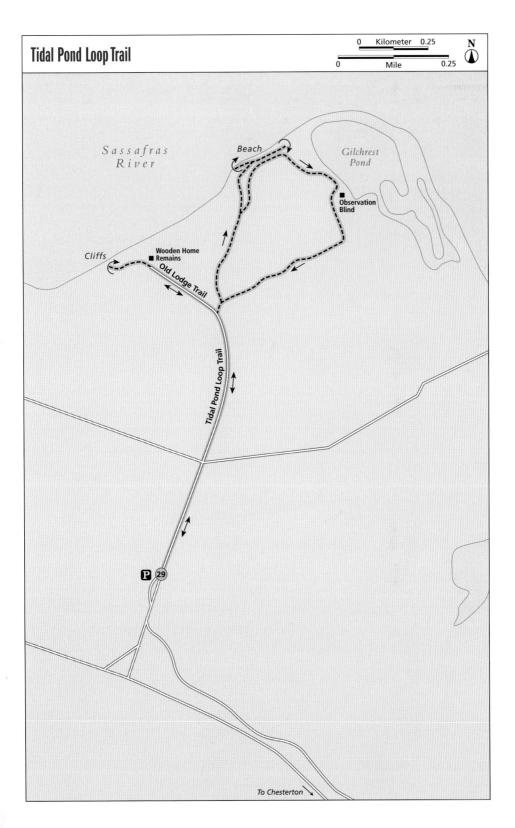

Tidal Pond Loop Trail

Sassafras
River

Beach

Gilchrest
Pond

Observation
Blind

Cliffs

Wooden Home
Remains

Old Lodge Trail

Tidal Pond Loop Trail

P 29

To Chesterton

0   Kilometer   0.25

0   Mile   0.25

N

At the end of the Old Lodge Trail, take in the views of 60-foot-tall bluffs that dramatically overlook the shoreline.

Enjoy a walk along the beach and enjoy far-reaching views across the Sassafras River.

for your own safety and the health of the cliffs to stay on the trail. Keep your eyes open. Eagles can frequently be seen soaring over the Sassafras River.

Imagine how, 400 years ago, the Tockwogh Indians would have seen Captain John Smith and his crew rowing and sailing up the river, greeted him, and invited him to visit their fortified town. Captain Smith wrote about his visit in his journal and how he and his men were treated to a feast and gift-giving. The town has not yet been uncovered by modern archaeologists.

From here, retrace your steps, then turn right at the 3.0-mile mark to continue on the Tidal Pond Loop Trail for the return hike to the parking area. At the 3.5-mile mark, your hike is complete.

MILES AND DIRECTIONS

0.0 Begin on the dirt trail just past the trail kiosk on the north end of the parking area.

0.3 At the four-way junction, continue straight ahead on the dirt trail.

0.6 Stay to the right on the trail, then veer left to begin the loop section of the hike.

0.8 Proceed left again to walk out to the sandy beach on the Sassafras River. Retrace your steps.

1.5 Turn left to reenter the loop trail.

1.8 Arrive at an observation blind overlooking Gilchrest Pond.

2.3 Close the loop, then in a few more steps, turn right onto the Old Lodge Trail.

2.5 Reach a small, dilapidated wooden home overtaken by nature.

2.7 Arrive at 60-foot-tall cliffs overlooking the Sassafras River. Retrace your steps to the start of the Old Lodge Trail.

3.0 Turn right to proceed to the parking area.

3.5 Arrive back at the parking area. Your hike is complete.

30 TURKEY POINT LIGHTHOUSE TRAIL

The historic Turkey Point Lighthouse wows visitors with far-reaching views across the Chesapeake Bay and Elk River from a vantage point more than 100 feet above the waters. On seasonal weekends, visitors can climb to the lantern room for even more spectacular views from high atop the sandstone bluffs.

Start: Parking area at the southern end of Elk Neck State Park
Elevation gain: 197 feet
Maximum grade: 12%
Distance: 2.0-mile lollipop
Difficulty: Easy
Hiking time: 1.5 to 2 hours
Best seasons: Year-round
Fees and permits: Free
Trail contact: Elk Neck State Park, 4395 Turkey Point Rd., North East, MD; (410) 287-5333; dnr.maryland.gov/publiclands/Pages/central/elkneck.aspx

Dogs: Yes, on a leash no longer than 6 feet
Trail surface: Mostly dirt, gravel, and grass trails
Land status: State park
Nearest town: North East
Maps: National Geographic Trails Illustrated Topographic Map 772 (Delmarva Peninsula). A trail map can also be found online at dnr.maryland.gov/publiclands/Pages/central/elkneck.aspx.
Amenities: Porta-potties, gift shop, benches
Cell service: Reliable

FINDING THE TRAILHEAD

The trailhead for the Turkey Point Lighthouse Trail is located in the northwest corner of the parking area, to the right of a large trail kiosk. GPS: N39°27'34.7" / W76°00'22.0"

THE HIKE

Set on the Chesapeake Bay, Elk Neck State Park in North East is home to six forested hiking trails. Unfortunately, three of the trails have been closed to visitors since a tornado with winds nearing 100 mph touched down in Cecil County in June 2019. The impact to the state park was so severe that downed and damaged trees are still being removed from the park. Thankfully, one of the park's gems, the Turkey Point Lighthouse Trail, was not affected by the tornado.

The trail begins in the parking area on the far southwest section of Elk Neck State Park, on a peninsula that touches both the Chesapeake Bay and Elk River. A large trail kiosk educates visitors on the significance of lighthouses and the history of the Turkey Point Lighthouse, in particular, which guided ships to safe waters for nearly 175 years. The light was decommissioned in April 2000. Two years later, on December 2, 2002, the Turkey Point Light Station earned a spot on the National Register of Historic Places.

On weekends from May through October, visitors can climb forty steps to the top of the lighthouse—to a vantage point 129 feet above the choppy waters—to fill up on scenic views for miles from the confluence of the Elk River and Chesapeake Bay. There is

On the way to the lighthouse on the Turkey Point Lighthouse Trail, make a stop at the stone beach on the Chesapeake Bay.

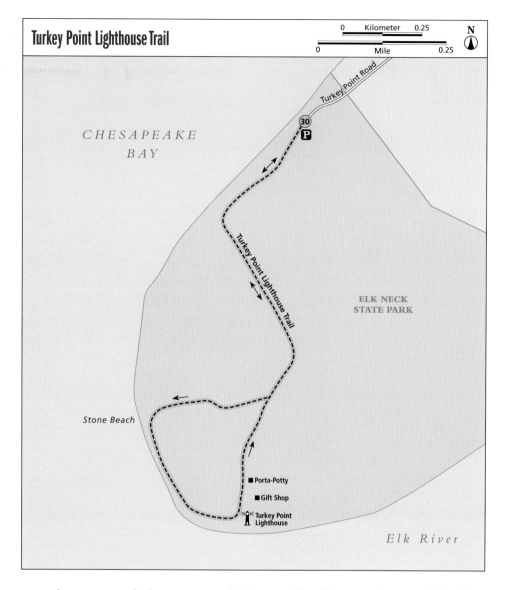

no charge to enter the lantern room, which is open from 10 a.m. to 2 p.m., as is the gift shop at the lighthouse. There are also two porta-potties a few steps from the lighthouse.

The hike to the Turkey Point Lighthouse begins with a gentle ascent on a wide gravel path, which is also used as a service road by state park employees. Several wooden benches along the way offer a respite on the way to the bluffs. There are also a handful of spots along the way where you can pop out to enjoy bay views, though in summer the dense foliage largely obscures the water views. Thankfully, there are wide-open views aplenty from the lighthouse.

You will reach a fork in the trail at the 0.6-mile mark. Note that much of the path up to this point is in full sun. Stay to the right to descend along a grass path and briefly regain welcome shade. At the 0.8-mile mark, a red trail marker on the left leads into the

forest. You will also see a welcoming bench and a stone beach on the right. Step out onto the beach to see how many stones you can skip across the bay water. From here, retrace your steps to reach the red trail marker and reconnect with the trail that leads back into the forest.

As you reenter the forest, ascend along a fairly tight dirt trail (mind the tree roots) until you reach the wide-open grounds of the lighthouse at the 1.1-mile mark. There's a lot to explore here, including the historic stucco-covered Turkey Point Lighthouse that dates back to 1833. The 31½-foot-tall lighthouse was visible for 13 miles when in operation. At one time, the bluff was also home to a keeper's quarters, fog bell tower, boat landing, wood shed, stable, and smokehouse, all of which have since been destroyed. The last keeper was Fannie May Salter, who served until August 1947 when she retired at age 65. Today, a couple of placards share the lighthouse's story, and benches allow visitors to relish the views.

From the lighthouse, continue on a loop, descending along a gravel trail that leads back into the forest. At the 1.4-mile mark, take pause for a large Hawk Watch placard on the right. There are also a couple of picnic tables. Here you'll learn about the migratory hawks that frequent the area, including falcons (year-round), eagles (late October to November), and osprey (mid-September). For best viewing, the park suggests looking to the skies between 9 a.m. and noon.

From here, you will close the loop on this lollipop hike and begin to retrace your steps to the parking area. You will arrive at the lot at the 2.0-mile mark. Note that while the

Dating back to 1833, the historic Turkey Point Lighthouse watches over the Chesapeake Bay and Elk River in Maryland.

parking area can accommodate fifteen to twenty cars, this is a popular hike and the lot can fill to capacity, especially on fair-weather weekends.

MILES AND DIRECTIONS

0.0 Begin at the trailhead in the northwest corner of the parking area. You will see a wide gravel trail to the right of a large trail kiosk.

0.6 Reach a fork in the trail. Stay to the right on the grassy path.

0.8 Arrive at a stone beach. Explore, then retrace your steps to reconnect with the trail by way of a red trail marker that guides visitors into the woods.

1.1 Reach the grounds of the lighthouse. Once you've taken in the views, continue on a wide gravel path that descends into the forest.

1.4 Arrive at the Hawk Watch placard. Close the loop, then retrace your steps to the parking area.

2.0 Arrive back at the parking area. Your hike is complete.

31 BACK BAY NATIONAL WILDLIFE REFUGE

Back Bay National Wildlife Refuge in Virginia Beach is a coastal refuge for migratory birds, providing them with a safe place to rest and feed during their travels along the Atlantic Flyway. More than 8 miles of scenic hiking trails allow visitors to view wildlife, including waterfowl and migratory birds, as well as enjoy access to the beach for fishing.

Start: Visitor center parking lot
Elevation gain: 43 feet
Maximum grade: 3%
Distance: 3.6-mile lollipop with spurs
Difficulty: Easy
Hiking time: 1.5 to 2.5 hours
Best seasons: Year-round
Fees and permits: $
Trail contact: Back Bay National Wildlife Refuge, 4005 Sandpiper Rd., Virginia Beach, VA; (757) 301-7329; fws.gov/refuge/back_bay

Dogs: No
Trail surface: Mostly sand and gravel trails, some boardwalk
Land status: National wildlife refuge
Nearest town: Virginia Beach
Maps: National Geographic Trails Illustrated Topographic Map 772 (Delmarva Peninsula)
Amenities: Restrooms, visitor center
Cell service: Reliable

FINDING THE TRAILHEAD

The trailhead is at the back of the front parking lot, to the left of the visitor center. GPS: N36°40'17.9" / W75°54'53.7"

THE HIKE

Back Bay National Wildlife Refuge is a beautiful coastal wildlife refuge, but it's not without rules. As in, no swimming, no sunbathing, and no pets allowed. It's a scenic refuge to explore. The hiking trails are flat, easy, and replete with spectacular bay and ocean views. Even better, it's a stone's throw from Sandbridge, an uncrowded sandy hideaway known for its colorful beach houses.

If you've got Back Bay National Wildlife Refuge on your mind, start in the visitor center, then stroll along one or more of these coastal hiking trails. Or, take on this 3.6-mile hike that incorporates three of the four hiking trails at this 9,250–plus-acre coastal refuge.

Start at the back of the front parking lot along a gravel service road (West Dike Trail). After 0.1 mile, you will reach a large trail kiosk. Stay to the right to continue on the West Dike Trail. A canal is on your left as you walk. At the 0.6-mile mark, the trail splits. Stay left, then turn right onto the East Dike Trail at the 0.7-mile mark.

Continue on this gravel trail to 1.0-mile mark for the Wildlife Viewing Window, which is basically an observation blind, allowing you to see wildlife (without them seeing you). There is also a restroom. Once you've taken in the views, retrace your steps. Stay right for the East Dike Trail at the 1.3-mile mark. Proceed along this full-sun trail until you reach the Dunes Trail on the right at the 1.6-mile mark. You'll also see a bench and a bike rack.

The easy Seaside Trail at Back Bay National Wildlife Refuge in Virginia Beach begins with a stretch of wooden boardwalk that leads to the ocean.

Turn right to ascend the wooden boardwalk. The Dunes Trail is almost entirely fully accessible. At the 1.7-mile mark, you will arrive at the wooden overlook, which allows you to see over the dunes to the ocean. From here, it's another 0.1-mile walk on sand to the beach. From the beach, retrace your steps to return to the East Dike Trail, then turn right to continue back to the visitor center.

Once you reach the parking lot, continue to the front of the lot, where you will see a sign for the Seaside Trail on the right. This accessible hike leads to a sandy, windswept refuge beach and the Atlantic Ocean. The hike begins on a wooden boardwalk, guiding visitors through a freshwater marsh and alongside sand dunes. You will pass one or two benches on the way to the beach.

Keep your eyes open for songbirds and seabirds, even mammals like white-tailed deer and raccoons. You may also see reptiles and amphibians like the northern cottonmouth, one of Virginia's three venomous snake species. The wooden boardwalk ends after 0.1 mile, but then is replaced by a mesh walkway over the dunes to aid mobility-impaired visitors with beach access. From the beach, retrace your steps along the Seaside Trail to the front parking lot to complete this short, breezy hike at the 2.6-mile mark.

From here, cross the parking lot diagonally to reach the Raptor Trail, which begins at a trail kiosk just behind the visitor center. The Raptor Trail guides visitors through a delightful wetlands area, even alongside a small bald cypress swamp, on a mostly gravel

The wooden overlook on the Dunes Trail offers pristine views of the Atlantic Ocean.

trail. There are several overlooks along the way with views across the freshwater Back Bay.

At the 2.8-mile mark, turn right onto the Sunset Point Overlook Loop. This short boardwalk trail wows with west-facing views that are just right for sunset (of course). You'll also find a bench or two along the way to settle in for the views. At the 3.2-mile mark, you will complete the loop and be back to your starting point. From here, turn right to continue on the Raptor Trail.

You'll reach another bayside overlook at the 3.3-mile mark. Then, a wooden boardwalk leads to the final overlook over the shimmering bay. Retrace your steps on the Raptor Trail to the trailhead, bypassing the turnoff for the Sunset Point Overlook Loop. Your hike is complete when you arrive at the parking area just past the trailhead for the Raptor Trail at the 3.6-mile mark.

MILES AND DIRECTIONS

0.0   The West Dike Trail begins at the back of the front parking lot, guiding you along a gravel service road.

0.1   Arrive at a large trail kiosk. Stay to the right for the West Dike Trail.

0.6   The trail splits. Stay to the left to loop around, then turn right onto the East Dike Trail.

1.0   Reach the Wildlife Viewing Window. Retrace your steps to the East Dike Trail.

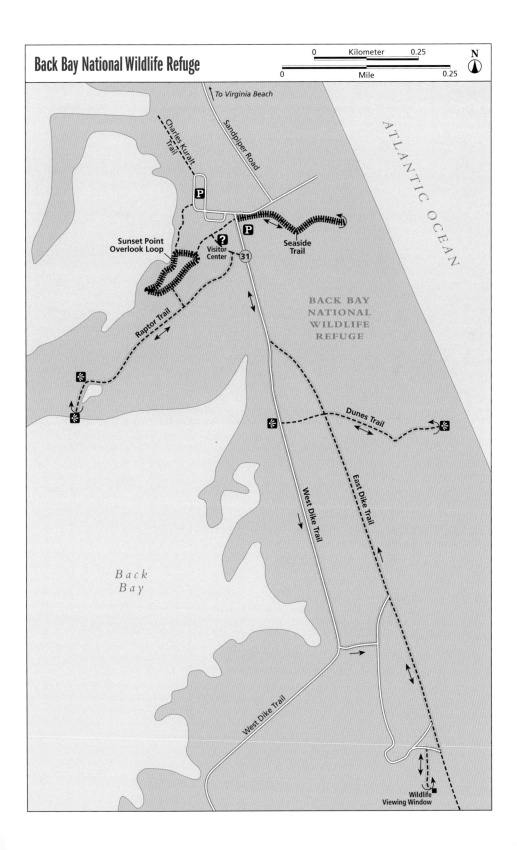

Back Bay National Wildlife Refuge

0   Kilometer   0.25

0   Mile   0.25

N

To Virginia Beach

ATLANTIC OCEAN

Charles Kuralt Trail

Sandpiper Road

P

P

Sunset Point Overlook Loop

Visitor Center

31

Seaside Trail

Raptor Trail

BACK BAY NATIONAL WILDLIFE REFUGE

Dunes Trail

West Dike Trail

East Dike Trail

Back Bay

West Dike Trail

Wildlife Viewing Window

Enjoy views across shimmering Back Bay from the wooden overlook on the Raptor Trail at Back Bay National Wildlife Refuge.

1.3   At the trail split, stay right for the East Dike Trail.

1.6   Turn right onto the Dunes Trail.

1.7   Arrive at the wooden overlook. Continue on to the shores of the Atlantic Ocean, then retrace your steps to the East Dike Trail.

1.9   Turn right onto the East Dike Trail.

2.1   The trail reconnects with the West Dike Trail. Take this to the end, then to the front of the parking lot for the Seaside Trail.

2.2   Turn right onto the Seaside Trail.

2.4   Arrive at the Atlantic Ocean. Retrace your steps to the parking lot.

2.6   Cross over the parking lot to the Raptor Trail, just behind the visitor center.

2.8   Turn right onto the Sunset Point Overlook Loop.

3.2   Complete the loop, then turn right onto the Raptor Trail.

3.3   Arrive at a wooden overlook on Back Bay. Retrace your steps to the parking area, bypassing the exit for the Sunset Point Overlook Loop.

3.6   Arrive back at the parking area. Your hike is complete.

32 BALD CYPRESS TRAIL

This enchanting loop hike over tree-filled swamps and across wooden bridges at First Landing State Park, the most-visited state park in Virginia, will leave visitors of all ages wide-eyed as they home in on the curious "knees" of quirky bald cypress trees protruding from dark, murky waters.

Start: First Landing State Park trail center
Elevation gain: 30 feet
Maximum grade: 2%
Distance: 1.8-mile loop
Difficulty: Easy
Hiking time: About 1 hour
Best seasons: Year-round
Fees and permits: $$
Trail contact: First Landing State Park, 2500 Shore Dr., Virginia Beach, VA; (757) 412-2300; dcr.virginia.gov/state-parks/first-landing
Dogs: Yes, on a leash no longer than 6 feet

Trail surface: Mostly sand and gravel trail, some wooden bridges to cross over swamps
Land status: State park
Nearest town: Virginia Beach
Maps: National Geographic Trails Illustrated Topographic Map 772 (Delmarva Peninsula). Trail maps are also available at the visitor center and online at dcr.virginia.gov/state-parks/first-landing.
Other trail users: Cyclists, when the loop merges with the Cape Henry Trail at the 1.6-mile mark
Amenities: Restrooms, picnic tables, trail center, water fountains
Cell service: Reliable

FINDING THE TRAILHEAD

The trail begins to the right of the trail center on the south side of Shore Drive. GPS: N36°54'57.71564" / W76°2'26.29422"

THE HIKE

This easygoing hike is easy to find, situated immediately to the right of the trail center at First Landing State Park in Virginia Beach. Take your first steps along an engaging trail that charms visitors with an enchanting wooden bridge over a freshwater cypress swamp teeming with curious bald cypress trees.

Once you cross the bridge, turn left at the trail sign. You will immediately see two cozy wooden benches on the left. Take a short break, but don't settle in. Many more bald cypress trees await along this meandering wooded (and well-shaded) trail.

A few steps ahead, a swampy scenic overlook on the right nudges you to stop over to ogle the moss-covered deciduous conifers. Bald cypress trees have flat needles, like conifers, which turn from yellow-green to rusty-brown and then fall off in winter, like deciduous trees. Near the 0.4-mile mark, you'll reach a fork on this soft trail composed primarily of dirt, sand, and fine gravel. Stay to the right to connect with the red-blazed Bald Cypress Trail. Then, stay right again in a few more steps.

As you continue along, you will be awed by the bald cypress trees that grow up in swamps, completely immersed in mucky waters. Look for the "knees," or knobby tree roots, that have sprouted up above the water. These help the trees deliver much-needed oxygen to their roots.

Curious bald cypress trees charm and puzzle visitors eager to know how they seemingly grow up out of the murky swamp.

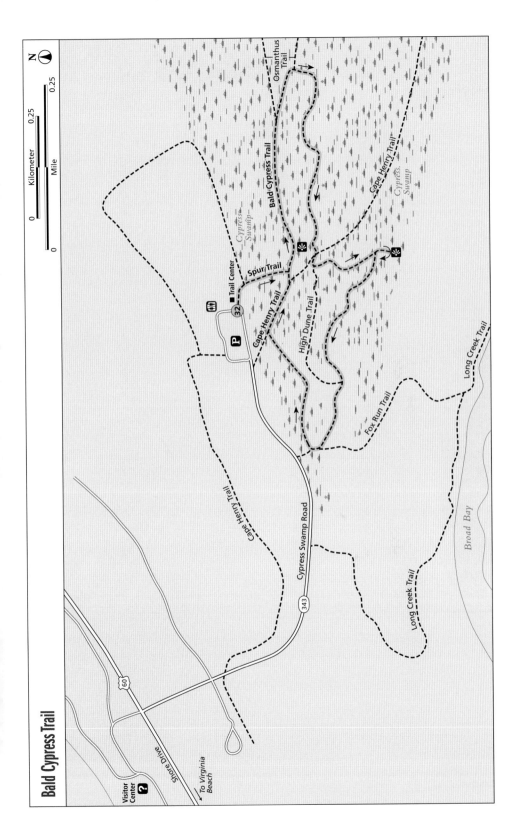

Bald Cypress Trail

Visitor Center

To Virginia Beach

Shore Drive

60

Cape Henry Trail

343

Cypress Swamp Road

Long Creek Trail

Long Creek Trail

Broad Bay

Fox Run Trail

High Dune Trail

Cape Henry Trail

P

32

Trail Center

Spur Trail

Cypress Swamp

Bald Cypress Trail

Cape Henry Trail

Cypress Swamp

Osmanthus Trail

N

Kilometer

0   0.25

0   0.25

Mile

Walk along a delightful boardwalk trail over a freshwater cypress swamp on the Bald Cypress Trail.

At the 0.8-mile mark, you will reach a junction of trails. Continue straight ahead to stay on the Bald Cypress Trail. Look both ways before crossing over the Cape Henry Trail. This mostly flat, multiuse trail is a popular path with area bicyclists. In another 0.1 mile, you will reach what looks like a fork in the trail. It's not. Proceed straight ahead to step out onto a delightfully scenic wooden overlook over the cypress swamp. From here, retrace your steps to the trail, and turn left at the junction.

At the 1.2-mile mark, you will spy a marker for the High Dune Trail on the right, but bypass this trail and proceed straight ahead for the Bald Cypress Trail. In a few more steps, prepare to be bowled over by the very best views of the freshwater cypress swamps at trail markers M, N, and P. These are the views you'll want to snap and share on social media.

The Cape Henry Trail reappears at the 1.6-mile mark. This time, turn right to merge onto this multiuse trail. In less than 0.1 mile, turn left at the trail sign. In a few more steps, the wooden bridge over the cypress swamp comes into the view. Turn left to return to the trail center. At the 1.8-mile mark, your hike is complete.

MILES AND DIRECTIONS

0.0 Begin at the trailhead to the right of the trail center on the south side of Shore Drive.

0.1 Turn left at the T-intersection after crossing a wooden bridge over a cypress swamp.

0.4 The trail splits. Veer right to continue on the red-blazed Bald Cypress Trail. Then stay to the right again in a few more steps.

0.8 Approach a junction of trails. Continue straight ahead, cutting across the Cape Henry Trail.

0.9 Reach a scenic overlook over the freshwater cypress swamp.

1.6 Turn right onto the Cape Henry Trail.

1.7 Turn left to cross over the wooden bridge.

1.8 Arrive back at the trail center. Your hike is complete.

33 BEACH TRAIL, SAVAGE NECK DUNES NATURAL AREA PRESERVE

This hike at Savage Neck Dunes Natural Area Preserve on Virginia's Eastern Shore highlights three restoration zones: coastal grassland, coastal shrub, and maritime forest. When you arrive at the beach, prepare to be awed by driftwood that seems to grow right out of the sand, as well as the tiny house just to the north on the beach.

Start: Savage Neck Dunes Natural Area Preserve parking area
Elevation gain: 16 feet
Maximum grade: 1%
Distance: 1.3 miles out and back
Difficulty: Easy
Hiking time: 1 to 1.5 hours
Best seasons: Year-round
Fees and permits: Free
Trail contact: Virginia Department of Conservation and Recreation, Eastern Shore Region Steward; (757) 787-5989; dcr.virginia.gov/natural

-heritage/natural-area-preserves/savage
Dogs: Yes, on a leash no longer than 6 feet
Trail surface: Mostly dirt, grass, and sand trails
Land status: Natural area preserve
Nearest town: Cape Charles
Maps: National Geographic Trails Illustrated Topographic Map 772 (Delmarva Peninsula)
Amenities: None
Cell service: Reliable

FINDING THE TRAILHEAD

The trailhead is located toward the back of the parking area, to the right of a large trail kiosk. GPS: N37°19'40.5" / W76°00'15.0"

THE HIKE

For a delightful coastal hike through a migratory songbird habitat, look to the Beach Trail at Savage Neck Dunes Natural Area Preserve in Cape Charles. This 1.3-mile out-and-back hike guides visitors through coastal grassland, coastal shrub, and maritime forest environments.

It's okay to wear flip-flops or sandals on this hike, too. You may even prefer to wear beach-appropriate footwear since the last 0.2 mile of this trail is soft sand, so you may be thankful to skip the sneakers or hiking boots on this hike. The Beach Trail, which leads to a sandy beach, is one of three trails at Savage Neck Dunes. The other two short trails are the Field Loop and the Woodland Loop.

A small eight-car parking lot for Savage Neck Dunes Natural Area Preserve sits alongside Savage Neck Road, a country road that divides up local farms. Parallel parking is not allowed on Savage Neck Road. There's a large kiosk at the front of the parking area. The trailhead for all three trails is just to the right of the trail kiosk. You will see a trail marker, too.

The hike begins on a grass trail through a meadow. This is the coastal grassland section and is made up of perennial grasses for nesting birds, like sparrows and quail. At the 0.1-mile mark, you will have the option to turn left onto the Field Loop. For the Beach Trail, continue straight ahead to enter the coastal shrubland. This section is replete with wax

An easy walk along the Beach Trail at Savage Neck Dunes Natural Area Preserve guides visitors through three restoration zones: coastal grassland, coastal shrub, and maritime forest.

myrtles. This fast-growing native shrub (3 to 5 feet of upward growth in a year) produces small berries. These trees provide plenty of food and perches for birds.

At the 0.2-mile mark, you can turn left for the Woodland Loop, but instead continue forging ahead on the Beach Trail. In a few more steps, you will arrive at Custis Pond, a 4.6-acre freshwater pond. It's one of only a few naturally occurring interdune ponds on Virginia's Eastern Shore. Keep your eyes open for green tree frogs and southern painted turtles. There are three interdune ponds in the preserve. The other two are located along the Woodland Loop.

At this point, you will enter a mixed maritime forest with deciduous, coniferous, and broadleaf evergreen trees. Coastal pines dominate this forested section. The trail quickly turns to soft sand as you cross the maritime forest. The closer you get to the beach, the sandier the trail becomes. You may even decide to take off your shoes and carry them to the beach.

At the 0.6-mile mark, turn left for a short walk on a boardwalk trail to the Dune Overlook for a peek at a secondary dune ridge that parallels the shoreline for 1 mile and features some of the highest elevation points on Virginia's Eastern Shore. From here, retrace your steps to the Beach Trail, then turn left to continue on to the beach.

As you approach the beach, you will see a sign educating visitors about the rare northeastern beach tiger beetle. The tiger beetle is so rare that it can now only be found at two sites outside the Chesapeake Bay. These beetles are vulnerable to any kind of beach sand disruptions, like digging doggos.

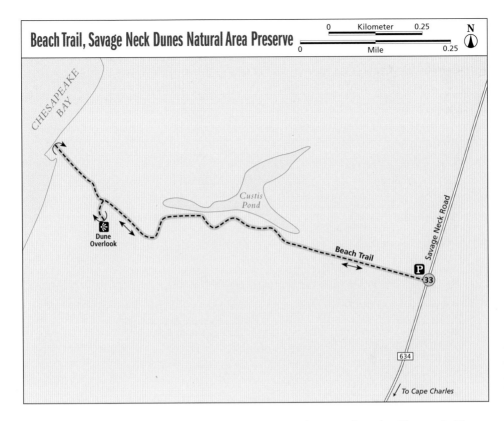

Beach Trail, Savage Neck Dunes Natural Area Preserve

You will arrive at the beach at the 0.7-mile mark. The water from the Chesapeake Bay is shallow and gentle. Enjoy the calmly lapping waves. The white sand beach is littered with weathered driftwood, largely on the north end. Some of the driftwood appears to grow right out of the sandy beach. Walk north on the beach and you will spot an adorable tiny home with mad west-facing views. The sunsets here are exceptional.

Enjoy your time on this largely secluded beach in Cape Charles, then retrace your steps to the parking area for Savage Neck Dunes Natural Area Preserve.

MILES AND DIRECTIONS

0.0 Begin at the trailhead in the back of the parking area, adjacent to the large trail kiosk.

0.2 Arrive at Custis Pond.

0.6 Turn left onto a short boardwalk trail to the Dune Overlook. Retrace your steps to the Beach Trail and turn left.

0.7 Reach the sandy beach. Retrace your steps to return to the parking area.

1.3 Arrive back at the parking area. Your hike is complete.

34 BELLE ISLE STATE PARK LOOP

This delightful coastal hike at Belle Isle State Park on Virginia's Northern Neck wows visitors of all ages with a small sandy beach, coastal marshes, and a large water-facing picnic area.

Start: Parking area at the end of Creek Landing Road
Elevation gain: 56 feet
Maximum grade: 2%
Distance: 5.8-mile loop
Difficulty: Easy
Hiking time: 3 to 4 hours
Best seasons: Year-round
Fees and permits: $
Trail contact: Belle Isle State Park, 1632 Belle Isle Rd., Lancaster, VA; (804) 462-5030; dcr.virginia.gov/state-parks/belle-isle
Dogs: Yes, on a leash no longer than 6 feet

Trail surface: Mostly dirt, gravel, and sand trails; some boardwalk stretches
Land status: State park
Nearest town: Warsaw
Maps: National Geographic Trails Illustrated Topographic Map 772 (Delmarva Peninsula). Trail maps are also available at the visitor center and online at dcr.virginia.gov/state-parks/belle-isle.
Other trail users: Cyclists, equestrians
Amenities: Vault toilets, picnic tables, playground
Cell service: Reliable

FINDING THE TRAILHEAD

The trail begins at the back of the parking area at the end of Creek Landing Road. GPS: N37°46'57.2" / W76°36'11.9"

THE HIKE

Belle Isle State Park in coastal Lancaster may be one of the state's smaller parks, but it certainly makes up for its size with far-reaching views across the Rappahannock River and Mulberry Creek. This scenic state park has fewer than 10 miles of hiking trails. For this hike, begin on the Mud Creek Trail, the longest hiking trail in the park at 1.9 miles.

When you arrive at the park, continue on Creek Landing Road to the end and you will dead-end in the parking lot. Here you'll find a couple dozen parking spaces, as well as the launch area for canoes and kayaks. You'll also find restrooms and a picnic table.

Look for the large canoe/kayak launch sign in the northwest corner of the parking lot. A colorful trail marker heralds the start of this hike. Walk past the trail marker on a gravel road. This road is used by vehicles looking to drop their canoes and kayaks into Mulberry Creek. You are now on the burgundy-blazed Mulberry Creek Boardwalk Trail, though the actual boardwalk doesn't begin until after you pass the boat launch.

Look left and you'll see a delightful stretch of fully accessible boardwalk. Along this section, you'll encounter several walk-out overlooks for water views across Mulberry Creek. At one of the overlooks, near the 0.2-mile mark, there is a set of mounted binoculars just right for observing waterfowl, like ospreys, blue herons, and bald eagles. In a few more steps, you'll see picnic tables to the left of the boardwalk trail, each with views across scenic Mulberry Creek.

Just ahead, there is a trail marker and a gravel trail. Proceed straight ahead to reconnect with the yellow-blazed Mud Creek Trail. At the 0.6-mile mark, you'll reach an open

This loop hike begins with a stroll along the Mulberry Creek Boardwalk Trail, which features several wooden overlooks for far-reaching water views at Belle Isle State Park.

field. At first, it may seem confusing. However, once you walk a few steps in, you'll note that the trail casually skirts around the open space on the right. At the 0.7-mile mark, you'll reach another trail marker and a dead end. Turn right for the Watch House Trail, which leads to a delightful small beach on the gently flowing Rappahannock River.

This red-blazed trail may feel like a gravel service road, but you will enjoy gorgeous views of coastal marshes on both sides of the trail. In a few more steps, you can proceed straight ahead for a direct route to the small sandy beach. Or, you can turn right or left for the Watch House Loop. Turn left here for some extra mileage and water views.

At the 1.4-mile mark, you will reach the small sandy beach. The views across the Rappahannock River are truly spectacular. Once you exit the beach area, turn left to continue on the Watch House Loop. As an option, and to subtract a few steps, you can walk straight ahead for the Watch House Trail. Both trails will meet. At the 2.0-mile mark, the loop trail reconnects with the Watch House Trail. Turn left to retrace your steps to and then past the Mud Creek Trail.

When you reach the Porpoise Creek Trail at the 2.3-mile mark, turn right. This trail continues on to dead end at a picnic area with restrooms and a playground. This is the perfect spot to break for lunch with a view. Enjoy the refreshing views across the Rappahannock River, then cut across the parking area and walk along Belle Isle Road. At the 3.5-mile mark, turn left on the paved road that leads into the campground (even if it's closed). In a few more steps, you'll see a trail marker on the right.

In the fall and winter, the murky waters along the White Oak Swamp Loop may surprise you with a rainbow of colors as sunlight magically transforms the water filled with decomposing leaves.

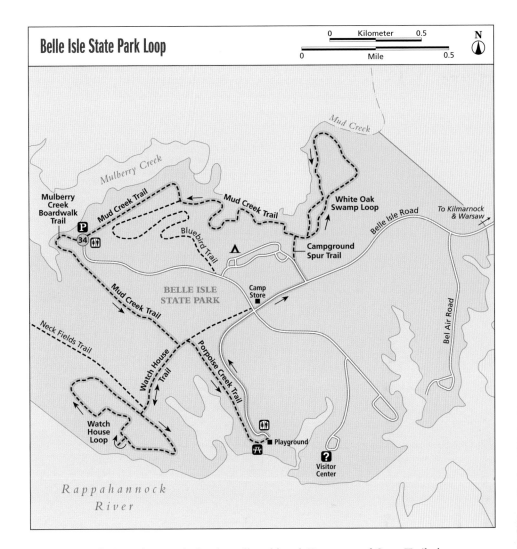

Belle Isle State Park Loop

0 Kilometer 0.5
0 Mile 0.5

N

Mud Creek

Mulberry Creek

Mulberry
Creek
Boardwalk
Trail

Mud Creek Trail

P
34

Mud Creek Trail

Bluebird Trail

White Oak
Swamp Loop

Belle Isle Road

To Kilmarnock
& Warsaw

Campground
Spur Trail

BELLE ISLE
STATE PARK

Camp
Store

Bel Air Road

Mud Creek Trail

Neck Fields Trail

Watch House Trail

Porpoise Creek Trail

Watch
House
Loop

Playground

Visitor
Center

*Rappahannock
River*

Turn right into the woods for the yellow-blazed Campground Spur Trail, then turn right onto the Mud Creek Trail. At the 3.8-mile mark, stay right for the white-blazed White Oak Swamp Loop. In late fall or winter, you may be in for a surprise when you reach the short boardwalk. You may spy a rainbow sheen across the murky waters caused by the sun's rays hitting natural oils released by decomposing leaves.

Close the loop at the 4.7-mile mark. In a few more steps, stay right to exit this section of the park by way of the Mud Creek Trail. As you continue along, you'll see lots of nice lookouts across the grasses in Mulberry Creek. You'll also see a few benches along the way to settle in and enjoy the scenery. At the 5.4-mile mark, there is a dead end (on the far side of the open field). Turn left for the final steps to the parking area. Your hike is complete at the 5.8-mile mark.

A walk along the Watch House Loop at Belle Isle State Park leads to a small, scenic beach with views across the Rappahannock River.

MILES AND DIRECTIONS

0.0 The trail begins at the back of the parking area at the end of Creek Landing Road.

0.1 Turn left to continue on the Mulberry Creek Boardwalk Trail.

0.2 Reconnect with the Mud Creek Trail.

0.7 Turn right onto the Watch House Trail.

1.0 Turn left onto the Watch House Loop.

1.3 Turn left onto a spur trail to reach a small beach on the Rappahannock River. Retrace your steps to return to the Watch House Loop, then turn left to continue on the loop.

2.0 Turn left onto the Watch House Trail.

2.3 Turn right onto the Porpoise Creek Trail.

2.8 Walk to the front of the parking area, then exit by walking alongside Belle Isle Road.

3.5 Turn left on the road leading into the campground.

3.6 Turn right at the trail marker for the Campground Spur Trail. Then, turn right again in a few steps for the Mud Creek Trail.

3.8 Stay right for the white-blazed White Oak Swamp Loop.

4.7 Close the loop. Then, stay right to exit by way of the Mud Creek Trail.

5.4 Turn left to stay on the Mud Creek Trail to return to the parking area.

5.8 Arrive back at the parking area. Your hike is complete.

35 BIG MEADOW TRAIL

This forested hike at Westmoreland State Park in Montross has a big payoff when you reach the sandy beach and you can try your luck hunting for fossils, like shark teeth. Take a seat on the wooden bench to take in all the views of the gorgeous sandstone cliffs.

Start: Westmoreland State Park visitor center
Elevation gain: 144 feet
Maximum grade: 9%
Distance: 1.4 miles out and back
Difficulty: Easy
Hiking time: 1 to 1.5 hours
Best seasons: Year-round
Fees and permits: $$
Trail contact: Westmoreland State Park, 145 Cliff Rd., Montross, VA; (804) 493-8821; dcr.virginia.gov/state-parks/westmoreland

Dogs: Yes, on a leash no longer than 6 feet
Trail surface: Mostly dirt and sand trails
Land status: State park
Nearest town: Montross
Maps: Trail maps are available at the visitor center and online at dcr.virginia.gov/state-parks/westmoreland.
Amenities: Restrooms, picnic tables, visitor center, camp store
Cell service: Reliable

FINDING THE TRAILHEAD

The trailhead is located in the parking area for the visitor center. You will see a large sign that reads Fossil Beach. GPS: N38°10'10.3" / W76°51'47.9"

THE HIKE

Westmoreland State Park is north of historic Montross on Virginia's Northern Neck. You'll find nearly 8 miles of hiking trails, including the Big Meadow Trail. This popular trail leads to Fossil Beach. As a bonus, the trailhead is a stone's throw from Campground A for tent campers and those with RVs and travel trailers. Bring along a sieve or colander to hunt for fossils, like shark teeth, while at Fossil Beach. Even a simple spaghetti colander is just right for sifting sand in search of treasures.

The hike along the Big Meadow Trail begins with an easy and gradual descent under a forest canopy. Signs along the way point out trees, like black cherry and pawpaw. The red blazes are impossible to miss as you make your way to Fossil Beach. At the 0.3-mile mark, you'll reach a comfy bench for those eager to take a quick break.

At the 0.6-mile mark, you will arrive at a tidal marsh that—from April to June—is filled with bright yellow flag irises. These flowers are numerous in wet areas and along shorelines. The showy yellow flowers are beautiful, but they are also invasive. Sadly, they are also known to crowd out native vegetation. In a few more steps, you'll reach what was once a trail that led to a boardwalk, an observation tower, and the Turkey Neck Trail. This has been closed for some time, and there are no indications that it will reopen in the future.

You'll then arrive at a perpetually muddy area. Thankfully, a short boardwalk and wooden planks allow you to cross this section and keep your shoes clean at the same time. At the 0.7-mile mark, you will arrive at Fossil Beach. There is a bench on the left

As you approach Fossil Beach on the Big Meadow Trail, you will pass a tidal marsh overflowing with plant life.

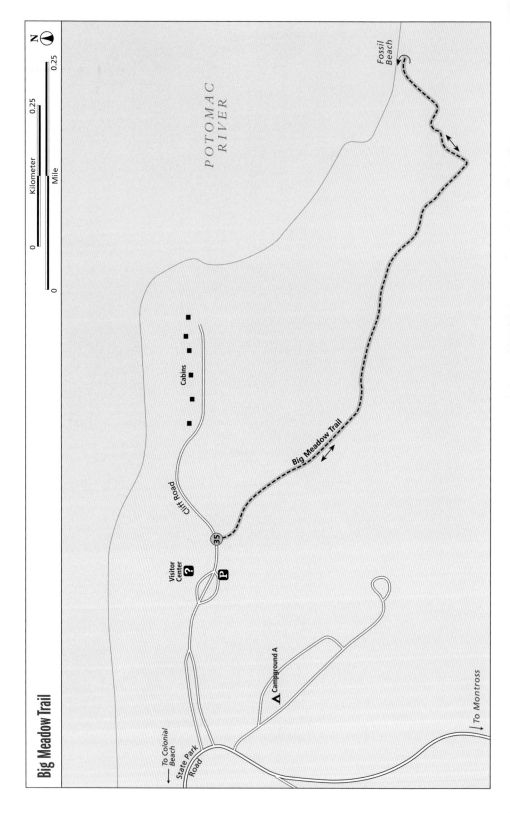

Big Meadow Trail

Visitor Center

35

Cliff Road

Cabins

Big Meadow Trail

POTOMAC
RIVER

Fossil
Beach

To Colonial
Beach

State Park
Road

Campground A

To Montross

Kilometer
0   0.25

Mile
0   0.25

N

Bring a sieve or colander to sift sand in search of fossils, like shark teeth, at Fossil Beach.

and a small sandy beach on the right. Due to erosion, you cannot access the sandy beach and sandstone cliffs on the left.

If you plan to hunt for fossils, low tide is the best time to go to scoop up fossil-like shells, maybe a shark tooth or two. Plan to bring your patience as well. If you don't have much luck, you can always savor scenic views of the beautiful sandstone cliffs. They are gorgeous.

Once you've finished fossil hunting, retrace your steps to the trailhead. Note that the trailhead shares a parking lot with the visitor center, so plan to walk out behind the visitor center to take in panoramic views across the Potomac River from atop the famed Horsehead Cliffs.

MILES AND DIRECTIONS

0.0   Begin at the Fossil Beach sign that marks the trailhead in the parking area for the visitor center.

0.3   There is a wooden bench for those eager to take a quick break.

0.6   Arrive at a tidal marsh filled with yellow flag irises.

0.7   Reach Fossil Beach. Retrace your steps to the parking area.

1.4   Arrive back at the parking area. Your hike is complete.

36 BOYD'S HOLE TRAIL

This shaded hike guides you through an old-growth forest and on to the Potomac River for a perfect picnic on the sandy shore. Bring a hammock and a good book. The riverside picnic area is an ideal spot to laze the day away in the shade.

Start: Caledon State Park visitor center
Elevation gain: 171 feet
Maximum grade: 8%
Distance: 3.3-mile lollipop
Difficulty: Easy
Hiking time: 1.5 to 2 hours
Best seasons: Year-round
Fees and permits: $
Trail contact: Caledon State Park, 11617 Caledon Rd., King George, VA; (540) 663-3861; dcr.virginia.gov/state-parks/caledon

Dogs: Yes, on a leash no longer than 6 feet
Trail surface: Mostly dirt and gravel trails
Land status: State park
Nearest town: Dahlgren
Maps: Trail maps are available at the visitor center and online at dcr.virginia.gov/state-parks/caledon.
Other trail users: Cyclists
Amenities: Restrooms, picnic tables, gift shop, visitor center
Cell service: Reliable

FINDING THE TRAILHEAD

Start at the "Explore Your Chesapeake" sign to the left of the visitor center. GPS: N38°20'30.3" / W77°09'20.2"

THE HIKE

Located in King George County, Caledon State Park is a coastal state park on the Potomac River in the northeast section of Virginia's Northern Neck, the northernmost of three peninsulas on the Chesapeake Bay's western shore. There are more than a dozen hiking trails, many with woodsy names like Laurel Glen, Cedar Ridge, and Fern Hollow. This National Natural Landmark is best known for its majestic bald eagles, and the best trails for seeing bald eagles are the Boyd's Hole Trail and Jones Pond Loop.

The hike begins at the "Explore Your Chesapeake" sign and gently descends along a gravel road through an old-growth forest of tulip poplar and oak trees. A wooden bench appears at the 0.1-mile mark, then the trail forks a few steps later at the 0.2-mile mark. The trail on the right leads to the park's primitive hike-in campground by way of the purple-blazed Hampstead Road Trail.

Stay on the blue-blazed Boyd's Hole Trail. You'll reach another relaxing bench at the 0.4-mile mark. Then, the loop on this lollipop hike begins at the 0.7-mile mark. It doesn't matter which way you begin on the loop, but for this hike, stay to the left for a clockwise loop.

At the 1.4-mile mark, a wooden bench swing turns up on the right. On the left, you'll see the foundation of what was once a colonial plantation in the 1600s. The plantation and farm were owned by the Alexander family. The family later spent more of their time in Northern Virginia. The town of Alexandria was named for them when it was founded in 1749.

A walk on the Boyd's Hole Trail at Caledon State Park in King George County guides you through old-growth forest to the Potomac River.

Mallows Marsh, a scenic wetland area, appears on the right at the 1.6-mile mark. A few steps later, you will arrive at a small picnic area on the Potomac River. You'll find five picnic tables, as well as a wooden overlook, a trash can, and a recycling bin. Since this trail is also open to bikes, you'll find a couple of bike racks, too.

There are no designated swimming areas at Caledon State Park, but you can wade into the river at the shaded picnic area. Consider bringing a hammock, too. There are several trees that are just right for hanging a hammock. This is the perfect spot to laze the day away in the shade. From here, continue along the gravel loop trail. You will close the loop at the 2.7-mile mark. Turn left on the gravel trail to retrace your steps to the trailhead. Your hike is complete at the 3.3-mile mark.

MILES AND DIRECTIONS

0.0   Begin at the "Explore Your Chesapeake" sign to the left of the visitor center. Walk past the sign, then descend along the gravelly Boyd's Hole Trail.

0.2   Arrive at a junction with the Hampstead Road Trail. Continue straight ahead on the Boyd's Hole Trail.

0.7   Reach the loop section of the hike. Stay left on the Boyd's Hole Trail.

1.4   Arrive at a swinging bench as well as the brick foundation of a colonial plantation.

Stop in the visitor center at Caledon State Park for bald eagle exhibits and historical artifacts.

Bring a picnic lunch and a hammock for a full afternoon of relaxation at the picnic area on the Potomac River that you reach midway along the Boyd's Hole Trail.

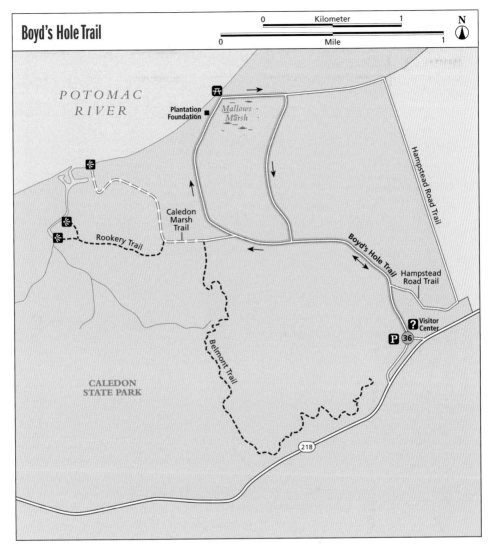

Kilometer

0   1

Mile

0   1

N

POTOMAC
RIVER

Plantation
Foundation

Mallows
Marsh

Caledon
Marsh
Trail

Rookery Trail

Boyd's Hole Trail

Hampstead Road Trail

Hampstead
Road Trail

Visitor
Center

P 36

Belmont Trail

CALEDON
STATE PARK

218

1.6   Reach Mallows Marsh, a scenic wetland area. Then, arrive at a picnic area on the Potomac River in a few more steps.

2.7   Close the loop, then turn left to retrace your steps to the trailhead.

3.3   Arrive back at the trailhead. Your hike is complete.

37 BOYKIN'S LANDING TRAIL

At Crow's Nest Natural Area Preserve in Stafford County, revel in a forested hike to breathtaking views across Potomac Creek from Boykin's Landing. An easy hike, mostly along the Boykin's Landing Trail, drops you off at two wooden benches for plentiful water views.

Start: Crow's Nest Natural Area Preserve, Raven Road access
Elevation gain: 246 feet
Maximum grade: 8%
Distance: 3.6 miles out and back
Difficulty: Easy
Hiking time: 1.5 to 2 hours
Best seasons: Year-round
Fees and permits: Free
Trail contact: Virginia Department of Conservation and Recreation, Division of Natural Heritage, Stafford, VA; (540) 658-8690; dcr.virginia

.gov/natural-heritage/natural-area-preserves/crowsnest
Dogs: Yes, on a leash no longer than 6 feet
Trail surface: Mostly sand and dirt trails, some grass
Land status: Nature preserve
Nearest town: Stafford
Maps: Trail maps are available online at dcr.virginia.gov/natural-heritage/natural-area-preserves/crowsnest.
Amenities: Porta-potty
Cell service: Reliable

FINDING THE TRAILHEAD

The trailhead is located on the east side of the parking area off Raven Road, to the right of a large trail kiosk. GPS: N38°21'43.8" / W77°20'31.9"

THE HIKE

There's a hidden gem tucked away in Stafford County, and it's called Crow's Nest Natural Area Preserve. You'll find five hiking trails on this 895-acre peninsula made up of tidal and non-tidal wetlands in between two tidally influenced creeks, Potomac Creek and Accokeek Creek.

There are two ways to enter Crow's Nest Natural Area Preserve, the most popular being Raven Road given its access to four of the five hiking trails. However, the Raven Road access point is only open Thursday through Sunday, so keep this in mind if you plan to explore this forested nature preserve on foot. From Raven Road, a 2-mile gravel road leads to a parking area with eighteen parking spaces. This nature preserve may be lesser-known, but the lot can fill up quickly.

Three trails set off from the parking area: the Crow's Nest Point Trail, Accokeek Loop Trail, and Potomac Overlook Trail. To hike to Boykin's Landing, follow the Crow's Nest Point Trail. The trailhead is located on the east side of the parking area. You will see a large kiosk and a green sign marking the start of the trail.

The hike begins under a lush canopy of bright-green leaves, guiding you into a mature hardwood forest. The trail is wide, on a base of mostly dirt and sand, with some gravel. On some sections of trail, the foliage is so dense that the hike can feel quite dark and shady, even on cloudless days.

At the 0.7-mile mark, you'll reach a fork in the trail. Stay right for the red-blazed Boykin's Landing Trail. The trail veers right again and narrows at the 1.2-mile mark. In a

Wooden steps guide you to the grand viewpoint across Potomac Creek at Crow's Nest Natural Area Preserve.

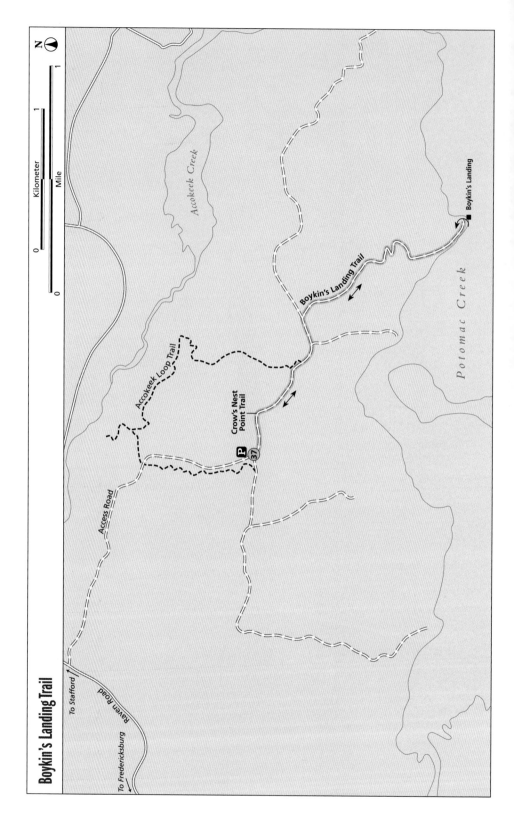

Boykin's Landing Trail

Accokeek Creek

Boykin's Landing

Boykin's Landing Trail

Potomac Creek

Accokeek Loop Trail

Crow's Nest Point Trail

Access Road

To Stafford

Raven Road

To Fredericksburg

Kilometer

Mile

N

37

P

At Crow's Nest Natural Area Preserve, the red-blazed Boykin's Landing Trail leads to big views across Potomac Creek.

few more steps, you'll catch your first glimpses of Potomac Creek through the leafy trees. Then, the hiking trail sidles up against the water for pristine views.

At the 1.8-mile mark, you will arrive at Boykin's Landing. A few wooden steps guide you to the viewpoint, and what a viewpoint it is. There are two benches at Boykin's Landing, encouraging you to sit and stay a while. Rehydrate here and take in the breathtaking views across Potomac Creek. Since this is an out-and-back hike, retrace your steps to the parking area once you've soaked in all the views. Your hike is complete at the 3.6-mile mark.

MILES AND DIRECTIONS

- **0.0** Begin on the green-blazed Crow's Nest Point Trail, which is located on the east side of the parking area at the Raven Road entrance.
- **0.7** Arrive at a fork in the trail. Stay right for the red-blazed Boykin's Landing Trail.
- **1.8** Reach Boykin's Landing. Retrace your steps to the parking area.
- **3.6** Arrive back at the trailhead and parking area. Your hike is complete.

38 BUTTERFLY TRAIL

Those eager for a quick leg-stretcher hike after crossing the 17.6-mile Chesapeake Bay Bridge-Tunnel to Virginia's Eastern Shore will want to look to the Butterfly Trail. Located at the Eastern Shore of Virginia National Wildlife Refuge visitor center, it's one of the first stops to make after crossing the bridge-tunnel, and it's well worth a stop for the history alone.

Start: Eastern Shore of Virginia National Wildlife Refuge visitor center
Elevation gain: 36 feet
Maximum grade: 5%
Distance: 1.4 miles out and back
Difficulty: Easy
Hiking time: 1 to 1.5 hours
Best seasons: Year-round
Fees and permits: Free
Trail contact: Eastern Shore of Virginia National Wildlife Refuge, 32205 Seaside Rd., Cape Charles,
VA; (757) 331-2760; fws.gov/refuge/Eastern_Shore_of_Virginia
Dogs: Yes, on a leash no longer than 6 feet
Trail surface: Mostly dirt, grass, and sand trails
Land status: Natural area preserve
Nearest town: Cape Charles
Maps: National Geographic Trails Illustrated Topographic Map 772 (Delmarva Peninsula)
Amenities: Restrooms, visitor center
Cell service: Reliable

FINDING THE TRAILHEAD

The trailhead is located to the right of the Eastern Shore of Virginia National Wildlife Refuge visitor center. Look for the sign with the bright orange butterfly. GPS: N37°08'12.3" / W75°57'55.0"

THE HIKE

This easy coastal trail is located at the 1,123-acre Eastern Shore of Virginia National Wildlife Refuge, which sits between the Atlantic Ocean and the Chesapeake Bay. Situated at the southernmost tip of the Delmarva Peninsula, the refuge is an important stopover for migratory birds. The area also has a military history that dates back to World War II.

The Butterfly Trail can be accessed from the wildlife refuge's visitor center. The trailhead is steps from a parking area that has room for at least a dozen cars. Note that the visitor center (including on-site restrooms) is not open every day. In the off-season, the center is only open Saturday from 10 a.m. to 2 p.m. You can also access the Butterfly Trail by way of a connector trail from the bridge-tunnel welcome center, just off US 13.

Shortly after the start of the hike, you will arrive at a couple of educational kiosks with a map and the scoop on what you'll find in the visitor center and at the refuge. As you continue on, you'll notice placards every so often, like the first one on seasonal birds, including ospreys, tree swallows, and pine warblers, that can be seen in each season.

Another small placard encourages visitors to use their senses, including sight, smell, and hearing, as birds and butterflies do. The placards provide an education for children. If you arrive on a day when the visitor center is open, pop in to pick up a Junior Refuge

Manager activity booklet. Children can complete learning games and tasks to earn an official patch.

At the 0.2-mile mark, you will arrive at the connector trail from the bridge-tunnel welcome center. Proceed straight ahead to stay on the Butterfly Trail. The trail takes a historic turn when you reach a tunnel and learn that military were once stationed here to protect the Chesapeake Bay, area naval bases, and even our nation's capital, Washington, DC.

During World War II, 800 soldiers patrolled the grounds at what was briefly called Fort Custis during the height of the war. The military installation closed in 1948, but was revived in 1950 as the Cape Charles Air Force Station, serving as part of a national radar network until 1981, when the site was shut down for good. Today, through the tunnel, you'll see the remains of the Winslow Battery, which once had two 16-inch guns. Each gun could hurl a one-ton projectile up to 25 miles.

As you continue on, the trail turns from mostly grass to gravel. At the 0.6-mile mark, veer left to reach a fenced-in historic cemetery on the right. A small placard notes that this is the private burial site of the Fitchett and Hallett families. Both families played important roles in farming on Virginia's Eastern Shore.

At the 0.7-mile mark, you will reach a marsh overlook. A placard points out the Cape Charles Lighthouse in the distance that welcomes travelers to the Eastern Shore. Once you've taken in the views, retrace your steps. At the 0.8-mile mark, ascend a few dozen steps to the observation deck to see Fisherman Island, one of Virginia's twenty-three barrier islands. Fisherman Island is Virginia's southernmost barrier island. Today, the island is

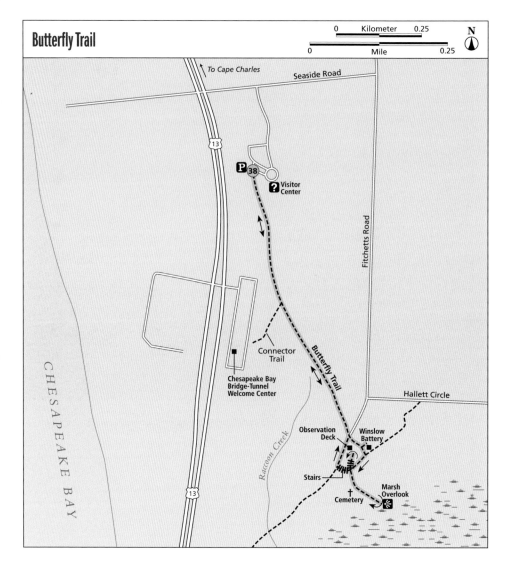

a crucial habitat for migrating and nesting shorebirds. Each fall, like colorful clockwork, the refuge is host to millions of songbirds and monarch butterflies, as well as thousands of raptors, as they come together on their southbound journey. Favorable weather patterns push migrating species through the area in waves.

In the late 1800s, Fisherman Island was the site of a marine hospital and quarantine station for immigrants on their way to Baltimore and Newport News. The island also served as a key harbor defense in World War I and World War II. Today, the barrier island chain serves as the mainland's first defense against natural forces. From the observation deck, retrace your steps back down and turn right at the bottom of the stairs. Turn left at the 0.9-mile mark and continue on to the parking area to complete your hike.

A military base to protect the Chesapeake Bay was once located at the Eastern Shore of Virginia National Wildlife Refuge. Today, former military artilleries, like the Winslow Battery, remain.

MILES AND DIRECTIONS

0.0 Begin at the trailhead to the right of the visitor center. You will see a sign with a bright orange butterfly that marks the start of the trail.

0.5 Arrive at the remains of the Winslow Battery from World War II.

0.6 Stay to the left to reach a fenced-in historic cemetery.

0.7 Reach a marsh overlook. Retrace your steps to the main trail.

0.8 Ascend a few dozen steps to the observation deck to see Fisherman Island. Retrace your steps. Turn right at the bottom of the stairs.

0.9 Turn left to continue on to the parking area.

1.4 Arrive back at the parking area. Your hike is complete.

39 **GEORGE WASHINGTON BIRTHPLACE NATIONAL MONUMENT**

In Colonial Beach, the George Washington Birthplace National Monument is a surprising and engaging destination with two scenic nature trails that loop around the property and wow with far-reaching views across Popes Creek.

Start: National monument visitor center
Elevation gain: 72 feet
Maximum grade: 4%
Distance: 1.9-mile loop
Difficulty: Easy
Hiking time: 1 to 1.5 hours
Best seasons: Year-round
Fees and permits: Free
Trail contact: George Washington Birthplace National Monument, 1732 Popes Creek Rd., Colonial Beach, VA; (804) 224-1732, ext. 227; nps.gov/gewa

Dogs: Yes, on a leash no longer than 6 feet
Trail surface: Mostly grass, dirt, and gravel trails
Land status: National monument
Nearest town: Colonial Beach
Maps: Trail maps are available at the visitor center and online at nps.gov/gewa.
Amenities: Restrooms, picnic tables, visitor center
Cell service: Reliable

FINDING THE TRAILHEAD

The trailhead is located behind the visitor center. GPS: N38°11'00.3" / W76°55'04.2"

THE HIKE

The George Washington Birthplace National Monument in Colonial Beach is set on 550 acres of the Popes Creek Plantation, which was once home to the Washington family. Of course, it's also where George Washington was born. It's worth the drive, too. For one, there are two hiking trails. You'll also find the Memorial House Museum, a delightful garden from the Colonial Revival era (1860–1940), and a farm building, as well as cows, hogs, and sheep.

The two on-property trails are the Nature Trail and the Dancing Marsh Trail. It's easy to cobble these two trails together to create a scenic 1.9-mile loop around the property. To get started, park in front of the visitor center for the George Washington Birthplace National Monument. There are lots and lots of parking spaces.

When facing the building, walk to the left. There are restrooms on the left side of the visitor center. From here, the trailhead is just a few steps closer to the Potomac River. The trailhead is not marked, at least not with a name. It also doesn't totally match up with the park's map, but this hike is all on trails and it's well worth your time.

Begin just behind the visitor center. You'll see a path made of grave and oyster shells that leads out to a wide-open area with very tall trees. At the 0.2-mile mark, a wooden bench turns up on the left. It's the perfect spot to stop and savor the water views across

Take a break on one of several wooden benches along the trails that cross George Washington Birthplace National Monument in Colonial Beach, Virginia.

Popes Creek. As you continue along, you'll arrive at a second wooden bench at the peninsula. This spot at the 0.3-mile mark is another nice place to take a break and enjoy the scenery.

The trail then meanders alongside Popes Creek. At the 0.4-mile mark, you'll be in front of the Memorial House Museum and Colonial Revival Garden. Take time to explore. There's another wooden bench here, too. Explore the manicured grounds, then take a seat for a sip of water or a light snack. In a few more steps, you'll reach a placard titled "Artery of Commerce," which outlines the role of sailing ships to tidewater planta- tions in Virginia and Maryland.

At the 0.5-mile mark, a wooden pedestrian footbridge crosses over Popes Creek. The views along this stretch are first-rate. Once you cross the creek, a sign indicates that the Nature Trail spans left and right, and that the picnic area is to the right. Proceed to the right for more views across Popes Creek. At the 0.7-mile mark, you will arrive at a picnic area as well as wooden steps that lead to a small fishing area.

Explore the fishing area, then retrace your steps and continue on into the picnic area. You will see a parking lot, too. On the other side of the lot there is a Nature Trail placard. The placard suggests that you imagine you are a young George Washington exploring the wooded plantation more than 250 years ago as you hike along the leafy trail.

From here, the trail turns inland into the woods. You'll cross over the park road at the 1.2-mile mark, then come to a short stretch of boardwalk trail. At the 1.4-mile mark,

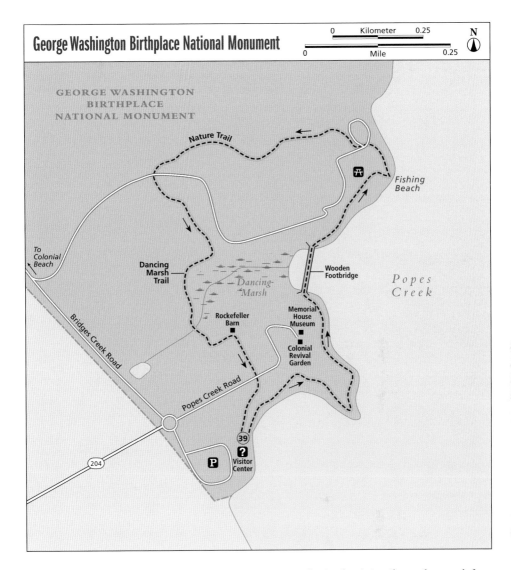

0   Kilometer   0.25

N

0   Mile   0.25

GEORGE WASHINGTON
BIRTHPLACE
NATIONAL MONUMENT

Nature Trail

Fishing
Beach

To
Colonial
Beach

Dancing
Marsh
Trail

Dancing
Marsh

Wooden
Footbridge

Popes
Creek

Bridges Creek Road

Rockefeller
Barn

Memorial
House
Museum

Colonial
Revival
Garden

Popes Creek Road

39

204

P

Visitor
Center

walk across a wooden footbridge over Dancing Marsh. At the 1.6-mile mark, turn left to walk up a small grassy hill. There is snake-rail fencing on both sides of the trail. Keep your eyes open for cows grazing in the pasture. At the top of the hill is Rockefeller Barn. In a few more steps, turn right to proceed on a mostly gravel and crushed oyster shell trail. The trail ends at the 1.9-mile mark, when you return to the visitor center. Your hike is complete.

MILES AND DIRECTIONS

0.0   Begin at the trailhead behind the visitor center.

0.4   Arrive at the Memorial House Museum and Colonial Revival Garden. Take time to explore.

A wooden footbridge guides hikers across Popes Creek at George Washington Birthplace National Monument.

0.5   Cross a wooden pedestrian footbridge over Popes Creek.

0.7   Arrive at a wooden fishing pier. Retrace your steps to the trail, then turn right to continue on. Walk across a picnic area and parking lot to reach a Nature Trail placard.

1.2   Cross over the park road, then walk a short stretch of boardwalk trail.

1.4   Walk across Dancing Marsh on a wooden footbridge.

1.6   Turn left to walk up a grassy hill. Rockefeller Barn turns up on your left. Then, turn right to proceed on a mostly gravel trail.

1.9   Arrive back at the visitor center. Your hike is complete.

40 GOVERNMENT ISLAND PARK

This hiking trail at Government Island Park in Stafford wows with water views, as well as the history of a quarry that provided free-stone used in the original construction of the White House and the US Capitol building. It's no surprise that Government Island is "America's Historic Stone Quarry" and holds a well-deserved spot on the National Register of Historic Places.

Start: Large kiosk that orients visitors to Government Island
Elevation gain: 23 feet
Maximum grade: 5%
Distance: 1.7-mile lollipop
Difficulty: Easy
Hiking time: About 1 hour
Best seasons: Year-round
Fees and permits: Free
Trail contact: Stafford Parks, Recreation and Community Facilities, PO Box 339, Stafford, VA 22555;

(540) 658-4871; staffordcountyva.gov
Dogs: Yes, on a leash no longer than 6 feet
Trail surface: Mix of paved, dirt, and boardwalk trails
Land status: County park
Nearest town: Stafford
Maps: A trail map can be found at alltrails.com.
Amenities: None
Cell service: Reliable

FINDING THE TRAILHEAD

The trailhead is located to the right of a large kiosk that orients visitors to Government Island. GPS: N38°26'49.1" / W77°23'17.1"

THE HIKE

Government Island in Stafford County has a long and storied history. In fact, this island was once owned by Westinghouse—as in, Westinghouse Electric Corporation. The forested hike around the 17-acre Government Island on a scenic heritage trail is shaded, easygoing, and rich with history.

As you enter Government Island Park, you are dropped into a large circular gravel parking area. There are no marked spaces. Simply park where you can. A large kiosk at the entrance orients visitors to Government Island, an early American quarry that was originally named Brent's Island or Wiggington's Island. In 1791, the federal government purchased the island to quarry freestone (Aquia stone) for use in the original construction of the White House and the US Capitol building. That noted, it's no surprise to learn that Government Island is "America's Historic Stone Quarry." It's also on the National Register of Historic Places.

From the kiosk, begin along a paved path on the right that leads east toward Government Island. For the first 0.3 mile, the trail sidles up against Austin Run. There are several spots along the way where you can dip down to Austin Run to skip stones across the water. You'll soon approach a wooden boardwalk.

The wooden boardwalk traverses a gorgeous wetland area. There are a couple of openings with benches and placards where you can sit and brush up on wildlife and history. Once you cross over the wetlands, the hiking trail becomes all dirt as you enter the largely shaded forest of Government Island. From here, it's a wooded loop. Since it's

The remains of a historic rock quarry can be found just off the trail at Government Island in Stafford County, Virginia.

a loop, you can go either way, of course, but for this hike, turn left for a clockwise hike around the historic island.

At the 0.5-mile mark, stop for what's left of the historic quarry. A placard illustrates how stone was quarried from the site in the late eighteenth and early nineteenth centuries. Another placard educates visitors on George Brent, the island's first owner, who purchased it in 1694.

Continue on to a wooden bench (which looks to be carved into a log) at the 0.7-mile mark. You are now at the highest point of the hike with views across Aquia Creek. Then, you will reach another placard that educates on how the stone was transported. As you can imagine, it was extremely labor-intensive. At the 0.9-mile mark, a spur trail veers left to an overlook. A single-family home subdivision is now on the other side of Aquia Creek from Government Island. Some homes even have wooden boat docks.

Retrace your steps from the overlook to a placard on the Native American presence in the area. A number of artifacts from the Patawomeck tribe have been recovered here. Stay left to continue looping around the island. At the 1.2-mile mark, you will reach the wooden boardwalk. Turn left, then retrace your steps to the parking area to complete your hike.

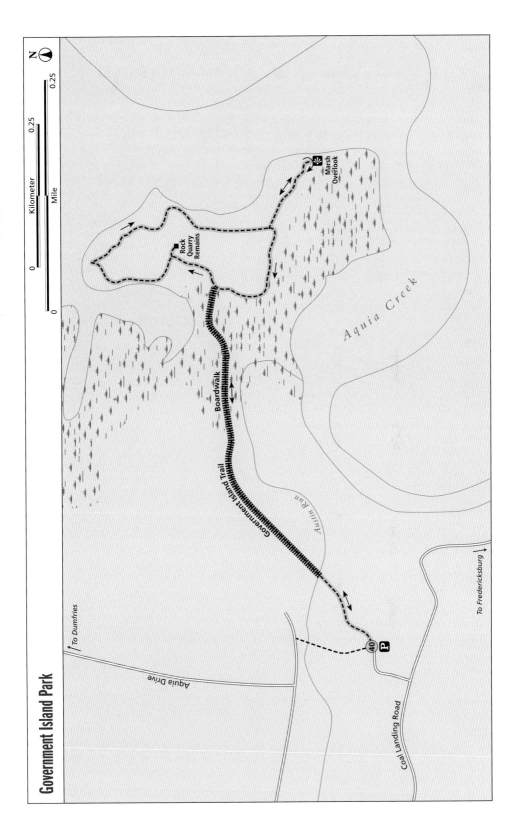

Government Island Park

N

Kilometer
0   0.25   0.25

Mile
0   0.25

To Dumfries

Aquia Drive

Coal Landing Road

To Fredericksburg

Austin Run

Government Island Trail

Boardwalk

Rock
Quarry
Remains

Marsh
Overlook

Aquia Creek

P 40

A wooden boardwalk traverses a beautiful wetland area on the way to Government Island.

MILES AND DIRECTIONS

0.0 Begin at the trailhead located to the right of a large kiosk that orients visitors to Government Island.

0.3 Arrive at a wooden boardwalk to cross over Austin Run. When the boardwalk ends, turn left to enter the loop on Government Island.

0.5 Arrive at the remains of a historic quarry on the right.

0.7 Reach a wooden bench at the highest point of the hike. Take in the views across Aquia Creek.

0.9 Veer left on a spur trail to walk out to an overlook across a marsh. Retrace your steps, then turn left to get back onto the main trail.

1.2 Close the loop, then turn left to recross the wooden boardwalk. Retrace your steps to the parking area.

1.7 Arrive back at the parking area. Your hike is complete.

Enjoy views across Aquia Creek from the forested trail that circumnavigates Government Island.

41 HUGHLETT POINT NATURAL AREA PRESERVE

On Virginia's Northern Neck, you'll find a true hidden gem tucked away in a rural county known for farming and fishing. In fact, Hughlett Point Natural Area Preserve wows with sandy beaches, coastal marshes, and towering loblolly pines, as well as far-reaching views across pristine Ingram Cove.

Start: Preserve parking lot
Elevation gain: 20 feet
Maximum grade: 1%
Distance: 1.8-mile loop
Difficulty: Easy
Hiking time: 1 to 1.5 hours
Best seasons: Year-round
Fees and permits: Free
Trail contact: Virginia Department of Conservation and Recreation, Chesapeake Bay Region Steward, VA; (804) 225-2303; dcr.virginia .gov/natural-heritage/natural-area -preserves/hughlett

Dogs: Yes, on a leash no longer than 6 feet
Trail surface: Mostly dirt, gravel, and sand trails; some boardwalk
Land status: Natural area preserve
Nearest town: Kilmarnock
Maps: National Geographic Trails Illustrated Topographic Map 772 (Delmarva Peninsula). Trail maps are also available online at dcr.virginia .gov/natural-heritage/natural-area -preserves/hughlett.
Amenities: None
Cell service: Reliable

FINDING THE TRAILHEAD

The trailhead is located in the northeast corner of the parking lot. GPS: N37°44'31.0" / W76°19'01.8"

THE HIKE

Situated on a small peninsula, the 204-acre Hughlett Point Natural Area Preserve is a hidden gem in rural Northumberland County. Driving to the parking area in Kilmarnock, passing acres upon acres of corn and soybean fields, you would have no idea this sandy shoreline and coastal hike even existed.

You will drive along small country roads, passing family farms all along the way, until at last you see a sign for the Hughlett Point Natural Area Preserve. The parking lot is small, with room for maybe a dozen cars. A sign adjacent to the trailhead notes that when the lot is full, it's full—as in, make plans to go elsewhere.

This easygoing 1.8-mile hike begins on a stretch of boardwalk trail across a wet coniferous forest. But first, read up on Jessie Ball duPont. At the start of the trail, a placard educates on Mrs. duPont's contributions to the area as a schoolteacher, philanthropist, and historic preservationist.

Walk along the shaded boardwalk trail until you reach a large trail kiosk at the 0.1-mile mark. You'll also see a trail marker. Turn right onto the Access Road Loop for the observation decks. The trail turns to dirt and gravel as it makes its way through a mostly shaded upland forest. Enjoy a mix of loblolly pines and hardwood varieties.

At the 0.4-mile mark, turn left for the north observation deck. It's a sunny walk along a boardwalk to a scenic platform with far-reaching views across the salt marsh. There are

Take off your shoes to walk the sandy shores before reconnecting with the shady, forested trail to the parking area.

This hike at Hughlett Point Natural Area Preserve begins on a stretch of boardwalk trail across a wet coniferous forest.

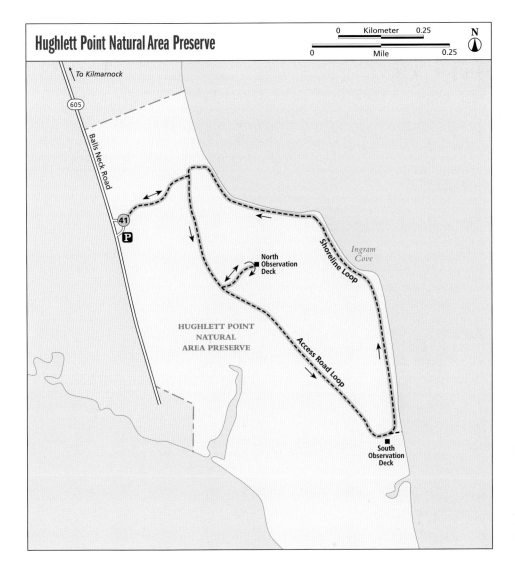

0   Kilometer   0.25

0   Mile   0.25

N

To Kilmarnock

605

Balls Neck Road

41

P

North
Observation
Deck

Shoreline Loop

*Ingram
Cove*

HUGHLETT POINT
NATURAL
AREA PRESERVE

Access Road Loop

South
Observation
Deck

two benches for you to sit and delight in the views. A placard educates on the challenges of the Chesapeake Bay to seafarers, like shifting winds and choppy waters.

Retrace your steps, then turn left to continue on the main trail. At the 0.9-mile mark, you'll reach the octagon-shaped south observation deck for another round of sweeping views. From the platform, turn right to get back on the main trail, then turn left to walk out onto the sandy shoreline at Ingram Cove. As the waves gently lap along the soft sands, proceed north on the Shoreline Loop. Take your shoes off to walk the sandy strip of beach in between lush wetlands on the left and the Chesapeake Bay on the right. You'll feel worlds away from farm fields.

Like the Savage Neck Dunes Natural Area Preserve on Virginia's Eastern Shore, this nature preserve is home to the threatened northeastern beach tiger beetle. The tiger beetle is so rare that it can now only be found at two sites outside the Chesapeake Bay. These beetles are vulnerable to any kind of beach sand disruptions.

At the 1.6-mile mark, keep your eyes open. There is no trail marker to indicate where the Shoreline Loop reconnects with the shady, forested trail to the parking area. The sandy trail on the left that leads into the forest is marked (informally) by a large, full loblolly pine. At the base is a narrow trail leading into the shaded forest.

If you miss this exit, you'll end up walking another 0.1 mile down the beach until you reach a sign that notes you can go no farther. Simply turn around and try again. Once you reach the main trail, note that it quickly veers to the left, at which point you will see the large trail kiosk. Turn right and retrace your steps to the parking area to complete this hike.

MILES AND DIRECTIONS

0.0 Begin at the trailhead in the northeast corner of the parking lot. The trail starts as a wooden boardwalk through the forest.

0.1 Arrive at a large trail kiosk. Turn right to proceed to the north and south observation decks.

0.4 Turn left for a short spur trail to the north observation deck. Retrace your steps, then turn left to continue on the main trail.

0.9 Arrive at the octagon-shaped south observation deck. Turn right to continue on the main trail, then turn left at the sandy beach to proceed north on the Shoreline Loop.

1.6 Turn left to reenter the forest and jump back on the main trail. Turn left, then turn right at the large trail kiosk to return to the parking area.

1.8 Arrive back at the parking area. Your hike is complete.

42 INTERPRETIVE TRAIL, MACHICOMOCO STATE PARK

At Machicomoco State Park, Virginia's fortieth state park, visitors can walk the Interpretive Trail. This coastal trail is steeped in history for those eager to learn about the role that Native Americans played in the growth of Virginia.

Start: Parking area in the far southeast section of the park
Elevation gain: 23 feet
Maximum grade: 4%
Distance: 0.9-mile loop with spurs
Difficulty: Easy
Hiking time: About 1 hour
Best seasons: Year-round
Fees and permits: $
Trail contact: Machicomoco State Park, 3601 Timberneck Farm Rd., Hayes, VA; (804) 642-2419; dcr.virginia.gov/state-parks/machicomoco

Dogs: Yes, on a leash no longer than 6 feet
Trail surface: Mostly gravel and paved trails
Land status: State park
Nearest town: Yorktown
Maps: National Geographic Trails Illustrated Topographic Map 772 (Delmarva Peninsula). Trail maps are also available at the visitor center and online at dcr.virginia.gov/state-parks/machicomoco.
Amenities: Flush toilets, picnic tables
Cell service: Reliable

FINDING THE TRAILHEAD

The trailhead is located to the left of the restrooms at the parking area in the far southeast section of the park. GPS: N37°17'55.3" / W76°32'13.2"

THE HIKE

Set on Virginia's Middle Peninsula, 645-acre Machicomoco State Park is a work in progress, but with a campground, three hiking trails, and a boat launch, it's coming along quite nicely. Virginia's fortieth state park is 10 miles down the York River from Werowocomoco, a village that was once home to Chief Powhatan, a political and spiritual leader. In fact, *Werowocomoco* roughly translates from the Virginia Algonquian language as "place of leadership." Chief Powhatan's daughter, Pocahontas, lived there, too.

It's a certainty that the state park's land was associated with *Tsenacommacah*, a name given by the Powhatan people to their native lands on the coast of Virginia. A celebration of this Native American heritage can be seen across Machicomoco State Park, most notably on the 0.9-mile Interpretive Trail. This is one of three hiking trails at this state park, the others being the Loop Trail (3.1 miles) and Forestry Trail (2.4 miles). The Loop Trail is a paved walk around the park, while the Forestry Trail is a shaded walk in the woods.

The Interpretive Trail is the best hiking trail at this state park for taking in both scenic views and state history. It begins at the parking area in the far southeast section of the park. Look for the red-blazed trail markers. A paved trail sets off to the left of the restrooms. Stay right at the split.

At the 0.1-mile mark, the trail veers to the right to connect with the Forestry Trail. However, you'll want to stay left until the 0.2-mile mark. You'll soon spy a short wooden

An open-air interpretive structure at Machicomoco State Park shares the story of Native American tribes in Virginia.

boardwalk on the right. Proceed to the fishing dock. The views across the York River are fantastic.

On the return, notice the wooden markers to the right of the dock. Each has a drawing of a native animal, like a crab. Look down at the dock and you will see the Algonquian word for each drawing. In this case, *tuttascuc*, or "crab." The English translation is written to the left of the word.

Retrace your steps to the path, then turn right to ascend the small hill. In a few steps, you will see the remains of Timberneck House, which dates back to 1800. But first, continue right to the end of the peninsula. At the 0.4-mile mark, you'll reach an interpretive stop, again showcasing the Algonquian language. The gravel trail splits in a few more feet, but you can go either way since the two reconnect in a few more feet. At the peninsula, enjoy views across Timberneck Creek. Here, the trail terrain changes to crushed oyster shells. A bench shares with visitors two more Algonquian words: *arrokoth* (sky) and *maraak* (cedar).

Retrace your steps. At the 0.8-mile mark, stay to the right to be front and center at Timberneck House. There is also an educational placard on the home's preservation. Your hike is complete at the 0.9-mile mark. However, you will want to stop for the large interpretive structure. A path leading to the open-air pavilion features a time line, which begins at 16,000 BC with the creation of channels that ultimately formed the Chesapeake Bay, the largest estuary in the United States. Included on the time line is the year

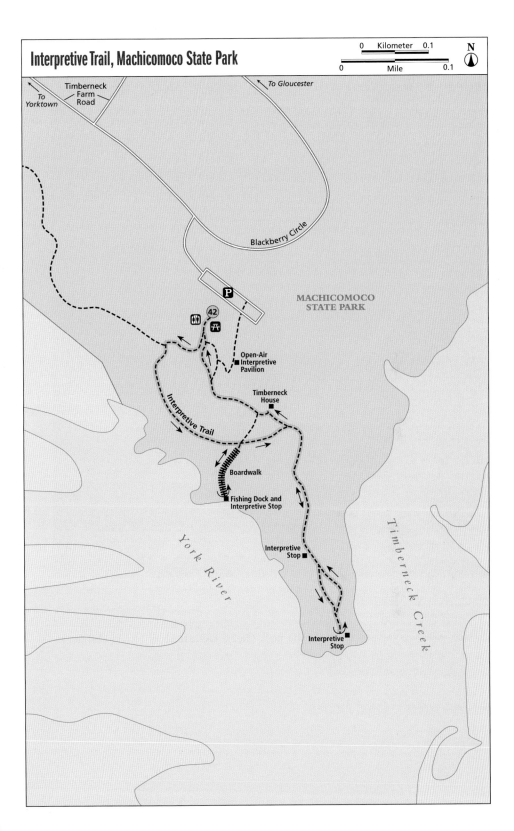

Interpretive Trail, Machicomoco State Park

0   Kilometer   0.1

0   Mile   0.1

N

To Yorktown

Timberneck Farm Road

To Gloucester

Blackberry Circle

P

MACHICOMOCO STATE PARK

42

Open-Air Interpretive Pavilion

Timberneck House

Interpretive Trail

Boardwalk

Fishing Dock and Interpretive Stop

York River

Interpretive Stop

Interpretive Stop

Timberneck Creek

Notice drawings on wooden markers along the dock on the Interpretive Trail. Each one is a native animal, like a crab.

the Powhatan Indians met the English colonists (1607), as well as dates when Virginia formally recognized local Native American tribes (1983–2010). Inside the structure, placards educate on the landscape and the role of the various Native American communities in the region.

MILES AND DIRECTIONS

0.0   Begin at the trailhead to the left of the restrooms at the parking area in the far southeast section of the park.

Enjoy far-reaching water views across the York River from the grounds of Machicomoco State Park.

0.2 Arrive at a wooden boardwalk. Walk out to the end, making note of the wooden markers with pictures of native animals and the Algonquian word for each drawing.

0.4 Reach an interpretive stop showcasing the Algonquian language.

0.5 Arrive at the peninsula. Retrace your steps.

0.8 Stay to the right at the fork and reach Timberneck House. A placard educates on the status of the home's preservation.

0.9 Arrive back at the parking area. Your hike is complete.

43 NOLAND TRAIL

The Noland Trail guides visitors around The Mariners' Lake, wowing with far-reaching lake views at several overlooks around this 167-acre reservoir in Newport News.

Start: Across Museum Drive from the Mariners' Museum parking lot
Elevation gain: 177 feet
Maximum grade: 4%
Distance: 5.6-mile loop
Difficulty: Easy
Hiking time: 2 to 3 hours
Best seasons: Year-round
Fees and permits: Free
Trail contact: The Mariners' Museum and Park, 100 Museum Dr., Newport News, VA; (757) 596-2222; marinersmuseum.org

Dogs: Yes, on a leash no longer than 6 feet
Trail surface: Mostly dirt trails
Land status: Private property
Nearest town: Newport News
Maps: National Geographic Trails Illustrated Topographic Map 772 (Delmarva Peninsula)
Amenities: Restrooms, picnic tables, benches, museum
Cell service: Reliable

FINDING THE TRAILHEAD

Pick up the Noland Trail across Museum Drive from the Mariners' Museum parking lot. GPS: N37°03'21.3" / W76°29'18.1"

THE HIKE

For a relaxing loop hike, set off for Mariners' Museum Park in Newport News for a shady walk around The Mariners' Lake. Previously named Lake Maury, the 168-acre reservoir was renamed in June 2020. The lake got caught up in controversy, as it had been named more than eighty years ago for a Confederate officer named Matthew Fontaine Maury.

The Noland Trail, a forested 5.6-mile loop, circumnavigates the lake with lots of benches, bridges, and overlooks. You may even catch views of the James River. On arrival, park in the large lot in front of the Mariners' Museum, a 60,000-square-foot museum that explores global maritime history. The trailhead is on the other side of Museum Drive from the parking lot. You will see a bench, a water fountain, and a colorful map that heralds the start of the Noland Trail.

From here, the trail quickly descends into the woods, then crosses the first of fourteen bridges that casually guide visitors over The Mariners' Lake. The Noland Trail starts out as paved, but then turns to mostly dirt and sand after the first bridge over an inlet of The Mariners' Lake (on a clockwise hike).

At the 0.2-mile mark, you'll reach a small peninsula with a wooden overlook and a couple of benches. From here, you can see across the lake to the museum. Continue on until you cross a bridge that parallels Warwick Boulevard at the 0.4-mile mark. Note that each bridge is marked with a number on both sides of the bridge.

It's rather noisy here with cars motoring north and south, but then you return to the quiet of the woods. You'll reach the Pine Tree Overlook at the 0.7-mile mark for more lake views. There are plenty of benches scattered across this trail, too. Also, keep your eyes open for a mile marker that turns up every 0.5 mile.

Multiple wooden benches around The Mariners'
Lake allow visitors to rest and rehydrate
before continuing along the Noland Trail.

The Mariners' Lake, a 167-acre reservoir, is the centerpiece of this delightful loop hike at Mariners' Museum and Park in Newport News.

At the 1.8-mile mark, you'll pass Williams Field Park on the left, with a ball field and a wide-open space to run and play, as well as a few dilapidated picnic tables. The Noland Trail sidles up against a park road at the 2.0-mile mark, then proceeds to the Oak Tree Overlook. This lake overlook is large and has benches. From the overlook (which you access by way of a short spur trail), retrace your steps to the Noland Trail, then turn right to continue on the hiking trail.

At the 2.5-mile mark, you'll reach two picnic tables by the lake. It's a great stop to enjoy a picnic lunch in the outdoors before proceeding along the trail. Cross over bridge number seven, and keep walking until you reach the 3.3-mile mark. Here you can walk right out to the edge of The Mariners' Lake. In a few more steps, cross over the famed Lions Bridge, which looks over the mighty James River. After you cross the bridge, the trail reenters the forest.

But first, pass a restoration of Anna Hyatt Huntington's statue *Conquering the Wild*. The statue overlooks The Mariners' Lake and the James River. At the 3.6-mile mark, a short spur trail that's easy to miss leads to a small grove of longleaf pine trees. The longleaf pine is one of nine native pine species in Virginia.

Retrace your steps, then turn left onto the trail. You'll reach one more wooden overlook with refreshing lake views at the 4.3-mile mark. This is the Holly Tree Overlook. At the 5.3-mile mark, you'll brush up against Museum Drive, then pass the NOAA

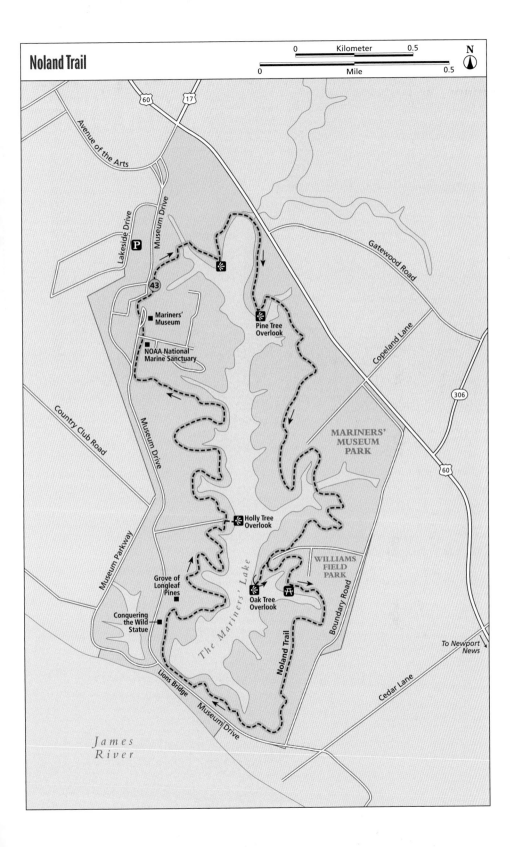

Noland Trail

0 — Kilometer — 0.5

0 — Mile — 0.5

N

Avenue of the Arts

60 17

Museum Drive

Gatewood Road

Lakeside Drive

P

Copeland Lane

43

Mariners' Museum

NOAA National Marine Sanctuary

Pine Tree Overlook

306

60

MARINERS' MUSEUM PARK

Country Club Road

Museum Drive

Holly Tree Overlook

Grove of Longleaf Pines

WILLIAMS FIELD PARK

Museum Parkway

Conquering the Wild Statue

Oak Tree Overlook

Boundary Road

To Newport News

The Mariners' Lake

Noland Trail

Lions Bridge

Museum Drive

Cedar Lane

James River

Numerous wooden bridges guide visitors over The Mariners' Lake on the Noland Trail.

National Marine Sanctuary and the Mariners' Museum, both on your right. In a few more steps, you'll arrive at the trailhead and your hike is complete.

MILES AND DIRECTIONS

0.0 Pick up the trail on the opposite side of Museum Drive from the parking area.

0.2 Arrive at a wooden overlook on a small peninsula.

0.7 Reach the Pine Tree Overlook.

1.8 Pass Williams Field Park on the left.

2.1 Arrive at the Oak Tree Overlook.

3.3 Cross over the famed Lions Bridge, then stay right to walk back into the forest.

3.6 A short spur trail on the left leads to a small grove of longleaf pine trees. Retrace your steps to the main trail.

4.3 Arrive at the Holly Tree Overlook.

5.3 The trail brushes up against Museum Drive. Pass the NOAA National Marine Sanctuary and the Mariners' Museum on the right.

5.6 Arrive at the trailhead. Your hike is complete.

44 PLEASURE HOUSE POINT NATURAL AREA

This delightful walk across Pleasure House Point Natural Area in Virginia Beach guides visitors across tidal marsh, sandy beaches, and maritime forest. Keep your eyes open for oysters growing on the shores at low tide. It's a wildly curious sight to behold from the trail.

Start: Trailhead on Marlin Bay Drive
Elevation gain: 7 feet
Maximum grade: 1%
Distance: 2.0-mile lollipop
Difficulty: Easy
Hiking time: 1 to 1.5 hours
Best seasons: Year-round
Fees and permits: Free
Trail contact: City of Virginia Beach, Parks and Recreation, 2408 Courthouse Dr., Virginia Beach, VA; (757) 385-1100; www.vbgov.com/

government/departments/parks-recreation/Pages/default.aspx
Dogs: Yes, on a leash no longer than 6 feet
Trail surface: Mostly sand, some gravel
Land status: City park
Nearest town: Virginia Beach
Maps: National Geographic Trails Illustrated Topographic Map 772 (Delmarva Peninsula)
Amenities: None
Cell service: Reliable

FINDING THE TRAILHEAD

The trailhead is located on Marlin Bay Drive, roughly 0.1 mile from Shore Drive on the right (when driving east along Marlin Bay Drive). A large trail sign marks the trailhead. GPS: N36°54'20.5" / W76°06'21.2"

THE HIKE

At the 118-acre Pleasure House Point Natural Area in Virginia Beach, you'll find two hiking trails—the Meadow Trail and the Beach Trail. Together, they form a 2-mile loop that encircles the natural area with views aplenty of maritime forest and tidal marsh.

There isn't much signage, but generally, if you stay to the right, you'll be on the correct path. With an elevation gain of 7 feet, it's not upsetting to veer off-course now and again. There is also no designated parking lot for Pleasure House Point Natural Area, but, thankfully, plenty of parallel parking spots are available along Marlin Bay Drive. Once you make the turn from Shore Drive, you'll immediately see cars parked on the side of the road.

The trailhead is roughly 0.1 mile from Shore Drive on the right (when driving east along Marlin Bay Drive). A large trail sign marks the trailhead. The Beach Trail starts out as soft sand, so keep this in mind. At the 0.1-mile mark, turn right to go around a small coastal pond. The trail is flat and sandy, with pine needles scattered across the path from coastal pines. At the 0.3-mile mark, you'll be around the pond.

A sign nudges you to stay right for the Meadow Trail and Beach Trail. A tidal marsh turns up on the left with more coastal loblolly pines as you continue walking on the sandy trail. Pleasure House Creek is now on your right. Interestingly, oysters grow at the water's edge. They are especially plentiful at low tide.

The trail is flat and sandy, with pine needles scattered across the path from coastal pines.

At the 0.6-mile mark, stay right to continue along the perimeter of the natural area. Marsh grasses and coastal pines flank either side of the hiking trail. A small sandy beach turns up at the 1.0-mile mark. You may see small children and active pups living their best lives splashing and running in the shallow waters of Crab Creek.

Continue alongside Crab Creek to reach several free-standing placards set up by the Chesapeake Bay Foundation to educate visitors on climate change and its impact on the health of the Chesapeake Bay. At the 1.2-mile mark, there is a comfy bench where the trail splits in two. Stay to the right to continue on. Then, another delightful small pond shows up on the left. Even better—for children, at least—a nice playground is on the right just past the pond. You are now passing through Loch Haven Park.

In a few more steps, enjoy a brief break from sandy trail as you step foot on a brick-paved path that leads to the Brock Environmental Center. The path then picks back up as a gravel trail, veering off to the right. At the 1.6-mile mark, you reach Marlin Bay Drive. This is the same road where you likely parked your car. You can either walk along the sidewalk to return to your car or stay left to return to the path. Opting to return to the path, you'll return to a familiar trail at the 1.7-mile mark. Turn right and retrace your steps from here to your car parked on Marlin Bay Drive. Your hike is complete.

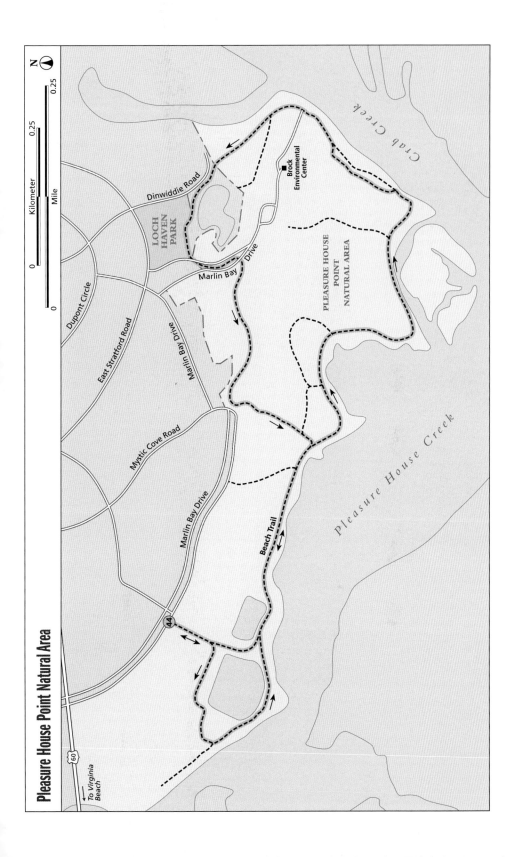

Pleasure House Point Natural Area

N

0	0.25	Kilometer
0		Mile
	0.25	

Dupont Circle

East Stratford Road

Mystic Cove Road

Marlin Bay Drive

Marlin Bay Drive

Dinwiddie Road

LOCH HAVEN PARK

Marlin Bay Drive

Brock Environmental Center

PLEASURE HOUSE POINT NATURAL AREA

Crab Creek

Pleasure House Creek

Beach Trail

44

60

To Virginia Beach

The Meadow Trail and Beach Trail link up to circumnavigate Pleasure House Point Natural Area in Virginia Beach.

MILES AND DIRECTIONS

0.0 Begin at the trailhead that starts next to the large trail sign on Marlin Bay Drive.

0.1 Turn right to walk the perimeter of a small coastal pond.

0.3 Stay right at the sign for the Meadow and Beach Trails to walk alongside Pleasure House Creek.

0.6 Stay to the right when the trail splits.

1.0 Arrive at a small sandy beach.

1.2 The trail splits again. Stay right to proceed to a small pond and children's playground at Loch Haven Park. In a few more steps, arrive at a path for the Brock Environmental Center. Turn right for a gravel path to continue this hike.

1.6 Reach Marlin Bay Drive. Turn left to reconnect with the path.

1.7 Turn right to retrace your steps to the trailhead.

2.0 Arrive back at the trailhead. Your hike is complete.

A relaxing 2-mile hiking loop encircles Pleasure House Point Natural Area in Virginia Beach.

45 RAGGED ISLAND WILDLIFE MANAGEMENT AREA

Across the James River from Newport News sits an unspoiled gem called the Ragged Island Wildlife Management Area. An easygoing coastal hike crosses over brackish marsh on a wooden boardwalk and alongside the river to reach two sandy beaches worthy of tossing down a blanket to enjoy a savory picnic lunch.

Start: Ragged Island parking area
Elevation gain: 7 feet
Maximum grade: 1%
Distance: 2.3 miles out and back
Difficulty: Easy
Hiking time: 1.5 to 2 hours
Best seasons: Year-round
Fees and permits: $
Trail contact: Virginia Department of Wildlife Resources, Region 1 Office, 3801 John Tyler Memorial Hwy., Charles City, VA; (804) 829-6580; dwr.virginia.gov/wma/ragged-island

Dogs: Yes, on a leash no longer than 6 feet
Trail surface: Mix of gravel, grass, sand, and wooden boardwalk
Land status: Wildlife management area
Nearest Town: Newport News
Maps: National Geographic Trails Illustrated Topographic Map 772 (Delmarva Peninsula)
Amenities: None
Cell service: Reliable

FINDING THE TRAILHEAD

The trailhead is located to the left of the large trail sign in the parking area. GPS: N36°57'54.8" / W76°30'50.8"

THE HIKE

The 1,537-acre Ragged Island Wildlife Management Area in Isle of Wight County is located across the James River Bridge from Newport News. It sits up against the lower James River. Here you'll find unspoiled wetlands, wooden boardwalk, coastal pines and reeds, even a couple of small sandy beaches.

The parking area is a good size, with room for at least a dozen cars. At the trailhead, you may notice trash bags as well as a handwritten sign encouraging hikers to pick up their trash. It's true that some cans and bottles washed ashore, while others were left behind by thoughtless visitors. If you can, bring along plastic gloves and a trash bag to help keep the trail clean.

The trailhead is easy to find—it's to the left of a large trail kiosk. The trail is neither marked nor named, but it's fairly simple to follow. Your best bet is to go at low tide. Some sections of the trail closest to the water can become hard to traverse when the tide comes in. Even better, at low tide you're more likely to see teeny-tiny crabs scurrying into and out of holes, on the prowl for scrumptious low-tide treasures.

The trail begins as a mostly gravel trail through a grove of coastal pines. At the 0.2-mile mark, turn left onto a wooden boardwalk. Peer out into the brackish marsh to see dozens, if not hundreds, of tiny crabs. Continue along the boardwalk that leads across the tidal marsh.

A second sandy beach on this hike wows with cool dead trees with roots that appear to have grown out of the sand.

At the 0.4-mile mark, you will reach a small fishing pier as the wooden boardwalk ends at the James River. Step down onto the sand. From here, you can walk along the water or on a reed-lined trail. In some areas of the trail, the reeds can be pared back, depending on the season you complete this hike. Thankfully, there are plenty of sections where you can step out closer to the water to continue on.

At the 0.8-mile mark, you'll reach the first of two sandy beaches. It's kind of oasis-like, since it just seems to appear out of nowhere. Feel free to sit down and enjoy a snack or a sip of water. From here, you may wonder whether to continue on through the reeds, but the second sand-covered beach is waiting for you.

At the 1.0-mile mark, a second beach awes with peculiar trees whose roots are curiously above the sand. You'll also find the only shade on the entire hike. You can see Newport News off in the distance, as well as the James River Bridge. It's very relaxing. The trail concludes at the end of the second beach, at around the 1.1-mile mark. The coastal reeds here are quite dense, and you can tell that this is the end. From here, retrace your steps to the parking area to complete your hike.

MILES AND DIRECTIONS

0.0   The trail begins to the left of a large trail kiosk in the parking area.

0.2   Turn left onto a wooden boardwalk.

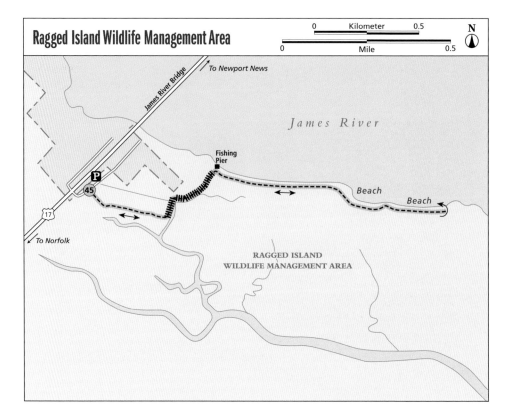

Ragged Island Wildlife Management Area

0   Kilometer   0.5

0   Mile   0.5

N

To Newport News

James River Bridge

James River

Fishing Pier

P

45

Beach

Beach

17

To Norfolk

RAGGED ISLAND
WILDLIFE MANAGEMENT AREA

0.4   Arrive at a small fishing pier where the wooden boardwalk ends. Turn right to walk along the shoreline adjacent to the James River.

0.8   Reach the first sandy beach.

1.0   Arrive at the second sandy beach.

1.1   The beach ends. Retrace your steps to the parking area.

2.3   Arrive back at the parking area. Your hike is complete.

46 TASKINAS CREEK TRAIL

An easy wetlands loop hike at York River State Park in Williamsburg wows with plenty of delightful water-filled views across winding Taskinas Creek.

Start: Taskinas Creek Overlook and picnic shelters
Elevation gain: 243 feet
Maximum grade: 11%
Distance: 2.9-mile lollipop
Difficulty: Easy
Hiking time: 1.5 to 2 hours
Best seasons: Year-round
Fees and permits: $
Trail contact: York River State Park, 9801 York River Park Rd., Williamsburg, VA; (757) 566-3036; dcr.virginia.gov/state-parks/york-river

Dogs: Yes, on a leash no longer than 6 feet
Trail surface: Mostly sand and dirt trails, some wooden boardwalk
Land status: State park
Nearest town: Williamsburg
Maps: Trail maps are available at the visitor center and online at dcr .virginia.gov/state-parks/york-river.
Amenities: Restrooms, picnic tables, visitor center, playground
Cell service: Reliable

FINDING THE TRAILHEAD

The trailhead begins south of the Taskinas Creek Overlook and picnic shelters. GPS: N37°24'46.4" / W76°42'50.1"

THE HIKE

At York River State Park in Williamsburg, the hike along the Taskinas Creek Trail wows with sweeping views across this small tributary of the York River. This relaxing hike includes forested views, wooden bridges, boardwalk sections, and several overlooks for scenic views of the Taskinas Creek watershed.

You'll find a large central parking lot at York River State Park. There are plenty of parking spaces. Even on weekends, parking should not be a problem. As you drive in, park on the left side of the parking area, near a picnic shelter and a large playground. You'll also see a large trail kiosk and will be steps from the visitor center.

A paved trail runs south until you reach a sign for the Taskinas Creek Trail. The coastal forests and freshwater swamps that surround the creek are critical habitats. The red-blazed trail begins as paved surface, but quickly guides past an equestrian parking area and descends into the forest along a mostly dirt and sand trail.

At the 0.3-mile mark, you will climb, then quickly reach a trail sign. Here, the Taskinas Creek Trail becomes a loop. You can go either way, but a left turn for a clockwise hike delivers you more quickly to the primary overlook.

As you continue on, you'll arrive at a spur trail to the main overlook for Taskinas Creek at the 0.8-mile mark. It's a 0.3-mile walk downhill to a wooden overlook. There's a nice bench, too. It's the perfect place to stop to rehydrate and take in the views, especially since it's an uphill walk to return to the main loop.

Once you return to the main trail, turn left to continue on the loop. From here, you'll cross over several wooden bridges and boardwalk sections, as well as ascend steps. You

Savor the views across Taskinas Creek on this easygoing loop hike at York River State Park.

Plan to encounter wooden bridges, sections of boardwalk, and sweeping overlooks along the Taskinas Creek Trail.

Taskinas Creek Trail

will also reach three more wooden overlooks for bonus views across Taskinas Creek. One or two even have benches for relaxing and wildlife-watching. At the 2.7-mile mark, the loop closes. Turn left for the final steps to the trailhead. Your hike is complete at the 2.9-mile mark.

MILES AND DIRECTIONS

0.0   Begin on the Taskinas Creek Trail, just south of the Taskinas Creek Overlook.

0.3   Arrive at a T-intersection. Turn left for a clockwise loop hike.

0.8   Stay left for a spur trail to reach the main overlook for Taskinas Creek.

1.1   Reach the wooden overlook with sweeping views across Taskinas Creek. Retrace your steps to the Taskinas Creek Trail.

1.4   Arrive at the Taskinas Creek Trail. Turn left to return to the clockwise loop. As you continue on, you will reach three more wooden overlooks for bonus views across Taskinas Creek.

2.7   Close the loop. Turn left to exit for the final steps back to the trailhead.

2.9   Arrive back at the trailhead. Your hike is complete.

47 WHITE OAK NATURE TRAIL

The White Oak Nature Trail at Newport News Park is a delightful wooded trail that crosses the Lee Hall Reservoir twice, offering views of coastal wetlands and cypress swamps. Plan to spend the whole day here thanks to playgrounds, disc golf, a campground, and more.

Start: Newport News Park, Dam Bridge #1
Elevation gain: 62 feet
Maximum grade: 4%
Distance: 2.7-mile loop
Difficulty: Easy
Hiking time: 1 to 1.5 hours
Best seasons: Year-round
Fees and permits: Free
Trail contact: Newport News Park, 13560 Jefferson Ave., Newport News, VA; (757) 886-7912; nnparks.com

Dogs: Yes, on a leash no longer than 6 feet
Trail surface: Mostly dirt trails, some wooden bridges
Land status: City park
Nearest town: Newport News
Maps: National Geographic Trails Illustrated Topographic Map 772 (Delmarva Peninsula)
Amenities: Restrooms, picnic tables, playground
Cell service: Reliable

FINDING THE TRAILHEAD

The trailhead is located to the left of the large trail sign at Dam Bridge #1, to the left of the parking area. GPS: N37°10'58.8" / W76°32'12.4"

THE HIKE

The White Oak Nature Trail at Newport News Park in Newport News is one of sixty-five trail loops that make up the Virginia Bird and Wildlife Trail. These trail loops are spread across three regions, including mountain, piedmont, and coastal, and all feature multiple wildlife and birding sites and overlooks. In Virginia's coastal region, there are eighteen trail loops, including the White Oak Nature Trail. These hiking trails allow exploration of windswept barrier islands, cypress swamps, and scenic seashores.

Enter Newport News Park by way of Constitution Way. From here, it's a short drive to the parking area at Dam Bridge #1. As you drive in, you'll pass picnic areas, fishing piers, boat launches, playgrounds, and restrooms. There's a lot to do at this park, including disc golf, archery, and a ropes course. There's also a campground, which boasts 188 wooded campsites.

The hike along the White Oak Nature Trail begins at Dam Bridge #1, a wooden bridge that crosses over the Lee Hall Reservoir. But first, a bit of Civil War history. Before you step foot on the wooden bridge, notice several placards and monuments. Read up on the Battle of Dam #1 (April 16, 1862). Dam #1 is one of three dams constructed by Confederate soldiers, which successfully transformed the slow-moving Warwick River into a defensive barrier. There is also a monument to the Union Army's 3rd Vermont Infantry Regiment, a volunteer division that led the charge during the Battle of Dam #1.

Cross Dam Bridge #1 over the Lee Hall Reservoir. You may see turtles swimming in the reservoir, as well as small children squealing in delight at the sight of the turtles. At the 0.2-mile mark, you'll be on the other side of the reservoir and at a trail junction. Stay right for the wooded White Oak Nature Trail. In a few steps, cross over a small bridge.

There are plenty of wooden bridges and boardwalk trails to cross all along the White Oak Nature Trail.

Step out onto a wooden overlook at the 0.6-mile mark to see a murky swamp of bald cypress trees. As you continue along, cross bridges over more small creeks, including Sycamore Creek and Greenbriar Creek. You'll also see benches along the trail so you and your crew can take a rest every now and again.

At the 1.5-mile mark, you'll reach Swamp Bridge, which will take you over a wetlands-dominated section of the Lee Hall Reservoir. As you cross over, you will encounter two walk-out overlooks, each with four or five steps to reach an elevated overlook. The first turns up on the right; the second is on the left.

At the 1.9-mile mark, a sign indicates that the Swamp View Point is only 0.1 mile off the trail. Here you'll find a nice platform with two benches, though the views are superior from Swamp Bridge. At this point, you're also walking alongside the Newport News Golf Club at Deer Run. Thankfully, this golf course on the left is mostly hidden by the woods.

At the 2.3-mile mark, turn right for more views of bald cypress trees from a small wooden overlook. From here, a few more bridges and boardwalks lead to the end. Your hike is complete at the 2.7-mile mark.

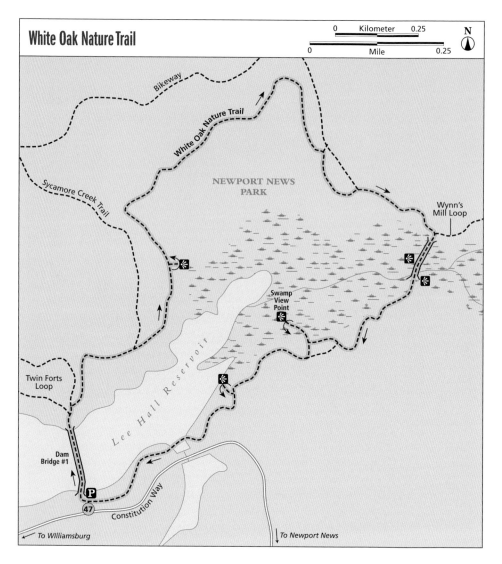

White Oak Nature Trail

MILES AND DIRECTIONS

0.0 The trail begins to the left of the large trail sign at Dam #1, to the left of the parking area.

0.2 Arrive at a trail junction. Turn right for the White Oak Nature Trail.

0.6 Reach a wooden overlook for views of bald cypress trees in a swamp.

1.5 Cross Swamp Bridge. Make stops for the two wooden overlooks.

1.9 Turn right onto a spur trail to Swamp View Point. Retrace your steps, then turn right onto the main trail.

2.3 Reach a small overlook for more views of bald cypress trees.

2.7 Arrive at the trailhead. Your hike is complete.

48 WILLIAM B. CUMMINGS BIRDING AND WILDLIFE TRAIL

At Brownsville Preserve in Nassawadox you'll find 1,000-plus acres of habitats, including wooded uplands and tidal marshes. A 3-mile hike on the William B. Cummings Birding and Wildlife Trail exposes visitors to salt marshes, hardwood forest, tidal creeks, and retired agricultural fields.

Start: Brownsville Preserve parking area
Elevation gain: 16 feet
Maximum grade: 1%
Distance: 3.0-mile lollipop
Difficulty: Easy
Hiking time: 1 to 2 hours
Best seasons: Year-round
Fees and permits: Free
Trail contact: Brownsville Preserve–Virginia Coast Reserve, 11332 Brownsville Rd., Nassawadox, VA; (757) 442-3049; dwr.virginia.gov/vbwt/sites/brownsville-preserve

Dogs: Yes (except during hunting season), on a leash no longer than 6 feet
Trail surface: Mostly grass, sand, and gravel trails; some wooden boardwalk
Land status: Private nature preserve
Nearest town: Cape Charles
Maps: National Geographic Trails Illustrated Topographic Map 772 (Delmarva Peninsula). Trail maps are also available at the on-site trail kiosk in the parking area.
Amenities: None
Cell service: Reliable

FINDING THE TRAILHEAD

The trailhead is located to the left of the large trail sign in the parking area. GPS: N37°28'11.4" / W75°50'05.8"

THE HIKE

Brownsville Preserve in Nassawadox is the headquarters for the Nature Conservancy's Virginia Coast Reserve. This coastal wildlife habitat features tidal wetlands and old-growth forest, as well as a scenic hiking trail. Pick up a printed trail guide on-site to read up on what you will see on the trail, as well as learn all about the nature preserve as you hike across the landscape.

It's wise to note that leashed pets are allowed, but no pets may enter Brownsville Preserve during hunting season—from October through early January. Visitor hours are also limited during this time period to between 9 a.m. and 3 p.m.

You'll find the parking area for Brownsville Preserve about halfway down Brownsville Road, a small country road in Nassawadox (25 minutes north of Cape Charles). Look for the trail parking sign on the right. You'll see a large trail kiosk with printed trail maps, scavenger hunts for kids, and guides to the Virginia Coast Reserve. At the back of the small parking area, a large sign welcomes visitors to the William B. Cummings Birding and Wildlife Trail. The trail begins to the left of this sign.

The hike starts on a mostly grass and gravel path, but quickly transforms into a narrow boardwalk that's just three boards wide. On the elevated wooden boardwalk, traverse salt

The hike across Brownsville Preserve in Nassawadox begins with a delightful walk across an elevated wooden boardwalk.

William B. Cummings Birding and Wildlife Trail

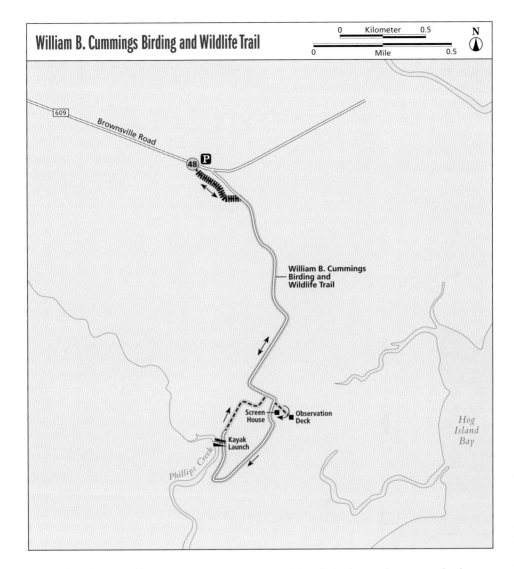

marshes dominated by salt-tolerant wax myrtles, high-tide bushes, and eastern redcedars. As you continue along, enter a mature pine-hardwood forest made up of loblolly pines, white oaks, sweet gums, and black cherry trees. Finally, tall salt marsh grasses, including saltmeadow cordgrass and narrowleaf cattail, are found along the boardwalk as it comes to an end at the 0.2-mile mark.

Turn right onto the trail (more like a service road) made up of gravel, sand, and crushed oyster shells. Retired farmlands turn up on the left side of the trail. Following crop failures from 2000 to 2006 due to saltwater intrusion, the fields were retired. Native trees and shrubs have since been planted to restore forested habitats. Near the 0.9-mile mark, you may see the effects of flooding from Hurricane Isabel in 2003. Many of the mature pines were killed by salt water that flooded the area.

As you continue along, you will see man-made wetlands on the left, including a small pond that attracts black-crowned night herons and egrets. At the 1.0-mile mark, walk straight ahead to see a screen house on the right, then a wooden observation deck across the clearing. Climb a few steps to enjoy a wide-reaching vista across the marsh. Keep your eyes open for egrets and waterfowl. It's hard to believe, but cattle once grazed here. Weathered cedar fence posts can be seen across the marsh, evidence that cows once grazed on the native saltmeadow cordgrass.

Retrace your steps from the observation deck and turn left at the screen house. At the 1.7-mile mark, you will see a kayak launch and tidal creek views. Here you can enjoy views across Phillips Creek and associated tidal marshes. There are three zones: high marsh, low marsh, and open water. Continue walking alongside Phillips Creek. At the 2.0-mile mark, you will reconnect with the hiking trail. Turn left to retrace your steps to the parking area.

An observation deck allows visitors to enjoy a wide-reaching vista across the marsh at Brownsville Preserve.

A hike on the William B. Cummings Birding and Wildlife Trail exposes visitors to hardwood forest, tidal creeks, and salt marshes.

MILES AND DIRECTIONS

0.0 The trail begins to the left of a large trail sign toward the back of the parking area. After a few steps, you will walk along an elevated wooden boardwalk.

0.2 The boardwalk ends. Turn right onto a gravel and crushed oyster shell trail.

1.0 Arrive at a screen house and a wooden observation deck across the clearing. Retrace your steps from the clearing, then turn left at the screen house to proceed on the trail.

1.7 Reach a kayak launch and tidal creek views.

2.0 Turn left to reconnect with the gravel trail and retrace your steps to the parking area.

3.0 Arrive back at the parking area. Your hike is complete.

49 WINDSOR CASTLE PARK TRAIL

This idyllic park trail has a lot to see, including tidal marshes, wooden bridges, picnic areas, and vernal pools, even scurrying fiddler crabs. Bring your doggo to this dog-friendly park with a water station just for your furry pup. There's even a small fenced-in dog park.

Start: Parking area across from Smithfield Station
Elevation gain: 125 feet
Maximum grade: 5%
Distance: 2.7-mile lollipop
Difficulty: Easy
Hiking time: 1.5 to 2 hours
Best seasons: Year-round
Fees and permits: Free
Trail contact: Windsor Castle Park, 705 Cedar St., Smithfield, VA; (757) 542-3109; windsorcastlepark.com

Dogs: Yes, on a leash no longer than 6 feet
Trail surface: Mostly dirt and crushed gravel trails, some wooden boardwalk crossings
Land status: Public park
Nearest town: Smithfield
Maps: Park maps are available online at windsorcastlepark.com.
Amenities: Porta-potties, playground, picnic tables
Cell service: Reliable

FINDING THE TRAILHEAD

Start at the dedicated parking area across from Smithfield Station. GPS: N36°58'55.1" / W76°37'27.2"

THE HIKE

There's just something about a town park called Windsor Castle Park. The name alone begs a visit to this picturesque 208-acre riverside park in Smithfield, Virginia. Yes, in fact this quaint town is home to Smithfield Foods, the world's largest pork producer. Situated midway between Williamsburg and Virginia Beach (one hour by car to either city), Smithfield is a charming village situated on the banks of the historic James River. It's also home to this exquisite park with a variety of easygoing hiking trails that make this small town worth the drive.

The Windsor Castle Park Trail encircles this delightful green space, forming two connected loops (a figure eight). There is also a dedicated mountain bike trail within the hiking loop. You can access this trail in different locations, including from within the park and from the parking area across the street from Smithfield Station, which features a quaint waterfront inn with specialty shops, fine dining, and a small marina.

This hiking route is 2.7 miles, but it's a snap to get in more or fewer steps along this scenic path that includes coastal marshes, wooden bridges, and curious vernal pools. From the Smithfield Station parking area, cross the Station Bridge over a tidal saltwater marsh (which later switches to freshwater marsh). At the 0.1-mile mark, turn right onto a trail made of sand and crushed gravel.

At the 0.2-mile mark, cross a second pedestrian bridge, Jericho Bridge, over the marsh. In a few more steps, cross over Jericho Road. The marsh is now on your right. Keep your eyes open for teeny-tiny fiddler crabs scurrying about on the flat, sandy trail. At the 0.4-mile mark, turn right onto the second park loop.

The first steps of this hike lead visitors across Station Bridge, a wooden pedestrian bridge.

You'll see the first of several benches overlooking the coastal marsh at the 0.8-mile mark. These benches are ideal for taking a quick break or rehydrating on the trail. In a few more steps, you'll see a boardwalk trail on the right. This leads to the Mason Street park entrance. Do not turn right, but instead continue straight on the path.

At the 1.4-mile mark, you'll see peculiar vernal pools. It's as if trees were growing out of the watery basins. These are best seen in months with more precipitation. Vernal pools are unique seasonal wetland habitats, which create fantastic ecosystems for amphibians, like salamanders, frogs, and newts, and box turtles.

At the 1.5-mile mark, you will have a decision to make (at the #12 sign): turn left for a shaded trail, or continue straight for sun around the edge of the park. Both paths meet up in the main park area near the 2.0-mile mark. There are porta-potties, as well as a water bowl and a water pump for doggos. Here also is the main parking area for Windsor Castle Park.

As you continue on the wooded path, you will see a picnic area on the left. Near the 2.3-mile mark, turn right to retrace your steps to the parking lot. Be sure to turn left to cross back over Station Bridge to the parking area across the street from Smithfield Station. At the 2.7-mile mark, your hike is complete.

MILES AND DIRECTIONS

- **0.0** Begin at the dedicated parking area across the street from Smithfield Station. Immediately, cross a wooden pedestrian bridge over a tidal marsh.
- **0.1** Turn right onto the Windsor Castle Park Trail.
- **0.2** Cross a second pedestrian bridge, Jericho Bridge, over the tidal marsh.
- **0.3** Cross Jericho Road.
- **0.4** Veer right to access the park loop.

You will cross tidal marshes over wooden pedestrian bridges, like Jericho Bridge, on this hike.

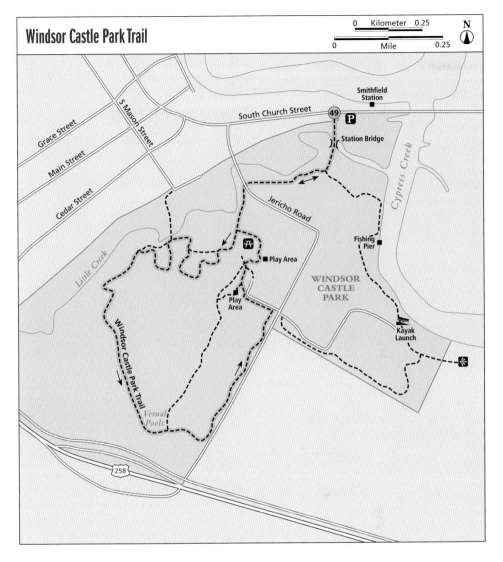

Windsor Castle Park Trail

0 Kilometer 0.25

0 Mile 0.25

N

Smithfield Station

South Church Street

49 P

Station Bridge

Grace Street

S Mason Street

Main Street

Cedar Street

Jericho Road

Cypress Creek

Little Creek

Play Area

Fishing Pier

WINDSOR CASTLE PARK

Play Area

Windsor Castle Park Trail

Kayak Launch

Vernal Pools

258

1.4   Reach vernal pools on the left.

1.5   Continue straight to remain on the loop. Do not turn left.

1.9   Turn left to stay on the loop trail.

2.0   Arrive at main park area with playscapes and picnic tables.

2.3   Close the loop and turn right to return to the parking area.

2.4   Cross back over Jericho Road.

2.5   Cross over Jericho Bridge.

2.6   Turn left to cross Station Bridge.

2.7   Arrive back at the parking area. Your hike is complete.

50 WOODLAND AND BIVALVE TRAILS

This popular coastal hike at Chincoteague National Wildlife Refuge offers up an overlook (and hopes of seeing wild horses), as well as scenic water views across Toms Cove.

Start: Parking area at the end of Woodland Trail Access Road, behind Wilgus Corral.
Elevation gain: 16 feet
Maximum grade: 1%
Distance: 2.3-mile loop
Difficulty: Easy
Hiking time: 1 to 2 hours
Best seasons: Year-round
Fees and permits: $$ per vehicle for a daily pass; no entry fee for pedestrians and cyclists
Trail contact: Chincoteague National Wildlife Refuge, 8231 Beach Rd.,
Chincoteague, VA; (757) 336-6122; fws.gov/refuge/chincoteague
Dogs: No
Trail surface: Mostly paved, plus crushed oyster shells and wooden boardwalk
Land status: National wildlife refuge
Nearest town: Chincoteague
Maps: National Geographic Trails Illustrated Topographic Map 772 (Delmarva Peninsula)
Other trail users: Cyclists
Amenities: Vault toilet
Cell service: Reliable

FINDING THE TRAILHEAD

The trailhead is located in back of the parking area, to the right of a large trail kiosk. GPS: N37°53'42.5" / W75°21'38.3"

THE HIKE

The Chincoteague National Wildlife Refuge is a short bike ride from the center of Chincoteague, which is home to bait shops, candy stores, and small inns, including the popular Refuge Inn, which has an on-property pony corral. Inside the refuge, plan to pedal around Snow Goose Pool on the Wildlife Loop before setting out on a refuge hike, like the easy 2.3-mile hike on the Woodland Trail and Bivalve Trail. The hike promises wetlands, coastal pines, maybe even a wild pony or two. You know, Misty of Chincoteague and the like.

As you proceed to the parking area, there is a bike rack on the left, adjacent to the pony corral. There is also a restroom. The lot can hold at least a dozen or so cars. The paved Woodland Trail begins to the left of the large trail kiosk on the southeast side of the parking area. This trail is for both hikers and bikers.

Proceed past the trail kiosk. The loop trail splits at the 0.1-mile mark. You can turn right for the pony overlook or turn left for the Bivalve Trail. For those eager to see ponies, turn right for a counterclockwise loop hike. There's not a lot of shade on this trail, so keep this in mind.

At the 0.2-mile mark, you will reach a comfy wooden bench. It's a nice place to stop, but it's also in full sun. A partially shaded bench turns up at the 0.6-mile mark. Here you'll also reach a boardwalk trail to the pony overlook. Note that bicycles are not allowed on the boardwalk section of trail. It's a short walk to the overlook with views across the coastal wetlands. Keep your eyes peeled for ponies.

A boardwalk trail leads to a pony overlook on the Woodland Trail at Chincoteague National Wildlife Refuge in Virginia.

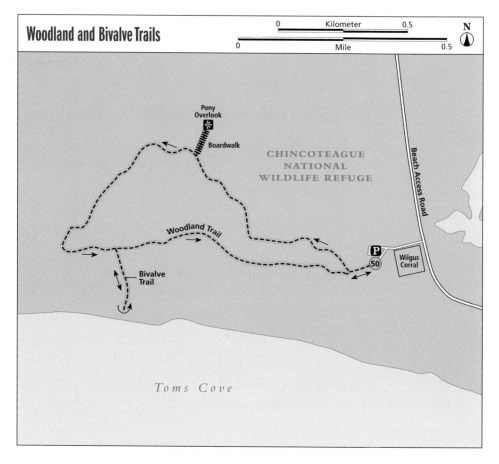

Woodland and Bivalve Trails

0   Kilometer   0.5

0   Mile   0.5

N

Pony Overlook

Boardwalk

CHINCOTEAGUE
NATIONAL
WILDLIFE REFUGE

Beach Access Road

Woodland Trail

Bivalve Trail

P
50

Wilgus Corral

Toms Cove

From the overlook, retrace your steps, then turn right onto the Woodland Trail. There's another wooden bench at the 1.2-mile mark. At the 1.4-mile mark, turn right onto the Bivalve Trail. This trail is made of crushed oyster shells and is for walking only. Bicycles are not allowed on this section either. Walk to the end for relaxing views across refreshing Toms Cove.

Savor the views, then retrace your steps to the paved Woodland Trail. Turn right to proceed to the trailhead. Naturally, you'll pass one more bench. Your hike is complete at the 2.3-mile mark.

MILES AND DIRECTIONS

0.0   Begin at the trailhead in the back of the parking area, adjacent to the large trail kiosk.

0.1   Reach a fork in the trail. Stay right to proceed to the pony overlook.

0.2   Arrive at a wooden bench.

0.6   Reach the boardwalk trail to the pony overlook. There is also a wooden bench here. Retrace your steps from the overlook to the Woodland Trail, then turn right onto the Woodland Trail.

Enjoy a change in terrain—crushed oyster shells—on the Bivalve Trail section of this hike.

1.2   Arrive at a wooden bench.

1.4   Turn right onto the Bivalve Trail to Toms Cove. Retrace your steps.

1.7   Turn right onto the Woodland Trail.

2.3   Arrive back at the parking area. Your hike is complete.

APPENDIX A: FOR MORE INFORMATION

The following are excellent sources of information on many of the trails, parks, recreation areas, and campgrounds referenced in this book.

Delaware Department of Natural Resources and Environmental Control (Delaware State Parks)
Richardson and Robbins Building
89 Kings Hwy. SW
Dover, DE 19901
(302) 739-9000
destateparks.com

Maryland Department of Natural Resources (Maryland Park Service)
580 Taylor Ave.
Annapolis, MD 21401
(410) 260-8367
dnr.maryland.gov/publiclands

The Nature Conservancy
4245 N. Fairfax Dr., Ste. 100
Arlington, VA 22203
(703) 841-5300
nature.org

Virginia Department of Conservation and Recreation (Virginia State Parks)
600 E. Main St., 24th Fl.
Richmond, VA 23219
(800) 933-7275
dcr.virginia.gov/state-parks

Virginia Department of Wildlife Resources
7870 Villa Park Dr., Ste. 400
Richmond, VA 23228
(804) 367-1000
dwr.virginia.gov

Park maps can often be found on-site at national, state, and regional parks as well as online for download before arriving at a trailhead. Alternatively, National Geographic creates a variety of Trails Illustrated topographic maps.

National Geographic Maps
212 Beaver Brook Canyon Rd.
Evergreen, CO 80439
(800) 962-1643
natgeomaps.com

APPENDIX B: FURTHER READING

The following books were helpful in the creation of this guidebook:

Burnham, Bill and Mary. *Hiking Virginia*. FalconGuides, 2013.

Connellee, Heather Sanders. *Best Easy Day Hikes Baltimore*. FalconGuides, 2013.

Cummings, Terry. *Hiking Maryland and Delaware*. FalconGuides, 2014.

The following online resources are also valuable in identifying and researching hiking trails:

AllTrails.com

HikingUpward.com

HikingProject.com

HIKE INDEX

THE TEN ESSENTIALS OF HIKING

American Hiking Society

American Hiking Society recommends you pack the "Ten Essentials" every time you head out for a hike. Whether you plan to be gone for a couple of hours or several months, make sure to pack these items. Become familiar with these items and know how to use them.

1. Appropriate Footwear
Happy feet make for pleasant hiking. Think about traction, support, and protection when selecting well-fitting shoes or boots.

2. Navigation
While phones and GPS units are handy, they aren't always reliable in the backcountry; consider carrying a paper map and compass as a backup and know how to use them.

3. Water (and a way to purify it)
As a guideline, plan for half a liter of water per hour in moderate temperatures/terrain. Carry enough water for your trip and know where and how to treat water while you're out on the trail.

4. Food
Pack calorie-dense foods to help fuel your hike, and carry an extra portion in case you are out longer than expected.

5. Rain Gear & Dry-Fast Layers
The weatherman is not always right. Dress in layers to adjust to changing weather and activity levels. Wear moisture-wicking cloths and carry a warm hat.

6. Safety Items (light, fire, and a whistle)
Have means to start an emergency fire, signal for help, and see the trail and your map in the dark.

7. First Aid Kit

Supplies to treat illness or injury are only as helpful as your knowledge of how to use them. Take a class to gain the skills needed to administer first aid and CPR.

8. Knife or Multi-Tool

With countless uses, a multi-tool can help with gear repair and first aid.

9. Sun Protection

Sunscreen, sunglasses, and sun-protective clothing should be used in every season regardless of temperature or cloud cover.

10. Shelter

Protection from the elements in the event you are injured or stranded is necessary. A lightweight, inexpensive space blanket is a great option.

Find other helpful resources at AmericanHiking.org/hiking-resources

PROTECT THE PLACES YOU LOVE TO HIKE.

Become a member today and take $5 off an annual membership using the code **Falcon5**.

AmericanHiking.org/join

American Hiking Society is the only national nonprofit organization dedicated to empowering all to enjoy, share, and preserve the hiking experience.

American Hiking Society